Documents for
Drama
and
Revolution

Documents for
Drama
and
Revolution
Bernard F. Dukore
CITY UNIVERSITY OF NEW YORK

HOLT, RINEHART AND WINSTON, INC.

NEW YORK   CHICAGO   SAN FRANCISCO   ATLANTA   DALLAS
MONTREAL   TORONTO

Preface

As its title implies, the purposes of this anthology are to supplement and provide background for plays in *Drama and Revolution*. To this end, it includes contemporary writings on the revolutions that are the subjects of these plays (composed in some instances by the authors of those plays), on the plays themselves, and where relevant on the revolutionary form of theatre they represent. The type of documents—selected on the basis of pertinence, availability, and space—of necessity varies in the case of each particular play and revolution. For each group of documents there is an introduction which relates them to the corresponding play in *Drama and Revolution*.

Bernard F. Dukore

July, 1970

72,623

Contents

Documents for
Drama
and
Revolution

The American Revolution

MY KINSMAN, MAJOR MOLINEUX

According to the first paragraph of the Declaratory Act (1766), the King of England, with the consent of Parliament, "had, hath, and of right ought to have full power and authority to make laws and statutes of sufficient force and validity to bind the colonies and people of America, subject of the Crown of Great Britain, in all cases whatsoever." England enacted laws taxing the colonists, quartering troops in the colonies in peacetime, establishing judicial decrees for the colonies that had no provisions for trial by jury—all without the advice or consent of the colonists, who had no representatives in Parliament. Rioting against these measures, American mobs sometimes destroyed the property and harmed the persons of the Crown's representatives. As in Robert Lowell's play, all classes of Americans joined in these mobs.

Massachusetts was considered an insidious center of seditious activity and Boston, its capital, was regarded as particularly subversive. Frequently fighting with British troops, Bostonians were also fired upon by them (as in the Boston Massacre, 1770). Sometimes tarring and feathering the Crown's representatives (as they do one such figure in *My Kinsman, Major Molineux*), they were at times arrested for treason. The Boston Tea Party (1773), in which Bostonians, protesting a tea tax, dumped 340 chests of tea into Boston Harbor, precipitated several such events in other American ports. In a series of repressive laws collectively known as the Coercive Acts, the Crown took its revenge on Boston. Apart from restricting the number of town hall meetings, quartering troops in the city, and ensuring that Crown representatives charged with crimes be tried anywhere but in that hostile colony, these acts closed the port of Boston until Bostonians reimbursed the East India Company for the tea dumped into the harbor. In the parliamentary debates on these bills, Colonel Barré warned Lord North, King George III's Prime Minister, "You point all your revenge at Boston alone; but I think you will very soon have the rest of the colonies on your back." His prophecy was accurate. Cities in other colonies, as well as in Massachusetts, sent supplies to the besieged Bostonians, many of whom were starving (more than 15,000, it has been estimated, by the middle of 1775). Protests against the Crown increased throughout the colonies.

In objecting to England's actions, the clergy joined the laity. In "Government Corrupted by Vice, and Recovered by Righteousness," which is representative of the revolutionary sermons, Reverend Samuel Langdon, President of Harvard College, inveighed against both the sinfulness of the English legislators and their unjust laws for the colonies. Hoping for a peaceful reconciliation between the colonists and the King, and a restoration of the former's "natural rights and civil and religious liberties," he was nevertheless under no illusion that these were likely to happen. Protesting therefore against "the arbitrary acts of legislators who are not our representatives" and approving the colonists' "noble stand for their natural and constitutional rights," he recounted the rebels' victories against the British troops at Lexington and Concord and proudly asked, "If God be for us, who can be against us?"

By the time of Lexington and Concord, as Thomas Paine said, the time for reconciliation was over. To remain tied to England, he argued in *Common Sense*, was not only disastrous to trade—an important motive of the American Revolution—but was also cowardly, since in delaying the inevitable it placed the burden on a future generation. According to Paine, "the period of debate is closed. Arms, as the last resource, decide the contest. . . ." Published anonymously in Philadelphia on January 10, 1776, the pamphlet *Common Sense* became overnight a best-seller and was a major influence in persuading Americans that reconciliation with England was "a fallacious dream." Three weeks after its appearance, George Washington remarked that its "sound doctrine and unanswerable reasoning," combined with such British actions as the burning of Falmouth and Norfolk, "will not leave numbers at a loss to decide upon the propriety of a separation." Although he himself was poor, Paine devoted the profits of *Common Sense* to the revolution. Accompanying Washington's troops during their retreat across New Jersey in December, 1776, Paine wrote the first of a series of sixteen pamphlets called *The American Crisis*, which began:

> *These are the times that try men's souls. The summer soldier and the sunshine patriot will, in this crisis, shrink from the service of his country; but he that stands by it now, deserves the love and thanks of man and woman. Tyranny, like hell, is not easily conquered; yet we have this consolation with us, that the harder the conflict, the more glorious the triumph. What we obtain too cheap, we esteem too lightly: 'tis dearness only that gives everything its value. Heaven knows*

how to put a proper price upon its goods; and it would be strange indeed, if so celestial an article as freedom should not be highly rated.

On Christmas eve, during a blizzard, before Washington and his men rowed across the Delaware River to surprise the Hessians stationed near Trenton, Washington had his troops listen to Paine read these words.

THE STAMP ACT RIOT

(Selection)

Cadwallader Colden

When the King's Order[1] in his Privy Council, of the 26th of July[2] arrived in September last it revived all the rage of the profession of the law, & they taking the advantage of the spirit of sedition which was raised in all the colonies against the act of Parliament for laying a stamp duty in the colonies, they turned the rage of the mob against the person of the Lieut. Governor, after all other methods which their malice had invented for that purpose had failed. The malice of the faction against the Lieut. Governor is so evident that their inclination to expose every failing in his administration cannot be doubted, & when they have nothing to charge him with besides his supporting the right of the subject to appeal to the King, it gives the strongest presumption in his favour that they cannot otherwise blame any part of his administration.

In the night of the 1st of November a great mob came up to the fort gate with two images carried on a scaffold: one representing their gray haired Governor, the other the Devil whispering him in the ear. After continuing thus at the gate, with all the insulting ribaldry that malice could invent, they broke open the Lieut. Governor's Coach House which was without the walls of the fort, carried his chariot round the streets of the town in triumph with the images—returned a second time to the fort gate, and in an open place near the fort, finished their insult with all the indignities that the malice of their leaders could invent. Their view certainly was to provoke the garrison, then placed on the ramparts, to some act which might be called a commencement of hostilities, in which case it cannot be said what was farther intended. Being disappointed in this, the mob expended their rage by destroying everything they found in the house of Major James of the Royal Artillery, for which no reason can be assigned other than his putting the fort in a proper state of defence as his duty in his department required of him.

[1] The Stamp Act.
[2] 1765.

From "The Account of the Lieutenant-Governor of New York, Cadwallader Colden, of the Stamp Act Riot, Sent to the Secretary of State and the Board of Trade in England," in *The Colden Letter Books: Collections for the Year 1877*, Volume II (New York: New York Historical Society, 1878).

GOVERNMENT CORRUPTED BY VICE, AND RECOVERED BY RIGHTEOUSNESS

Samuel Langdon

And I will restore thy judges as at the first, and thy counsellors as at the beginning; afterward thou shalt be called the city of righteousness, the faithful city.—Isaiah i. 26.

Shall we rejoice, my fathers and brethren, or shall we weep together, on the return of this anniversary, which from the first settlement of this colony has been sacred to liberty, to perpetuate that invaluable privilege of choosing from among ourselves wise men, fearing God and hating covetousness, to be honorable counsellors, to constitute one essential branch of that happy government which was established on the faith of royal charters?

On this day the people have from year to year assembled, from all our towns, in a vast congregation, with gladness and festivity, with every ensign of joy displayed in our metropolis, which now, alas! is made a garrison of mercenary troops, the stronghold of despotism. But how shall I now address you from this desk, remote from the capital, and remind you of the important business which distinguished this day in our calendar, without spreading a gloom over this assembly by exhibiting the melancholy change made in the face of our public affairs?[1]

We have lived to see the time when British liberty is just ready to expire, when that constitution of government which has so long been the glory and strength of the English nation is deeply undermined and

---

[1] May 31, 1775, the date this sermon was preached, was the anniversary, fixed by royal charter, for the election of counsellors. A month earlier, on the evening of April 18, 1775, English soldiers left Boston for Lexington, where they intended to arrest Samuel Adams and John Hancock, and for Concord, where they hoped to capture guns and ammunition stored by the American rebels. That night, Paul Revere and William Dawes rode to warn the populace. The next day, in battles at Lexington and Concord ("the shot heard round the world"), the Yankee patriots defeated the British troops. In Boston, General Gage, governor of the colony of Massachusetts, had troops at his command to enforce repressive regulations. Since the patriots were safer outside the colony's capital, they convened at Watertown.

From *The Pulpit of the American Revolution: or, The Political Sermons of the Period of 1776*, edited by John Wingate Thornton (Boston: Gould and Lincoln, 1860). This sermon was delivered on May 31, 1775, before the Congress of Massachusetts, assembled at Watertown.

5

ready to tumble into ruins, when America is threatened with cruel oppression, and the arm of power is stretched out against New England, and especially against this colony,[2] to compel us to submit to the arbitrary acts of legislators who are not our representatives, and who will not themselves bear the least part of the burdens which, without mercy, they are laying upon us. The most formal and solemn grants of kings to our ancestors are deemed by our oppressors as of little value; and they have mutilated the charter of this colony, in the most essential parts, upon false representations, and new-invented maxims of policy, without the least regard to any legal process. We are no longer permitted to fix our eyes on the faithful of the land, and trust in the wisdom of their counsels and the equity of their judgment; but men in whom we can have no confidence, whose principles are subversive of our liberties, whose aim is to exercise lordship over us, and share among themselves the public wealth, men who are ready to serve any master, and execute the most unrighteous decrees for high wages, whose faces we never saw before, and whose interests and connections may be far divided from us by the wide Atlantic, are to be set over us, as counsellors and judges, at the pleasure of those who have the riches and power of the nation in their hands, and whose noblest plan is to subjugate the colonies, first, and then the whole nation, to their will.

That we might not have it in our power to refuse the most absolute submission to their unlimited claims of authority, they have not only endeavored to terrify us with fleets and armies sent to our capital, and distressed and put an end to our trade, particularly that important branch of it, the fishery, but at length attempted, by a sudden march of a body of troops in the night,[3] to seize and destroy one of our magazines, formed by the people merely for their security, if, after such formidable military preparations on the other side, matters should be pushed to an extremity. By this, as might well be expected, a skirmish

---

[2] The statement is accurate. Massachusetts was given particularly harsh treatment, which in turn provoked more revolutionary activity. Partly as punishment for the Boston Tea Party (December 16, 1773), for example, Parliament passed several Coercive Acts, which restricted the number of town meetings in Massachusetts, permitted English troops to be quartered in Boston, allowed agents of the Crown charged with crimes to be tried in England or in other colonies, and closed Boston harbor until the East India Company was reimbursed for the tea dumped into that harbor. The act closing Boston harbor stated that "the opposition to the authority of Parliament had always originated in the colony of Massachusetts, and . . . the colony itself had ever been instigated to such conduct by the seditious proceedings of the town of Boston."

[3] April 18. See above, n. 1.

was brought on; and it is most evident, from a variety of concurring circumstances, as well as numerous depositions both of the prisoners taken by us at that time and our own men then on the spot only as spectators, that the fire began first on the side of the king's troops. At least five or six of our inhabitants were murderously killed by the regulars at Lexington before any man attempted to return the fire, and when they were actually complying with the command to disperse; and two more of our brethren were likewise killed at Concord bridge, by a fire from the king's soldiers, before the engagement began on our side. But, whatever credit falsehoods transmitted to Great Britain from the other side may gain, the matter may be rested entirely on this: that he that arms himself to commit a robbery, and demands the traveller's purse by the terror of instant death, is the first aggressor, though the other should take the advantage of discharging his weapon first, and killing the robber.

The alarm was sudden, but in a very short time spread far and wide. The nearest neighbors in haste ran together to assist their brethren and save their country. Not more than three or four hundred met in season, and bravely attacked and repulsed the enemies of liberty, who retreated with great precipitation. But, by the help of a strong reinforcement, notwithstanding a close pursuit and continual loss on their side, they acted the part of robbers and savages, by burning, plundering, and damaging almost every house in their way to the utmost of their power, murdering the unarmed and helpless, and not regarding the weaknesses of the tender sex, until they had secured themselves beyond the reach of our terrifying arms.[4]

That ever-memorable day, the nineteenth of April, is the date of an unhappy war openly begun by the ministers of the king of Great Britain against his good subjects in this colony, and implicitly against all the other colonies. But for what? Because they have made a noble stand for their natural and constitutional rights, in opposition to the machinations of wicked men who are betraying their royal master,

[4] Near the meeting-house in Menotomy [West Cambridge] two aged, helpless men, who had not been out in the action, and were found unarmed in a house where the regulars entered, were murdered without mercy. In another house, in that neighborhood, a woman, in bed with a new-born infant about a week old, was forced by the threats of the soldiery to escape, almost naked, to an open outhouse; her house was then set on fire, but was soon extinguished by one of the children which had laid concealed till the enemy was gone. In Cambridge, a man of weak mental powers, who went out to gaze at the regular army as they passed, without arms or thought of danger, was wantonly shot at and killed by those inhuman butchers as he sat on a fence. [—Samuel Langdon]

establishing Popery in the British dominions, and aiming to enslave and ruin the whole nation, that they may enrich themselves and their vile dependents with the public treasures and the spoils of America.

We have used our utmost endeavors, by repeated humble petitions and remonstrances, by a series of unanswerable reasonings published from the press—in which the dispute has been fairly stated, and the justice of our opposition clearly demonstrated—and by the mediation of some of the noblest and most faithful friends of the British constitution, who have powerfully plead our cause in Parliament, to prevent such measures as may soon reduce the body politic to a miserable, dismembered, dying trunk, though lately the terror of all Europe. But our king, as if impelled by some strange fatality, is resolved to reason with us only by the roar of his cannon and the pointed arguments of muskets and bayonets. Because we refuse submission to the despotic power of a ministerial Parliament, our own sovereign, to whom we have been always ready to swear true allegiance, whose authority we never meant to cast off, who might have continued happy in the cheerful obedience of as faithful subjects as any in his dominions, has given us up to the rage of his ministers, to be seized at sea by the rapacious commanders of every little sloop of war and piratical cutter, and to be plundered and massacred by land by mercenary troops, who know no distinction betwixt an enemy and a brother, between right and wrong, but only, like brutal pursuers, to hunt and seize the prey pointed out by their masters.

We must keep our eyes fixed on the supreme government of the Eternal King, as directing all events, setting up or pulling down the kings of the earth at his pleasure, suffering the best forms of human government to degenerate and go to ruin by corruption, or restoring the decayed constitutions of kingdoms and states by reviving public virtue and religion, and granting the favorable interpositions of his providence. To this our text leads us; and, though I hope to be excused on this occasion from a formal discourse on the words in a doctrinal way, yet I must not wholly pass over the religious instruction contained in them.

Let us consider—that for the sins of a people God may suffer the best government to be corrupted or entirely dissolved, and that nothing but a general reformation can give good ground to hope that the public happiness will be restored by the recovery of the strength and perfection of the state, and that Divine Providence will interpose to fill every department with wise and good men.

Isaiah prophesied about the time of the captivity of the Ten Tribes of Israel, and about a century before the captivity of Judah. The kingdom of Israel was brought to destruction because its iniquities were full; its counsellors and judges were wholly taken away because there remained no hope of reformation. But the sceptre did not entirely depart from Judah, nor a lawgiver from between his feet, till the Messiah came; yet greater and greater changes took place in their political affairs: their government degenerated in proportion as their vices increased, till few faithful men were left in any public offices; and at length, when they were delivered up for seventy years into the hands of the king of Babylon, scarce any remains of their original excellent civil polity appeared among them.

The Jewish government, according to the original constitution which was divinely established, if considered merely in a civil view, was a perfect republic. The heads of their tribes and elders of their cities were their counsellors and judges. They called the people together in more general or particular assemblies, took their opinions, gave advice, and managed the public affairs according to the general voice. Counsellors and judges comprehend all the powers of that government; for there was no such thing as legislative authority belonging to it, their complete code of laws being given immediately from God by the hand of Moses. And let them who cry up the divine right of kings consider that the only form of government which had a proper claim to a divine establishment was so far from including the idea of a king, that it was a high crime for Israel to ask to be in this respect like other nations; and when they were gratified, it was rather as a just punishment of their folly, that they might feel the burdens of court pageantry, of which they were warned by a very striking description, than as a divine recommendation of kingly authority.

Every nation, when able and agreed, has a right to set up over themselves any form of government which to them may appear most conducive to their common welfare. The civil polity of Israel is doubtless an excellent general model, allowing for some peculiarities; at least, some principal laws and orders of it may be copied to great advantage in more modern establishments.

When a government is in its prime, the public good engages the attention of the whole; the strictest regard is paid to the qualifications of those who hold the offices of the state; virtue prevails; everything is managed with justice, prudence, and frugality; the laws are founded on principles of equity rather than mere policy, and all the people are happy. But vice will increase with the riches and glory of an empire; and this gradually tends to corrupt the constitution, and in time bring on its dissolution. This may be considered not only as the natural effect of vice, but a righteous judgment of Heaven, especially upon a nation which has been favored with the blessings of religion and liberty, and is guilty of undervaluing them, and eagerly going into the gratification of every lust.

In this chapter the prophet describes the very corrupt state of Judah in his day, both as to religion and common morality, and looks forward to that increase of wickedness which would bring on their desolation and captivity. They were "a sinful nation, a people laden with iniquity, a seed of evil-doers, children that were corrupters, who had forsaken the Lord, and provoked the Holy One of Israel to anger." The whole body of the nation, from head to foot, was full of moral and political disorders, without any remaining soundness. Their religion was all mere ceremony and hypocrisy; and even the laws of common justice and humanity were disregarded in their public courts. They had counsellors and judges, but very different from those at the beginning of the commonwealth. Their princes were rebellious against God and the constitution of their country, and companions of thieves—giving countenance to every artifice for seizing the property of the subjects into their own hands, and robbing the public treasury. Every one loved gifts, and followed after rewards; they regarded the perquisites more than the duties of their office; the general aim was at profitable places and pensions; they were influenced in everything by bribery; and their avarice and luxury were never satisfied, but hurried them on to all kinds of oppression and violence, so that they even justified and encouraged the murder of innocent persons to support their lawless power and increase their wealth. And God, in righteous judgment, left them to run into all this excess of vice, to their own destruction, because they had forsaken him, and were guilty of wilful inattention to the most essential parts of that religion which had been given them by a well-attested revelation from heaven.

The Jewish nation could not but see and feel the unhappy consequences of so great corruption of the state. Doubtless they complained much of men in power, and very heartily and liberally reproached them for their notorious misconduct. The public greatly suffered, and the people groaned and wished for better rulers and better management; but in vain they hoped for a change of men and measures and better times when the spirit of religion was gone, and the infection of vice was become universal. The whole body being so corrupted, there could be no rational prospect of any great reformation in the state, but rather of its ruin, which accordingly came on in Jeremiah's time. Yet if a general reformation of religion and morals had taken place, and they had turned to God from all their sins, if they had again recovered the true spirit of their religion, God, by the gracious interpositions of his providence, would soon have found out methods to restore the former virtue of the state, and again have given them men of wisdom and integrity, according to their utmost wish, to be counsellors and judges. This was verified in fact after the nation had been purged by a long captivity, and returned to their own land humbled and filled with zeal for God and his law.

By all this we may be led to consider the true cause of the present remarkable troubles which are come upon Great Britain and these colonies, and the only effectual remedy.

We have rebelled against God. We have lost the true spirit of Christianity, though we retain the outward profession and form of it. We have neglected and set light by the glorious gospel of our Lord Jesus Christ, and his holy commands and institutions. The worship of many is but mere compliment to the Deity, while their hearts are far from him. By many the gospel is corrupted into a superficial system of moral philosophy, little better than ancient Platonism; and, after all the pretended refinements of moderns in the theory of Christianity, very little of the pure practice of it is to be found among those who once stood foremost in the profession of the gospel. In a general view of the present moral state of Great Britain it may be said, "There is no truth, nor mercy, nor knowledge of God in the land. By swearing, and lying, and killing, and stealing, and committing adultery," their wickedness breaks out, and one murder after another is committed, under the connivance and encouragement even of that authority by which such crimes ought to be punished, that the purposes of oppression and despotism may be answered. As they have increased, so have they sinned; therefore God is changing their glory into shame. The general prevalence of vice has changed the whole face of things in the British government.

The excellency of the constitution has been the boast of Great Britain and the envy of neighboring nations. In former times the great departments of the state, and the various places of trust and authority, were filled with men of wisdom, honesty, and religion, who employed all their powers, and were ready to risk their fortunes and their lives, for the public good. They were faithful counsellors to kings; directed their authority and majesty to the happiness of the nation, and opposed every step by which despotism endeavored to advance. They were fathers of the people, and sought the welfare and prosperity of the whole body. They did not exhaust the national wealth by luxury and bribery, or convert it to their own private benefit or the maintenance of idle, useless officers and dependents, but improved it faithfully for the proper purposes—for the necessary support of government and defence of the kingdom. Their laws were dictated by wisdom and equality, and justice was administered with impartiality. Religion discovered its general influence among all ranks, and kept out great corruptions from places of power.

But in what does the British nation now glory? In a mere shadow of its ancient political system, in titles of dignity without virtue, in vast public treasures continually lavished in corruption till every fund is exhausted notwithstanding the mighty streams perpetually flowing in, in the many artifices to stretch the prerogatives of the crown beyond all constitutional bounds, and make the king an absolute monarch, while the people are deluded with a mere phantom of liberty. What idea must we entertain of that great government, if such a one can be found, which pretends to have made an exact counter-balance of power between the sovereign, the nobles and the commons, so that the three branches shall be an effectual check upon each other, and the united wisdom of the whole shall conspire to promote the national felicity, but which, in reality, is reduced to such a situation that it may be managed at the sole will of one court favorite? What difference is there betwixt one man's choosing, at his own pleasure, by his single vote, the majority of those who are to represent the people, and his purchasing in such a majority, according to his own nomination, with money out of the public treasury, or other effectual methods of influencing elections? And what shall we say if, in the same manner, by places, pensions, and other bribes, a minister of the crown can at any time gain over a nobler majority likewise to be entirely subservient to his purposes, and, moreover, persuade his royal master to resign himself up wholly to the direction of his counsels? If this should be the case of any nation, from one seven years' end to another, the bargain and sale being made sure for such a period, would they still have reason to boast of their excellent constitution? Ought they not rather to think it high time to restore the corrupted, dying state to its original perfection? I will apply this to the Roman senate under Julius Caesar, which retained all its ancient formalities, but voted always only as Caesar dictated. If the decrees of such a senate were urged on the Romans, as fraught with all the blessings of Roman liberty, we must suppose them strangely deluded if they were persuaded to believe it.

The pretence for taxing America has been that the nation contracted an immense debt for the defence of the American colonies, and that, as they are now able to contribute some proportion towards the discharge of this debt, and must be considered as part of the nation, it is reasonable they should be taxed, and the Parliament has a right to tax and govern them, in all cases whatever, by its own supreme authority. Enough has been already published on this grand controversy, which now threatens a final separation of the colonies from Great Britain. But can the amazing national debt be paid by a little trifling sum, squeezed from year to year out of America, which is continually drained of all its cash by a restricted trade with the parent country, and which in this way is taxed to the government of Britain in a very large proportion? Would it not be much superior wisdom, and sounder policy, for a distressed kingdom to retrench the vast unnecessary expenses continually incurred by its enormous vices; to stop the prodigious sums paid in pensions, and to numberless officers, without the least advantage to the public; to reduce the number of devouring servants in the great family; to turn their minds from the pursuit of pleasure and the boundless luxuries of life to the important interests of their country and the salvation of the commonwealth? Would not a reverend regard to the authority of divine revelation, a hearty belief of the gospel of the grace of God, and a general reformation of all those vices which bring misery and ruin upon individuals, families, and kingdoms, and which have provoked Heaven to bring the nation into such perplexed and dangerous circumstances, be the surest way to recover the sinking state, and make it again rich and flourishing? Millions might annually be saved if the kingdom were generally and thoroughly reformed; and the public debt, great as it is, might in a few years be cancelled by a growing revenue, which now amounts to full ten millions per annum, without laying additional burdens on any of the subjects. But the demands of corruption are constantly increasing, and will forever exceed all the resources of wealth which the wit of man can invent or tyranny impose.

Into what fatal policy has the nation been impelled, by its public vices, to wage a cruel war with its own children in these colonies, only to gratify the lust of power and the demands of extravagance! May God, in his great mercy, recover Great Britain from this fatal infatuation, show them their errors, and give them a spirit of reformation, before it is too late to avert impending destruction! May the eyes of the king be opened to see the ruinous tendency of the measures into which he has been led, and his heart inclined to treat his American subjects with justice and clemency, instead of forcing them still further to the last extremities! God grant some method may be found out to effect a happy reconciliation, so that the colonies may again enjoy the protection of their sovereign, with perfect security of all their natural rights and civil and religious liberties.

But, alas! have not the sins of America, and of New England in particular, had a hand in bringing down upon us the righteous judgments of Heaven? Wherefore is all this evil come upon us? Is it not because we have forsaken the Lord? Can we say we are innocent of crimes against God? No, surely. It becomes us to humble ourselves under his mighty hand, that he may exalt us in due time. However unjustly and cruelly we have been treated by man, we certainly deserve, at the hand of God, all the calamities in which we are now involved. Have we not lost much of that spirit of genuine Christianity which so remarkably appeared in our ancestors, for which God distinguished them with the signal favors of providence when they fled from tyranny and persecution into this western desert? Have we not departed from their virtues? Though I hope and am confident that as much true religion, agreeable to the purity and simplicity of the gospel, remains among us as among any people in the world, yet, in the midst of the present great apostasy of the nations professing Christianity, have not we likewise been guilty of departing from the living God? Have we not made light of the gospel of salvation, and too much affected the cold, formal, fashionable religion of countries grown old in vice, and overspread with infidelity? Do not our follies and iniquities testify against us? Have we not, especially in our seaports, gone much too far into the pride and luxuries of life? Is it not a fact, open to common observation, that profaneness, intemperance, unchastity, the love of pleasure, fraud, avarice, and other vices, are increasing among us from year to year? And have not even these young governments been in some measure infected with the corruptions of European courts? Has there been no flattery, no bribery, no artifices practised, to get into places of honor and profit, or carry a vote to serve a particular interest, without regard to right or wrong? Have our statesmen always acted with integrity, and every judge with impartiality, in the fear of God? In short, have all ranks of men showed regard to the divine commands, and joined to promote the Redeemer's kingdom and the public welfare? I wish we could more fully justify ourselves in all these respects. If such sins have not been so notorious among us as in older countries, we must nevertheless remember that the sins of a people who have been remarkable for the profession of godliness, are more aggravated by all the advantages and favors they have enjoyed, and will receive more speedy and signal punishment; as God says of Israel: "You only have I known of all the families of the earth, therefore will I punish you for all your iniquities."

The judgments now come upon us are very heavy and distressing, and have fallen with peculiar weight on our capital, where, notwithstanding the plighted honor of the chief commander of the hostile troops, many of our brethren are still detained, as if they were captives; and those that have been released have left the principal part of their substance, which is withheld, by arbitrary orders, contrary to an express treaty, to be plundered by the army.[5]

[5] Soon after the battle at Concord, General Gage stipulated, with the selectmen of Boston, that if the inhabitants would deliver up their arms, to be deposited in Fanueil Hall, and returned when circumstances would permit, they should have liberty to quit the town, and take with them their effects. They readily complied, but soon found themselves abused. With great difficulty, and very slowly, they

Let me address you in the words of the prophet: "O Israel! return unto the Lord thy God, for thou hast fallen by thine iniquity." My brethren, let us repent, and implore the divine mercy; let us amend our ways and our doings, reform everything which has been provoking to the Most High, and thus endeavor to obtain the gracious interpositions of providence for our deliverance.

If true religion is revived by means of these public calamities, and again prevails among us—if it appears in our religious assemblies, in the conduct of our civil affairs, in our armies, in our families, in all our business and conversation—we may hope for the direction and blessing of the Most High, while we are using our best endeavors to preserve and restore the civil government of this colony, and defend America from slavery.

Our late happy government is changed into the terrors of military execution. Our firm opposition to the establishment of an arbitrary system is called rebellion, and we are to expect no mercy, but to yield property and life at discretion. This we are resolved at all events not to do, and therefore we have taken up arms in our own defence, and all the colonies are united in the great cause of liberty.

But how shall we live while civil government is dissolved? What shall we do without counsellors and judges? A state of absolute anarchy is dreadful. Submission to the tyranny of hundreds of imperious masters, firmly embodied against us, and united in the same cruel design of disposing of our lives and subsistence at their pleasure, and making their own will our law in all cases whatsoever, is the vilest slavery, and worse than death.

Thanks be to God that he has given us, as men, natural rights, independent on all human laws whatever, and that these rights are recognized by the grand charter of British liberties. By the law of nature, any body of people, destitute of order and government, may form themselves into a civil society, according to their best prudence, and so provide for their common safety and advantage. When one form is found

---

obtain passes, but are forbidden to carry out anything besides household furniture and wearing apparel. Merchants and shopkeepers are obliged to leave behind all their merchandise, and even their cash is detained. Mechanics are not allowed to bring out the most necessary tools for their work. Not only their family stores of provisions are stopped, but it has been repeatedly and credibly affirmed that poor women and children have had the very smallest articles of this kind taken from them, which were necessary for their refreshment while they travelled a few miles to their friends; and that even their young children, in their mothers' arms, the cruel soldiery have taken the morsel of bread to prevent their crying, and thrown it away. How much better for the inhabitants to have resolved, at all hazards, to defend themselves by their arms against such an enemy, than suffer such shameful abuse! [Samuel Langdon]

by the majority not to answer the grand purpose in any tolerable degree, they may, by common consent, put an end to it and set up another— only, as all such great changes are attended with difficulty and danger of confusion, they ought not to be attempted without urgent necessity, which will be determined always by the general voice of the wisest and best members of the community.

If the great servants of the public forget their duty, betray their trust, and sell their country, or make war against the most valuable rights and privileges of the people, reason and justice require that they should be discarded, and others appointed in their room, without any regard to formal resignations of their forfeited power.

It must be ascribed to some supernatural influence on the minds of the main body of the people through this extensive continent, that they have so universally adopted the method of managing the important matters necessary to preserve among them a free government by corresponding committees and congresses, consisting of the wisest and most disinterested patriots in America, chosen by the unbiased suffrages of the people assembled for that purpose in their several towns, counties, and provinces. So general agreement, through so many provinces of so large a country, in one mode of self-preservation, is unexampled in any history; and the effect has exceeded our most sanguine expectations. Universal tumults, and all the irregularities and violence of mobbish factions, naturally arise when legal authority ceases. But how little of this has appeared in the midst of the late obstructions of civil government!—nothing more than what has often happened in Great Britain and Ireland, in the face of the civil powers in all their strength; nothing more than what is frequently seen in the midst of the perfect regulations of the great city of London; and, may I not add, nothing more than has been absolutely necessary to carry into execution the spirited resolutions of a people too sensible to deliver themselves up to oppression and slavery. The judgment and advice of the continental assembly of delegates have been as readily obeyed as if they were authentic acts of a long-established Parliament. And in every colony the votes of a congress have had equal effect with the laws of great and general courts.

It is now ten months since this colony has been deprived of the benefit of that government which was so long enjoyed by charter. They have had no General Assembly for matters of legislation and the public revenue; the courts of justice have been shut up, and almost the whole executive power has ceased to act; yet order among the people has been remarkably preserved. Few crimes have been committed, punishable by the judge; even former contentions betwixt one neighbor and another have ceased; nor have fraud and rapine taken advantage of the imbecility of the civil powers.

The necessary preparations for the defence of our liberties required not only the collected wisdom and strength of the colony, but an immediate, cheerful application of the wealth of individuals to the public service, in due proportion, or a taxation which depended on general consent. Where was the authority to vote, collect, or receive the large sums required, and make provision for the utmost extremities? A Congress succeeded to the honors of a General Assembly as soon as the latter was crushed by the hand of power. It gained all the confidence of the people. Wisdom and prudence secured all that the laws of the former constitution could have given; and we now observe with astonishment an army of many thousands of well-disciplined troops suddenly assembled, and abundantly furnished with all necessary supplies, in defence of the liberties of America.

But is it proper or safe for the colony to continue much longer in such imperfect order? Must it not appear rational and necessary, to every man that understands the various movements requisite to good government, that the many parts should be properly settled, and every branch of the legislative and executive authority restored to that order and vigor on which the life and health of the body politic depend? To the honorable gentlemen now met in this new congress as the fathers of the people, this weighty matter must be referred. Who knows but in the midst of all the distresses of the present war to defeat the attempts of arbitrary power, God may in mercy restore to us our judges as at the first, and our counsellors as at the beginning?

On your wisdom, religion, and public spirit, honored gentlemen, we depend, to determine what may be done as to the important matter of reviving the form of government, and settling all necessary affairs relating to it in the present critical state of things, that we may again have law and justice, and avoid the danger of anarchy and confusion. May God be with you, and by the influences of his Spirit direct all your counsels and resolutions for the glory of his name and the safety and happiness of this colony. We have great reason to acknowledge with thankfulness the evident tokens of the Divine presence with the former congress, that they were led to foresee present exigencies, and make such effectual provision for them. It is our earnest prayer to the Father of Lights that he would irradiate your minds, make all your way plain, and grant you may be happy instruments of many and great blessings to the people by whom you are constituted, to New England, and all the united colonies.

Let us praise our God for the advantages already given us over the enemies of liberty, particularly that they have been so dispirited by repeated experience of the efficacy of our arms; and that, in the late action at Chelsea, when several hundreds of our soldiery, the greater part open to the fire of so many cannon, swivels, and muskets, from a battery advantageously situated, from two armed cutters, and many barges full of marines, and from ships of the line in the harbor, not one man on our side was killed, and but two or three wounded; when, by the best intelligence, a great number were killed and wounded on the other side, and one of their cutters was taken and burnt, the other narrowly escaping with great damage.

If God be for us, who can be against us? The enemy has reproached us for calling on his name, and professing our trust in him. They have made a mock of our solemn fasts, and every appearance of serious Christianity in the land. On this account, by way of contempt, they call us saints; and that they themselves may keep at the greatest distance from this character, their mouths are full of horrid blasphemies, cursing, and bitterness, and vent all the rage of malice and barbarity. And may we not be confident that the Most High, who regards these things, will vindicate his own honor, and plead our righteous cause against such enemies to his government, as well as our liberties? O, may our camp be free from every accursed thing! May our land be purged from all its sins! May we be truly a holy people, and all our towns cities of righteousness! Then the Lord will be our refuge and strength, a very present help in trouble, and we shall have no reason to be afraid though thousands of enemies set themselves against us round about, though all nature should be thrown into tumults and convulsions. He can command the stars in their courses to fight his battles, and all the elements to wage war with his enemies. He can destroy them with innumerable plagues, or send faintness into their hearts, so that the men of might shall not find their hands. In a variety of methods he can work salvation for us, as he did for his people in ancient days, and according to the many remarkable deliverances granted in former times to Great Britain and New England when popish machinations threatened both countries with civil and ecclesiastical tyranny.

May the Lord hear us in this day of trouble, and the name of the God of Jacob defend us, send us help from his sanctuary, and strengthen us out of Zion! We will rejoice in his salvation, and in the name of our God we will set up our banners. Let us look to him to fulfill all our petitions.

COMMON SENSE

(Selection)

Thomas Paine

In the following pages I offer nothing more than simple facts, plain arguments, and common sense; and have no other preliminaries to settle with the reader, than that he will divest himself of prejudice and prepossession, and suffer his reason and his feelings to determine for themselves; that he will put on, or rather that he will not put off, the true character of a man, and generously enlarge his views beyond the present day.

Volumes have been written on the subject of the struggle between England and America. Men of all ranks have embarked in the controversy, from different motives, and with various designs; but all have been ineffectual, and the period of debate is closed. Arms, as the last resource, decide the contest; the appeal was the choice of the king, and the continent hath accepted the challenge,

It hath been reported of the late Mr. Pelham (who, though an able minister, was not without his faults), that on his being attacked in the house of commons on the score that his measures were only of a temporary kind, he replied: *"They will last my time."* Should a thought so fatal and unmanly possess the colonies in the present contest, the name of ancestors will be remembered by future generations with detestation.

The sun never shone on a cause of greater worth. 'Tis not the affair of a city, a county, a province, or a kingdom; but of a continent—of at least one eighth part of the habitable globe. 'Tis not the concern of a day, a year, or an age; posterity are virtually involved in the contest, and will be more or less affected, even to the end of time, by the proceedings now. Now is the seed-time of continental union, faith, and honor. The least fracture now will be like a name engraven with the point of a pin on the tender rind of a young oak; the wound will enlarge with the tree, and posterity read it in full-grown characters.

By referring the matter from argument to arms, a new era for politics is struck—a new method of thinking hath arisen. All plans, proposals, &c., prior to the 19th of April—*i. e.* to the commencement

From Thomas Paine, *Common Sense* (New York: Beacon Office, 1849). First published, anonymously, in Philadelphia on January 10, 1776.

of hostilities[1]—are like the almanacs of the last year, which, though proper then, are superseded and useless now. Whatever was advanced by the advocates on either side of the question then, terminated in one and the same point, viz., a union with Great Britain. The only difference between the parties was the method of effecting it—the one proposing force, the other friendship; but it hath, so far, happened that the first hath failed, and the second hath withdrawn her influence.

As much hath been said of the advantages of reconciliation, which like an agreeable dream, hath passed away and left us as we were, it is but right that we should examine the contrary side of the argument, and inquire into some of the many material injuries which these colonies sustain, and always will sustain, by being connected with, and dependent on, Great Britain—to examine that connection and dependence, on the principles of nature and common sense, to see what we have to trust if separated, and what we are to expect if dependent.

I have heard it asserted by some, that as America hath flourished under her former connection with Britain, that the same connection is necessary toward her future happiness, and will always have the same effect. Nothing can be more fallacious than this kind of argument; we may as well assert, that because a child hath thrived on milk, that it is never to have meat—or that the first twenty years of our lives are to become a precedent for the next twenty. But even this is admitting more than is true; for I answer, roundly, that America would have flourished as much, and probably much more, had no European power taken any notice of her. The commerce by which she hath enriched herself are the necessaries of life, and will always have a market while eating is the custom of Europe.

But she hath protected us, say some. That she hath engrossed us is true, and defended the continent at our expense as well as her own is admitted; and she would have defended Turkey from the same motive, viz., the sake of trade and dominion.

Alas! we have been long led away by ancient prejudices and made large sacrifices to superstition. We have boasted the protection of Great Britain, without considering that her motive was *interest*, not *attachment*; that she did not protect us from our enemies on our account, but from *her enemies* on *her own account*—from those who had no quarrel with us on any other account, and who will always be our enemies on the same account. Let Britain waive her pretensions to the continent, or the continent throw off the dependence, and we should be at peace with France and Spain were they at war with Britain.

[1] See p. 5, n. 1.

The miseries of Hanover, last war, ought to warn us against connections.

It hath lately been asserted in parliament that the colonies have no relation to each other but through the parent-country—i. e., that Pennsylvania and the Jerseys, and so on for the rest, are sister-colonies by the way of England. This is certainly a very round about way of proving relationship, but it is the nearest and only true way of proving enemyship, if I may so call it. France and Spain never were, nor perhaps ever will be, our enemies as Americans, but as our being the subjects of Great Britain.

But Britain is the parent-country, say some. Then the more the shame upon her conduct. Even brutes do not devour their young, nor savages make war upon their families; wherefore, the assertion, if true, turns to her reproach: but it happens not to be true, or only partly so; and the phrase "parent" or "mother" country hath been jesuitically adopted by the king, and his parasites, with a low, papistical design of gaining an unfair bias on the credulous weakness of our minds. Europe—and not England—is the parent-country of America. This new world hath been the asylum for the persecuted lovers of civil and religious liberty from every part of Europe. Hither have they fled, not from the tender embraces of the mother, but from the cruelty of the monster; and it is so far true of England, that the same tyranny which drove the first emigrants from home pursues their descendants still.

In this extensive quarter of the globe, we forget the narrow limits of three hundred and sixty miles (the extent of England), and carry our friendship on a larger scale; we claim brotherhood with every European Christian, and triumph in the generosity of the sentiment.

It is pleasant to observe by what regular gradations we surmount the force of local prejudice as we enlarge our acquaintance with the world. A man born in any town in England divided into parishes, will naturally associate most with his fellow-parishioners (because their interests, in many cases, will be common) and distinguish him by the name of *neighbor*; if he meet him but a few miles from home, he drops the narrow idea of a street, and salutes him by the name of *townsman*; if he travel out of the country and meet him in any other, he forgets the minor divisions of street and town, and calls him *country-man—i. e. country-man*; but if in their foreign excursions they should associate in France, or any other part of Europe, their local remembrance would be enlarged into that of *Englishmen*. And by a just parity of reasoning, all Europeans meeting in America, or any other quarter of the globe, are *countrymen*; for England, Holland, Germany, or Sweden, when compared with the whole, stand in the same places on a larger scale which the divisions of street, town, and country, do on the smaller ones; distinctions too limited for continental minds. Not one third of the inhabitants even of this province[2] are of English descent. Wherefore, I reprobate the phrase of parent or mother country, applied to England only, as being false, selfish, narrow, and ungenerous.

But admitting that we are all of English descent, what does it amount to? Nothing. Britain being now an open enemy, extinguishes every other name and title; and to say that reconciliation is our duty is truly farcical. The first king of England, of the present line (William the Conqueror), was a Frenchman, and half the peers of England, are descendants from the same country; wherefore, by the same method of reasoning, England ought to be governed by France.

Much hath been said of the united strength of Britain and the colonies, that in conjunction, they might bid defiance to the world. But this is mere presumption: the fate of war is uncertain; neither do the expressions mean anything, for this continent would never suffer itself to be drained of inhabitants to support the British arms in either Asia, Africa, or Europe.

Besides, what have we to do with setting the world at defiance? Our plan is commerce; and that well attended to, will secure us the peace and friendship of Europe, because it is the interest of all Europe to have America a *free port*. Her trade will always be a protection, and her barrenness of gold and silver will secure her from invaders.

I challenge the warmest advocate for reconciliation to show a single advantage that this continent can reap by being connected with Great Britain. I repeat the challenge, not a single advantage is derived. Our corn will fetch its price in any market in Europe, and our imported goods must be paid for, buy them where we will.

But the injuries and disadvantages we sustain by that connection are without number, and our duty to mankind at large, as well as to ourselves, instructs us to renounce the alliance; because any submission to, or dependence on, Great Britain, tends directly to involve this continent in European wars and quarrels. As Europe is our market for trade, we ought to form no political connections with any part of it. 'Tis the true interest of America to steer clear of European contentions, which she never can do while, by her dependence on Britain, she is made the make-weight in the scale of British politics.

Europe is too thickly planted with kingdoms to be long at peace; and whenever a war breaks out between England and any foreign power, the trade of America goes to ruin, *because of her connection with Britain*. The next war may not turn out like the last, and should

[2] Pennsylvania, where *Common Sense* was printed.

it not, the advocates for reconciliation now will be wishing for separation then, because neutrality in that case would be a safer convoy than a man-of-war. Everything that is right or reasonable pleads for separation. The blood of the slain—the weeping voice of nature—cries, 'TIS TIME TO PART. Even the distance at which the Almighty hath placed England from America, is a strong and natural proof that the authority of the other was never the design of Heaven. The time, likewise, at which the continent was discovered, adds weight to the argument, and the manner in which is was peopled increases the force of it. The Reformation was preceded by the discovery of America: as if the Almighty graciously meant to open a sanctuary to the persecuted in future years, when home should afford neither friendship nor safety.

The authority of Great Britain over this continent is a form of government which, sooner or later, must have an end. And a serious mind can draw no true pleasure by looking forward, under the painful and positive conviction that what he calls "the present constitution" is merely temporary. As parents, we can have no joy, knowing that *this government* is not sufficiently lasting to insure anything which we may bequeath to posterity: and by a plain method of argument, as we are running the next generation into debt, we ought to do the work of it, otherwise we use them meanly and pitifully. In order to discover the line of our duty rightly, we should take our children in our hand, and fix our station a few years further into life; that eminence will present a prospect which a few present fears and prejudices conceal from our sight.

Though I would carefully avoid giving unnecessary offence, yet I am inclined to believe, that all those who espouse the doctrine of reconciliation may be included within the following descriptions; interested men, who are not to be trusted; weak men, who *can not* see; prejudiced men, who *will not* see; and a certain set of moderate men, who think better of the European world than it deserves; and this last class, by an ill-judged deliberation, will be the cause of more calamities to this continent than all the other three.

It is the good fortune of many to live distant from the scene of present sorrow; the evil is not sufficiently brought to *their* doors to make *them* feel the precariousness with which all American property is possessed. But let our imaginations transport us for a few moments to Boston; that seat of wretchedness will teach us wisdom, and instruct us for ever to renounce a power in whom we can have no trust. The inhabitants of that unfortunate town, who but a few months ago were in ease and affluence, have now no other alternative than to stay and starve, or turn out to beg; endangered by the fire of their friends if they continue within the town, and plundered by government if they leave it.[3] In their present condition, they are prisoners without the hope of redemption; and in a general attack for their relief, they would be exposed to the fury of both armies.

Men of passive tempers look somewhat lightly over the offences of Great Britain, and, still hoping for the best, are apt to call out: *Come, come, we shall be friends again, for all this.* But examine the passions and feelings of mankind; bring the doctrine of reconciliation to the touchstone of nature; and then tell me whether you can hereafter love, honor, and faithfully serve, the power that hath carried fire and sword into your land. If you can not do all these, then are you only deceiving yourselves, and by your delay bringing ruin upon posterity. Your future connection with Britain, whom you can neither love nor honor, will be forced and unnatural, and, being formed only on the plan of present convenience, will in a little time fall into a relapse more wretched than the first. But if you say you can still pass the violations over, then I ask, hath your house been burned? Hath your property been destroyed before your face? Are your wife and children destitute of a bed to lie on or bread to live on? Have you lost a parent or a child by their hands, and yourself the ruined and wretched survivor? If you have not, then you are not to judge of those who have. But if you have, and still can shake hands with the murderers, then are you unworthy the name of husband, father, friend, or lover, and whatever may be your rank or title in life, you have the heart of a coward, and the spirit of a sycophant.

This is not inflaming or exaggerating matters, but trying them by those feelings and affections which nature justifies, and without which we should be incapable of discharging the social duties of life, or enjoying the felicities of it. I mean not to exhibit horror for the purpose of provoking revenge, but to awaken us from fatal and unmanly slumbers, that we may pursue determinately some fixed object. 'Tis not in the power of England or Europe to conquer America, if she doth not conquer herself by *delay* and *timidity*. The present winter is worth an age, if rightly employed; but if lost, or neglected, the whole continent will partake of the misfortune; and there is no punishment which that man doth not deserve—be he who, or what, or where he will—that may be the means of sacrificing a season so precious and useful.

'Tis repugnant to reason—to the universal order of things— to all examples from former ages, to suppose that this continent can

---

[3] The "unfortunate town" is Boston. See p. 6, n. 2. Paine's reference to starvation is accurate. Historians estimate that by the middle of 1775, 15,000 Bostonians were starving.

long remain subject to any external power. The most sanguine in Britain do not think so. The utmost stretch of human wisdom can not, at this time, compass a plan, short of separation, which can promise the continent even a year's security. Reconciliation is *now* a fallacious dream. Nature hath deserted the connection, and art can not supply her place. For, as Milton widely expresses, "never can true reconciliation grow where wounds of deadly hate have pierced so deep."

Every quiet method for peace hath been ineffectual. Our prayers have been rejected with disdain, and hath tended to convince us that nothing flatters vanity or confirms obstinacy in kings more than repeated petitioning; and nothing hath contributed more than that very measure to make the kings of Europe absolute. Witness Denmark and Sweden. Wherefore, since nothing but blows will do, for God's sake let us come to a final separation, and not leave the next generation to be cutting throats, under the violated, unmeaning names of parent and child.

To say they will never attempt it again, is idle and visionary: we thought so at the repeal of the stamp act; yet a year or two undeceived us. As well may we suppose that nations which have been once defeated will never renew the quarrel.

As to government matters, 'tis not in the power of Britain to do this continent justice. The business of it will soon be too weighty and intricate to be managed, with any tolerable degree of convenience, by a power so distant from us, and so very ignorant of us; for if they can not conquer us, they can not govern us. To be always running three or four thousand miles with a tale or a petition, waiting four or five months for an answer, which, when obtained, requires five or six more to explain it in, will in a few years be looked upon as folly and childishness. There was a time when it was proper, and there is a proper time for it to cease.

Small islands, not capable of protecting themselves, are the proper objects for government to take under their care; but there is something very absurd in supposing a continent to be perpetually governed by an island. In no instance hath nature made the satellite larger than its primary planet; and as England and America, with respect to each other, reverse the common order of nature, it is evident they belong to different systems; England to Europe—America to itself.

I am not induced by motives of pride, party, or resentment, to espouse the doctrine of separation and independence: I am clearly, positively, and conscientiously persuaded that it is the true interest of this continent to be so; that everything short of that is mere patchwork—that it can afford no lasting felicity; that it is leaving the sword to our children, and shrinking back, at a time when a little more, a little further, would have rendered this continent the glory of the earth.

72,623

As Britain hath not manifested the least inclination toward a compromise, we may be assured that no terms can be obtained worthy the acceptance of the continent, or any ways equal to the expense of blood and treasure we have been already put to.

The object contended for ought always to bear some just proportion to the expense. The removal of North,[4] or the whole detestable junto, is a matter unworthy the millions we have expended. A temporary stoppage of trade was an inconvenience which would have sufficiently balanced the repeal of all the acts complained of, had such repeals been obtained; but if the whole continent must take up arms—if every man must be a soldier, it is scarcely worth our while to fight against a contemptible ministry only. Dearly, dearly do we pay for the repeal of the acts, if that is all we fight for; for, in a just estimation, it is as great a folly to pay a Bunker-hill price for law as for land. As I have always considered the independency of this continent as an event which sooner or later must arrive, so, from the late rapid progress of the continent to maturity, the event could not be far off. Wherefore, on the breaking out of hostilities, it was not worth the while to have disputed a matter which time would have finally redressed, unless we meant to be in earnest. Otherwise, it is like wasting an estate on a suit at law, to regulate the trespasses of a tenant whose lease is just expiring. No man was a warmer wisher for reconciliation than myself, before the fatal 19th of April, 1775; but the moment the event of that day was made known, I rejected the hardened, sullen-tempered Pharaoh for ever, and disdain the wretch that, with the pretended title of FATHER OF HIS PEOPLE, can unfeelingly hear of their slaughter, and composedly sleep with their blood upon his soul.

But admitting that matters were now made up, what would be the event? I answer, the ruin of the continent: and that for several reasons.

First: The powers of governing still remaining in the hands of the king, he will have a negative over the whole legislation of this continent. And as he hath shown himself such an inveterate enemy to liberty, and discovered such a thirst for arbitrary power, is he, or is he not, a proper man to say to these colonies: *You shall make no laws but what I please?* And is there any inhabitant in America so ignorant as not to know, that, according to what is called the *present constitution,* this continent can make no laws but what the king gives leave to? And is there any man so unwise as not to see, that, considering what has happened, he will suffer no laws to be made here but such as suit his purpose? We may be as effectually enslaved by the want of laws

---

[4] Lord Frederick North, Prime Minister of England from 1770–82.

in America, as by submitting to laws made for us in England. After matters are made up, as it is called, can there be any doubt but the whole power of the crown will be exerted to keep this continent as low and humble as possible? Instead of going forward, we shall go backwards, or be perpetually quarreling or ridiculously petitioning. We are already greater than the king wishes us to be, and will he not hereafter endeavor to make us less? To bring the matter to one point, is the power who is jealous of our prosperity, a proper power to govern us? Whoever says *no* to this question is an *independent*; for independency means no more than whether we shall make our own laws, or whether the king, the greatest enemy this continent hath, or can have, shall tell us: *There shall be no laws but such as I like.*

But the king, you'll say, hath a negative in England: the people there can make no laws without his consent. In point of right and good order, there is something very ridiculous, that a youth of twenty-one (which hath often happened) shall say to six millions of people, older and wiser than himself: "I forbid this or that of yours to be law." But, in this place, I decline this sort of a reply, though I will never cease to expose the absurdities of it, and only answer, that England being the king's residence, and America not so, makes quite another case. The king's negative here is ten times more dangerous and fatal than it can be in England; for *there* he will scarcely refuse his consent to a bill for putting England into as strong a state of defence as possible, and here he would never suffer such a bill to be passed.

America is only a secondary object in the system of British politics. England consults the good of this country no further than it answers her own purpose. Wherefore, her own interest leads her to suppress the growth of ours in every case which doth not promote her own advantage, or in the least interfere with it. A pretty state we should soon be in, under such a second-hand government, considering what has happened! Men do not change from enemies to friends by the alteration of a game. And, in order to show that reconciliation *now* is a dangerous doctrine, I affirm, *that it would be policy in the king, at this time, to repeal the acts, for the sake of reinstating himself in the government of the provinces*—in order that HE MAY ACCOMPLISH BY CRAFT AND SUBTLETY IN THE LONG RUN, WHAT HE CAN NOT DO BY FORCE AND VIOLENCE IN THE SHORT ONE. Reconciliation and ruin are nearly related.

Secondly: That as even the best terms which we can expect to obtain, can amount to no more than a temporary expedient, or a kind of government by guardianship, which can last no longer than till the colonies come of age, so that general face and state of things in the interim will be unsettled and unpromising. Emigrants of property will not choose to come to a country whose form of government hangs but by a thread, and is every day tottering on the brink of commotion and disturbance. And numbers of the present inhabitants would lay hold of the interval to dispose of their effects, and quit the continent.

But the most powerful of all arguments is that nothing but independence—*i. e.*, a continental form of government—can keep the peace of the continent, and preserve it inviolate from civil wars. I dread the event of a reconciliation with Britain *now*, as it is more than probable that it will be followed by a revolt, somewhere or other, the consequences of which may be far more fatal than all the malice of Britain.

Thousands are already ruined by British barbarity—thousands more will probably suffer the same fate. Those men have other feelings than us who have nothing suffered. All they *now* possess is liberty; what they before enjoyed is sacrificed to its service; and, having nothing more to lose, they disdain submission. Besides, the general temper of the colonies toward a British government, will be like that of a youth who is nearly out of his time—they will care very little about her. And a government which can not preserve the peace is no government at all; and in that case we pay our money for nothing. And pray, what is it that Britain can do, whose power will be wholly on paper, should a civil tumult break out the very day after reconciliation? I have heard some men say, many of whom I believe spoke without thinking, that they dreaded an independence, fearing that it would produce civil wars. It is but seldom that our first thoughts are truly correct, and that is the case here; for there are ten times more to dread from a patched-up connection than from independence. I make the sufferer's case my own, and I protest, that, were I driven from house and home, my property destroyed, and my circumstances ruined, as a man sensible of injuries, I could never relish the doctrine of reconciliation, or consider myself bound thereby.

The colonies have manifested such a spirit of good order and obedience to continental government, as is sufficient to make every reasonable person easy and happy on that head. No man can assign the least pretence for his fears, on any other grounds than such as are truly childish and ridiculous, viz., that one colony will be striving for superiority over another.

Where there are no distinctions, there can be no superiority: perfect equality affords no temptation. The republics of Europe are all (and we may say always) in peace. Holland and Switzerland are without wars, foreign or domestic. Monarchical governments, it is true, are never long at rest; the crown itself is a temptation to enterprising ruffians at *home*; and that degree of pride and insolence ever attendant on regal authority swells into a rupture with foreign powers in instances where a republican government, by being formed on more natural principles, would negotiate the mistake.

If there is any true cause for fear respecting independence, it is because no plan is yet laid down. Men do not see their way out. Wherefore, as an opening into that business, I offer the following hints, at the same time modestly affirming that I have no other opinion of them, myself, than that they may be the means of giving rise to something better.

Could the straggling thoughts of individuals be collected, they would frequently form materials for wise and able men to improve into useful matter.

Let the assemblies be annual, with a president only; the representation more equal; the business wholly domestic, and subject to the authority of a continental congress.

Let each colony be divided into six, eight, or ten convenient districts, each district to send a proper number of delegates to congress, so that each colony send at least thirty. The whole number in congress will be at least three hundred and ninety. Each congress to sit, and to choose a president by the following method: when the delegates are met, let a colony be taken from the whole thirteen colonies by lot; after which let the whole congress choose (by ballot) a president from out of the delegates of that province. In the next congress, let a colony be taken by lot from twelve only, omitting that colony from which the president was taken in the former congress, and so proceeding on till the whole thirteen shall have had their proper rotation. And in order that nothing may pass into a law but what is satisfactorily just, not less than three fifths of the congress to be called a majority. He that will promote discord under a government so equally formed as this, would have joined Lucifer in his revolt.

But as there is a peculiar delicacy from whom, or in what manner, this business must first arise, and as it seems most agreeable and consistent that it should come from some intermediate body between the government and the governors—that is, between the congress and the people—let a CONTINENTAL CONFERENCE be held in the following manner and for the following purpose:—

A committee of twenty-six members of congress, viz., two for each colony; two members for each house of assembly, or provincial convention; and five representatives of the people at large, to be chosen in the capital city or town of each province, for and in behalf of the whole province, by as many qualified voters as shall think proper to attend from all parts of the province for that purpose; or, if more convenient, that representatives may be chosen in two or three of the most populous parts thereof. In this conference, thus assembled, will be united the two grand principles of business, *knowledge and power*. The members of congress, assemblies, or conventions, by having had experience in national concerns, will be able and useful counsellors; and the whole, by being empowered by the people, will have a truly legal authority.

The conferring members being met, let their business be to frame a continental charter, or charter of the United Colonies (answering to what is called the magna charta of England), fixing the number and manner of choosing members of congress, members of assembly, with their date of sitting, and drawing the line of business and jurisdiction between them, always remembering that our strength and happiness are continental, not provincial; securing freedom and property to all men, and, above all things, the free exercise of religion, according to the dictates of conscience; with such other matters as is necessary for a charter to contain. Immediately after which, the said conference to dissolve, and the bodies which shall be chosen conformable to the said charter, to be the legislators and governors of this continent, for the time being. Whose peace and happiness, may God preserve! Amen.

Should any body of men be hereafter delegated for this or some similar purpose, I offer them the following extracts from that wise observer on government, Dragonetti:

"The science," says he, "of the politician consists in fixing the true point of happiness and freedom. Those men would deserve the gratitude of ages who should discover a mode of government that contained the greatest sum of individual happiness, with the least national expense."—*Dragonetti on Virtue and Rewards.*

But where, some say, is the king of America? I'll tell you, friend, he reigns above—and doth not make havoc of mankind, like the royal brute of Great Britain. Yet, that we may not appear to be defective in earthly honors, let a day be solemnly set apart for proclaiming the charter; let it be brought forth, placed on the divine law, the word of God; let a crown be placed thereon, by which the world may know, that so far as we approve of monarchy, that in America THE LAW IS KING. For as in absolute governments the king is law, so in free countries the law *ought* to be king, and there ought to be no other. But, lest any ill use should afterward arise, let the crown, at the conclusion of the ceremony, be demolished and scattered among the people, whose right it is.

A government of our own is our natural right; and when a man seriously reflects on the precariousness of human affairs, he will become convinced that it is infinitely wiser and safer to form a constitution of our own, in a cool deliberate manner, while we have it in our power, than to trust such an interesting event to time and chance. If we omit it now, some Massanello[5] may hereafter arise, who, laying hold of popular disquietudes, may collect together the desperate and discontented, and, by assuming to themselves the powers of government, may sweep away the liberties of the continent like a deluge. Should the government of America return again into the hands of Britain, the tottering situation of things will be a temptation for some desperate adventurer to try his fortune; and in such a case, what relief can Britain give? Ere she could hear the news, the fatal business might be done, and ourselves suffering, like the wretched Britons, under the oppression of the conqueror. Ye that oppose independence now, ye know not what ye do; ye are opening a door to eternal tyranny, by keeping vacant the seat of government. There are thousands, and tens of thousands, who would think it glorious to expel from the continent that barbarous and hellish power which has stirred up the Indians and the negroes to destroy us. The cruelty hath a double guilt: it is dealing brutally by us, and treacherously by them.

To talk of friendship with those in whom our reason forbids us to have faith, and our affections, wounded through a thousand pores, instruct us to detest, is madness and folly. Every day wears out the little remains of kindred between us and them; and can there be any reason to hope that as the relationship expires the affection will increase, or that we shall agree better when we have ten times more and greater concerns to quarrel over than ever?

Ye that tell us of harmony and reconciliation, can ye restore to us the time that is past? Can ye give to prostitution its former innocence? Neither can ye reconcile Britain and America. The last cord now is broken; the people of England are presenting addresses against us. There are injuries which Nature can not forgive—she would cease to be Nature if she did. As well can the lover forgive the ravisher of his mistress, as the continent forgive the murderers of Britain. The Almighty hath implanted in us these unextinguishable feelings for good and wise purposes. They are the guardians of his image in our hearts. They distinguish us from the herd of common animals. The social compact would dissolve, and justice be extirpated the earth or have only a casual existence, were we callous to the touches of affec-

---

[5] Thomas Anello, otherwise Massanello, a fisherman of Naples, who, after spiriting up his countrymen, in the public market-place, against the oppression of the Spaniards—to whom the place was then subject—prompted them to revolt, and in the space of a day became king. [Footnote in 1849 edition.]

tion. The robber and the murderer would often escape unpunished, did not the injuries which our tempers sustain provoke us into justice.

O ye that love mankind! ye that dare oppose not only the tyranny but the tyrant! stand forth; Every spot of the old world is overrun with oppression. Freedom hath been hunted round the globe. Asia and Africa have long expelled her; Europe regards her like a stranger; and England hath given her warning to depart. O! receive the fugitive, and prepare in time an asylum for mankind.

The French Revolution

DANTON'S DEATH

In a letter to his family on July 28, 1835, Georg Büchner declared that the playwright is "nothing but a writer of history," though he is superior to the historian in that "He transplants us directly into the midst of the life of an era, giving us, instead of a dry account of it, characters rather than characteristics, and figures rather than descriptions."[1] It is of course impossible for a dramatist to be "nothing but a writer of history," since he must—even if he does nothing else—perform such interpretive acts as selecting and omitting dialogue to be spoken on stage. Although Büchner does far more than this, he nevertheless utilizes historical records in order to recreate the French Revolution and to transplant his audience into the middle of its life. Such statements as Danton's "Soon I shall live in the Void and my name in the Pantheon of History," for example, and "Life is a burden to me; tear it from me! I yearn to shake it off!" derive from actual statements of Georges Danton. The entire milieu of the play, moreover, has the atmosphere of authenticity.

Because Büchner has not altered the chronology of the historical events with which the play deals, the time sequence of *Danton's Death* can be precisely dated. Although the brooding and sense of fatalism of the play's principal character may suggest that a long period of time passes, the play's action spans only thirteen days. The play begins on the day the political extremist Jacques René Hébert is executed by his extremist opponents, March 24, 1794. Danton is arrested on March 31. He makes his first speech before the Revolutionary Tribunal on April 2. He is executed on April 5. These particular dates are important, for by then the French Revolution had entered a new phase. By that time the lower classes had replaced the bourgeoisie as the major force of the revolutionary government. Demagogues exploited their frustrations and fears. Internecine warfare characterized the increasingly radical course of the extremists who controlled the revolutionary government. Those who opposed them were in danger of being

[1] "From Georg Büchner's Letters," *Tulane Drama Review*, VI (Spring, 1962), 133.

sent to the guillotine. Formerly, the revolutionists had executed the king and aristocrats. By the time of *Danton's Death*, they were executing each other.

Only five years earlier, the French National Convention had passed the Declaration of the Rights of Man and of the Citizen, which was modeled in part on the United States' Declaration of Independence. Essentially a bill of rights, it declared that all men are born equal, proclaimed that the source of sovereignty is the people, and asserted that the aim of government is to preserve man's natural rights, which include freedom, security, and property. This libertarian document reflects both the humanistic and the middle-class nature of the early stages of the revolution.

Within a few years, the revolutionary government was in danger. The lower classes, still hungry and ragged, were restive. French soldiers were fighting counterrevolutionary troops sent by foreign powers to destroy the revolution. Partly because of principle, partly because of self-defense, France exported the revolution to other countries. In the Decree of November 19, 1792, the National Convention declared that it would help the peoples of other countries overthrow their kings and establish freedom for themselves. Only a free and popular republic, the Convention declared in its Decree of December 15, 1792, would be acceptable either at home or in occupied territories. In the same document it decreed that anyone who wished to keep or bring back the aristocracy would be considered a public enemy. Military setbacks occurred abroad, internal disorders increased at home. Political extremists consolidated their power and in the name of opposition to counterrevolution they tabled the Declaration of the Rights of Man and of the Citizen. In March and April, 1793, the National Convention enacted "Emergency Decrees" which created the Committee of Public Safety and the Revolutionary Tribunal. With executive and legislative powers centralized in these bodies, civil rights were guillotined along with the political opponents of the extremists in power.

Initially an extremist, Georges Danton argued vigorously that the Emergency Decrees be enacted and he himself served as a member of the Committee of Public Safety. In 1793 he demanded that the Revolutionary Tribunal be created, insisted that he would personally kill anyone expressing counterrevolutionary sentiments, and urged the Convention to deal swiftly and harshly with suspected subversives. When he served on the Committee of Public Safety, he sent many men to their death. A year later, disillusioned by the excesses he helped establish and perform, he urged moderation. But it was too late: Danton, no longer an extremist, became a victim of his extremist opponents.

DECLARATION OF THE RIGHTS OF MAN AND OF THE CITIZEN

(1789)

The representatives of the French people, organized as a National Assembly, upon considering that ignorance of, neglect of, or contempt for the rights of man are the only causes of public misfortunes and of governmental corruption, have resolved to expound in a solemn declaration the natural, inalienable, and sacred rights of man, so that this declaration, being continually present before all the members of the social body, may unceasingly remind them of their rights and their duties; so that the acts of the legislative power and those of the executive power, capable at each moment of being compared with the end of every political institution, may be more respected; so that the claims of citizens, henceforth based on simple and incontestable principles, may always shape the maintenance of the Constitution and the general welfare.

Consequently, the National Assembly recognizes and declares, in the presence and under the auspices of the Supreme Being, the following rights of man and of the citizen:

I. Regarding their rights, men are born and remain free and equal. Social distinctions may be based only on general usefulness.

II. The end of every political association is the preservation of the natural and inalienable rights of man. These rights are liberty, property, security, and resistance to oppression.

III. The source of all sovereignty resides essentially in the nation. No body of men and no individual man may exercise authority which does not expressly derive from it.

IV. Liberty consists of being able to do what does not injure others. Thus, the exercise of the natural rights of each man has only those limits which assure other members of society of the enjoyment of the same rights. Those limits may be determined only by law.

V. The law has the right to prohibit only those actions which may be injurious to society. What is not prohibited by law may not be impeded, and no one may be forced to do what the law does not prescribe.

VI. The law is an expression of the general will. All citizens have the right to concur personally or through their representatives in its

Translated by Richard Kerr. Printed with permission of translator.

formation. Whether it protects or whether it punishes, the law must be the same for all. Since all citizens are equal in its eyes, they are equally eligible for all public offices, positions, and employment, according to their capacity and with no distinctions other than those of virtues and talents.

VII. No man may be accused, arrested, or detained except in cases determined by the law, and according to the manner which it prescribes. Those who solicit, expedite, execute, or order the execution of arbitrary orders, must be punished; but every citizen summoned or apprehended in pursuance of the law must immediately obey; by resisting, he makes himself guilty.

VIII. The law must establish only those penalties that are absolutely and obviously necessary, and no one should be punished except in accordance with a law established and promulgated prior to the offence and legally applied.

IX. If it is judged indispensable to arrest a man, then, because every man is presumed innocent until he is found guilty, all severity which is unnecessary for securing his person must be severely curbed by law.

X. A man must not be molested for his opinions, even his religious opinions, unless their manifestation disturbs the public order established by the law.

XI. Free communication of thoughts and opinions is one of the most precious rights of man: every citizen may therefore speak, write, and print such thoughts and opinions freely, except that he is responsible for the abuses of this liberty in cases determined by law.

XII. To guarantee the rights of man and of the citizen, a public force is necessary: this force is therefore instituted for the good of all, and not for the particular benefit of those to whom it is entrusted.

XIII. To support the public force and to provide for the expenses of government, a general tax is indispensable; it must be apportioned equally among all citizens, according to their means.

XIV. All citizens have the right to ascertain by themselves or through their representatives the necessity of the public tax, to consent freely to it, to oversee its employment, and to determine its amount, its method of assessment, its method of obtaining payment, and its duration.

XV. Society has the right to hold every public agent accountable for his administration.

XVI. Every society in which a guarantee of rights is not ensured, or a separation of powers not fixed, has no Constitution whatever.

XVII. Since property is a sacred and inviolable right, no one may be deprived of it, except when clearly required by a legally determined public necessity, and conditioned by a just and previous indemnity.

DECREE OF NOVEMBER 19, 1792

In the name of the French nation, the National Convention declares that she will accord fraternity and assistance to all peoples who want to recover their liberty, and it charges the executive power to give the necessary orders to the generals to carry assistance to these peoples, and to defend those citizens who have been or may be intimidated for the cause of liberty.

The National Convention decrees that the executive power will give orders to the generals of the French Republic to have the preceding decree printed and proclaimed in different languages, in all the countries through which the armies of the Republic travel.

Translated by Saraleigh Carney. Copyright 1970 by Saraleigh Carney.

DECREE OF DECEMBER 15, 1792

I. In countries which are or will be occupied by the armies of the French Republic, the generals will immediately proclaim, in the name of the French nation, the abolition of: existing imposts or taxes, the tithe, fixed or occasional feudal rights, real or personal servitude, exclusive hunting rights, the nobility, and all privileges generally. They will declare to the people that they bring peace, assistance, fraternity, liberty, and equality to them.

II. They will proclaim the sovereignty of the people and the suppression of all existing authorities. They will immediately summon the people into primary or communal assemblies to create and organize a provisional administration. They will publish, post, and execute in the language or the idiom of the country, in each district, the supplemental proclamation to this present decree.

III. All of the agents and officers of the old government, as well as those individuals formerly called noble, or members of various corporations formerly privileged, will, for the first election only, be ineligible to hold administrative positions or provisional judicial powers.

IV. The generals will immediately put under the safeguard and protection of the French Republic all movable goods and real estate belonging to the treasury; to the prince; to his supporters, adherents, and voluntary satellites; to public establishments; and to religious and lay bodies and communities. They will without delay draw up a detailed statement, which they will send to the executive council, and will take all measures in their power so that these properties may be respected.

V. The provisional administration named by the people will be charged with the supervision and administration of what may be put under the safeguard and protection of the French Republic. It will vigorously execute the law regarding civil and criminal trials, the police, and public safety. It will be charged with the regulation and payment of local expenses and those which are necessary for the common defense. It will establish taxes, provided always that they are not borne by the indigent and working portion of the people.

VI. As soon as the provisional administration is organized, the National Convention will appoint commissioners from it to deliberate with the National Convention.

Translated by Saraleigh Carney. Copyright 1970 by Saraleigh Carney.

VII. The Executive Council will also appoint national commissioners, who will immediately go to these places to confer with the provisional administration elected by the people on measures to be taken for the common defense, and on the means of procuring needed clothing and provisions for the armies of the Republic and of paying the expenses which these armies incur and will incur during their stay in their territory.

VIII. Every fortnight, the national commissioners appointed by the provisional Executive Council will send it an account of their operations. They will add their observations, the Executive Council will approve or reject them, and will immediately send an account to the Convention.

IX. The provisional administration elected by the people, as well as the functions of the national commissioners, will cease as soon as the inhabitants, having declared for liberty, independence, and the people's sovereignty, will have organized a form of free and popular government.

. . . .

The People of France to the People of _____:

Brothers and friends, we have conquered for the cause of liberty, and we will maintain it: our unity and strength guarantee it. We offer you the enjoyment of this inestimable good, which has always belonged to you, and which your oppressors cannot steal from you without committing a crime. We came to drive away your tyrants; they have fled. Show yourselves to be free men, and we will protect you from their vengeance, their plans, and their return.

From this moment, the French Republic proclaims the suppression of all your civil and military magistrates, of all authorities who have governed you; it proclaims in this country the abolition of all taxes which you have borne, under whatever form they existed: feudal rights, the salt tax, tolls, tariffs, entrance and exit rights, the tithe, exclusive hunting and fishing rights, forced labor crews, the nobility, and generally every kind of taxation and slavery which your oppressors have laid upon you.

It also abolishes among you all noble, sacerdotal and other corporations, all prerogatives, and all privileges contrary to equality. From this moment, you are all brothers and friends, citizens, equal in rights, and with equal obligation to defend, govern, and serve your country.

Immediately form communal assemblies. Hasten to establish your provisional administrations. The agents of the French Republic will confer with them to assure your happiness and the brotherhood which must henceforth exist between us.

THE REVOLUTIONARY TRIBUNAL

(Decree of March 10, 1793)

Concerning the composition and the organization of an extraordinary tribunal:

I. There will be established in Paris an extraordinary criminal tribunal, which will take cognizance of all counterrevolutionary enterprises, of all criminal attempts against the liberty, equality, unity, and indivisibility of the Republic, the internal and external safety of the state, and of all conspiracies aiming to reestablish royalty or to establish all other authority dangerous to the liberty, equality, and the sovereignty of the people, whether the accused be civil or military functionaries, or private citizens.

II. The tribunal will be composed of a jury and of five judges who will direct the investigation and apply the law according to the jury's findings.

III. The judges cannot render any judgment unless at least three are present.

IV. The first judge to be elected will preside. If he is absent, he will be replaced by the oldest judge.

V. The judges will be appointed by the National Convention by a plurality of votes, which cannot in any case be fewer than one-quarter of the votes.

VI. The National Convention will also name a public prosecutor and two associates, or substitutes, who will be chosen in the same way as the judges.

VII. At tomorrow's session, the National Convention will appoint twelve citizens from the district of Paris and from the four districts which surround it. These citizens will fill the functions of the jury. The National Convention will also appoint from the same districts four substitutes who will replace the jurors in case of absence, challenges or illness. The jurors will remain in office until May 1. The National Convention will provide for their replacement and for the formation of a jury from among the citizens of all of the districts.

VIII. The functions of the police concerning general safety, ascribing to the municipalities and the administrative bodies by the decree of last August 11, will extend to all crimes and misdemeanors mentioned in Article I of the present law.

IX. The administrative bodies will direct to the National Convention all official reports of denunciation, information, and arrest. They in turn will refer them to a commission of its members who will examine the evidence and submit reports.

X. A commission of six members of the National Convention will be formed to examine all documents, to report on them, to draw up and present indictments, to oversee the investigation made by the extraordinary tribunal, to maintain a correspondence with the public prosecutor and the judges on all matters which are sent to the tribunal, and to render an account to the National Convention.

XI. Those accused who wish to challenge one or more of the jurors will be required to put forward the causes of the challenge in a single joint document, whose validity the tribunal will judge within twenty-four hours.

XII. The jurors will vote and make decisions publicly, by voice, and by an absolute majority of votes.

XIII. Decisions will be executed without recourse to a court of appeal.

XIV. Those accused who are in flight and who do not appear within three months of their trial will be treated as *émigrés* and subject to the same punishments, with regard to their persons or their property.

XV. The judges of the tribunal will by an absolute majority elect a court clerk and two bailiffs. The court clerk will have two assistant clerks who are acceptable to the court.

DANTON'S SPEECH OF MARCH 27, 1793

(Selections)

It is finally necessary for the National Convention to be a revolutionary body; it is necessary for it to be the people; it is time for it to declare war on internal enemies. Civil war has been raging everywhere, and the Convention remains immobile. A revolutionary tribunal has been created which ought to punish all conspirators, and this tribunal is not yet active! What will the people say? Because they are ready to rise *en masse*, they feel they must do it. They will say: "Our representatives shudder helplessly, and meanwhile the counterrevolutionists kill liberty."

I must finally speak the truth to you. I will tell it to you without diluting it. What do all the chimeras which can be spread against me matter, as long as I can serve my country! Yes, citizens, you are not doing your duty. You say the people are misled, but why are you so removed from them? Get closer to them. They will understand why. The revolution can only advance, can only be consolidated with the people. The people are the instrument of the revolution, and it is up to you to serve the revolution. In vain do you say that the popular societies swarm with absurd informers, dreadful informers. What is to be done? A nation in revolution is like brass boiling in a crucible. The statue of liberty is not cast. If you do not regulate this metal boiling in the furnace, you will all be burned.

How can it be that you do not feel that the Convention must decree today that all men shall have pikes at the nation's expense? The rich will pay for it; the law will make them pay; the legal proprieties will not be violated. Also, it must be decreed that wherever the revolution appears, whoever has the audacity to call for counterrevolution will be put outside the law. In Rome, Valerius Publicola had the courage to propose a law which carried the death penalty against whoever called for tyranny. I declare that since patriots are insulted in the streets and public places, since references in plays to the country's misfortunes are passionately applauded, I declare that whoever dares to call for the destruction of liberty shall perish by my very hand, though afterwards I may have to carry my head to the scaffold; I will be happy to have given an example of virtue to my country.

I ask that we move to the order of the day, to the motion which

Translated by Saraleigh Carney. Copyright 1970 by Saraleigh Carney.

impelled me to speak. I ask that throughout the Republic each citizen be given a pike at the nation's expense. I ask that the extraordinary tribunal be activated. I ask that the Convention declare to the French people, to Europe, and to the universe that it is a revolutionary body, that it is resolved to maintain liberty and to suffocate the serpents which rend the country's breast.

Show yourselves to be revolutionaries, show yourselves to be the people, and then liberty will no longer be in peril. Nations which want to be great must, like heroes, be raised in the school of unhappiness. We have had reverses; but if in September it had been said, "The tyrant's head will fall under the law's sword, the enemy will be driven from the Republic's territory, 100,000 men will be at Mayence, we will have an army at Tournai," you would have seen liberty triumphant. This is still our position. We have lost precious time; we must retrieve it. We believed that the revolution was completed. We cried out against factions. And these are the factions which fall under the assassins' knife. . . .

But let us close the curtain on the past. It is necessary to reunite. . . . It is necessary to kill enemies at home in order to defeat enemies abroad. If you do not save the Republic, you will become victims of your passions or your ignorance. The Republic is immortal! The enemy can still make some progress, he can still take some of our fortresses, but in doing so he will consume himself. May our reverses turn to our advantage! May each man of France, like the giant of the fable, regain his strength when he touches the soil of his country.

I insist on what is more than a single law, on what necessity commands you: be the people! May every man here who still carries a spark of liberty in his heart not remove himself from the people. We are not their fathers, we are their children. Reveal to them our needs and their resources; tell them that they will be inviolable, if they are united. Think back to the memorable and terrible time of the month of August. All passions clashed. No one in Paris would venture beyond its walls. I myself, I sometimes have to point out, I brought the executive council and all of the people's magistrates together at the city hall. The people saw us together again, they seconded our reunion, and the enemy was vanquished. If we reunite, if we love the popular societies, if we assist them, in spite of their defects, France will recover her strength, will again become victorious, and soon the despots will repent of their ephemeral triumphs which will only have been more fatal to them.

LAW OF SUSPECT PERSONS

(September 17, 1793)

I. Immediately following the publication of this decree, all suspect persons who are found in the territory of the Republic, and who are still at liberty, will be arrested.

II. The following are considered suspect persons: (1) those who, either by their conduct, by their associates, by their discourse, or by their writings, reveal themselves to be partisans of tyranny and federalism, and enemies of liberty; (2) those who cannot justify, in the manner prescribed by the law of last March 21, their means of existence and the discharge of their civic duties; (3) those who have been denied a certificate of devotion to the Revolution; (4) public functionaries suspended or relieved of their assignments by the National Convention or its commissioners, and not reinstated, notably those who have been or are to be discharged pursuant to the law of last August 12; (5) those former nobles, together with their husbands, wives, fathers, mothers, sons or daughters, brothers or sisters, and agents of *émigrés* who have not consistently demonstrated their devotion to the revolution; (6) those who emigrated in the interval between July 1, 1789, and the publication of the law of April 8, 1792, even if they returned to France during the time set either by that law or earlier ones.

III. The committees of surveillance established according to the law of last March 21, or those which were substituted for them either by the orders of the people's representatives to the armies and the districts, or by virtue of particular decrees of the National Convention, will be responsible for drawing up, each in its own district, a list of suspect persons, for issuing arrest warrants against them, and for having seals affixed to their papers. The commanders of the public force to whom these warrants shall be remitted will be required to execute them immediately, under pain of dismissal.

IV. Committee members will not order the arrest of any individual unless at least seven members are present and an absolute majority consents.

V. Individuals arrested as suspects will first be conducted to prison for their detention; if prisons are not available, they will be guarded in their respective homes.

VI. By the following week they will be transferred to the national buildings which, immediately following the receipt of this decree, the district administrations will be required to designate and prepare for this purpose.

VII. The detained persons will take to these national buildings only those furnishings which are absolutely necessary. They will remain under guard until the peace.

VIII. The expenses of custody will be charged to the detained persons and divided equally among them. This custody will be entrusted preferably to fathers of families and parents of citizens who are or who will be sent to the frontiers. The salary of each guard will be fixed at the value of a day and a half of labor.

IX. The committees of surveillance will send without delay to the Committee of General Security of the National Convention a list of the persons arrested, the reasons for their arrest, and relevant papers seized.

X. If there is cause, the civil and criminal tribunals may keep under arrest as suspect persons, and may send to the houses of detention stated above, those accused of misdemeanors even though it has been declared that there is no cause for the accusation or that they have been acquitted of the charges against them.

DANTON'S DEFENSE BEFORE THE
REVOLUTIONARY TRIBUNAL

(April 2, 1794)

PRESIDENT OF THE REVOLUTIONARY TRIBUNAL   Danton, the National Convention accuses you of having favored Dumouriez, of having failed to make known what he was, of having shared in his liberty-killing projects such as making an army march on Paris in order to destroy the republican government and to reestablish royalty.

DANTON   My voice, which so many times has made itself heard in the cause of the people, in order to support and defend their interests, will not have any difficulty in repelling calumny. The cowards who have heaped calumny upon me, do they dare to attack me in person? If they would show themselves, I could cover them with the ignominy, with the opprobrium which is theirs. I have said it and I repeat it: *"my home will soon be in nothingness, and my name in the Pantheon!"* Here is my head: it will answer all your charges! Life is a burden to me. I long to be delivered of it!

PRESIDENT   Danton, audacity is the hallmark of guilt, and moderation that of innocence. No doubt defense is a legitimate right, but this defense should be bounded by decency and moderation, which respects everyone, even its accusers. You are prosecuted here by the highest of authorities; you must obey its decrees and should only concern yourself with your defense against the particulars in the accusation made against you. I request that you respond to the questions with precision, and especially that you limit yourself to the facts.

DANTON   Individual audacity should no doubt be reprimanded, and never could I be reproached for it; but national audacity, of which I have so many times given examples, through which I have served the public, this type of audacity is permissible, even necessary in revolution, and it is this audacity that I am proud to have. When I find myself so grievously, so unjustly accused, can I control the feelings of indignation which rise in me against my detractors? From a revolutionist like me, a strongly pronounced one like me, do you expect a cool response? Men of my temper are invaluable. On their foreheads the seal of liberty, the republican genius are printed in indelible markings; and it is I who am accused of having fawned at the feet of vile despots, of having always been against the party of liberty, of having conspired with Mirabeau and Dumouriez! And it is I who am summoned to answer to inevitable, inflexible justice! And you, Saint-Just, you will have to answer to posterity for the defamation flung against the people's best friend, against their most ardent defender! When I go over this list of horrors, I feel my entire existence tremble.

PRESIDENT   Marat was accused like you. He felt the necessity to justify himself; he fulfilled this duty as a good citizen, established his innocence in a respectable manner, and as a result was loved more by the people, whose interests he had not ceased to support. Marat was not indignant against his slanderers; he did not contrast probabilities or semblances to the facts; he categorically answered the accusation brought against him, applied himself to the demonstration of its falsity, and succeeded. I could not propose a better model for you; it is in your own interest to conform to it.

DANTON   I will stoop to justify myself. I will follow the defense plan adopted by Saint-Just. Me, sold out to Mirabeau, to Orleans, to Dumouriez! Me, a partisan of the royalists and royalty! Has it been forgotten that I was appointed an administrator in opposition to the wishes of all the counterrevolutionists, who detest me? Correspondence from me to Mirabeau! But everybody knows that I fought Mirabeau, that I opposed all his projects every time I believed them to be fatal to liberty. Did I remain silent about Mirabeau when I defended Marat, who was attacked by this haughty man? Did I not do more than can rightfully be expected from an ordinary citizen? Was I not present when efforts were made to remove the tyrant by dragging him to Saint-Cloud? Did I not proclaim in the Cordelier district the necessity of rebellion? I have abundant self-possession when I challenge my accusers, when I ask that I be measured against them. Let them be brought before me and I will plunge them back into the nothingness from which they should never have emerged! Appear, vile imposters, and I will tear away the mask which hides you from public revenge!

PRESIDENT   Danton, indecent outbursts against your accusers will not succeed in convincing the jury of your innocence. Speak in a language they can understand, but do not forget that your accusers enjoy public esteem, and have done nothing which warrants taking it way from them.

DANTON   An accused man like myself, who knows men and affairs, replies before the jury, but does not address himself to it. I do defend myself and I do not slander. Never has ambition or greed had any power over me; never have these passions made me compromise public affairs. For my country alone I have made the generous sacrifice of my existence. It is in this spirit that I fought the infamous Pastoret, Lafayette, Bailly, and all the conspirators who wanted to insinuate themselves into the most important posts in order to better and more easily assassinate liberty. I must speak of the three rascals whom Robespierre has lost. I have vital things to reveal; I ask that I be heard in peace, as the safety of the country requires it as much as a law would.

PRESIDENT The accused person's duty and his own personal interest require that he explain himself in a clear and precise manner on the facts with which he is charged; that he establish clearly his defense for each charge made against him; and it is only when he has convinced his judges that he is worthy of some faith that he may be permitted to make denunciations against men invested with public confidence. I therefore request that you confine yourself to your defense, and not bring in anything extraneous. It is the entire Convention which has accused you, and I do not believe that your scheme includes making some people doubt this. Though the Convention admits the basis of these suspicions toward some individuals, the group's collective accusation is in no way weakened by this.

DANTON I will return to my defense. It is notorious public knowledge that I was named to the Convention by a very small minority of good citizens, and that I am odious to the bad ones. When Mirabeau wished to depart for Marseille, I suspected his perfidious schemes. I unmasked them and forced him to remain at his post, and it is thus that he managed to catch me, to open my mouth or close it. It is a very strange thing that the National Convention's blindness has miraculously undergone a sudden illumination on this day of my reckoning!

PRESIDENT The irony to which you resort does not destroy the reproach that you covered yourself publicly with the mask of patriotism in order to deceive your colleagues and sacretly favor royalty. Nothing is more common than wit, word play by accused persons who feel themselves pressed and crushed by their own deeds but are unable to eradicate them.

DANTON I actually recall having provoked the reestablishment of royalty, the resurrection of all monarchic power, having protected the flight of the tyrant—while at the same time opposing with all my energy his voyage to Saint-Cloud, while covering his passage with pikes and bayonets, while chaining his fiery chargers, as it were. If this is to declare oneself a partisan of royalty, to show oneself its friend, if in these traits you can recognize a man who favors tyranny, then by this hypothesis I swear I have been guilty of these crimes. . . .

PRESIDENT   Did you not emigrate on July 17, 1789? Did you not spend time in England?

DANTON   My brothers-in-law went to that country on business, and I profited by the opportunity. Who can make a crime of that? At that time despotism was still fully preponderant; then it was not yet permissible even to whisper in secret about the rule of liberty. I therefore exiled myself, I banished myself, and I swore that I would return to France only when liberty was admissible there.

PRESIDENT   Marat, whom you pretend to have defended, did not conduct himself thus when it was a question of laying the foundations of liberty; when liberty was in her cradle, surrounded by the greatest danger, he did not hesitate to share it.

DANTON   And I, I recall that Marat went to England twice, and that Ducos and Fonfrede owed their safety to him. At the time when royal power was still most redoubtable, I proposed the law of Valerius Publicola, which permitted the killing of a man on your own responsibility, by placing your own head in danger. I denounced Louvet; I defended the popular societies at the risk of my life, and at a time when patriots were very few in number. The ex-minister Lebrun, while he was still chairman—I unmasked him. In open court, I demonstrated his complicity with Brisson. They accuse me of having withdrawn to Acis-sur-Aube, at the time when the day of August 10 was foreseen, when free men would fight slaves. To this charge I reply that at that time I declared that the French people would be victorious or I would die. I ask that the citizen Payne[1] be produced as a witness. I also said that I should have either laurels or death. Where are all these men who were needed to force Danton to appear on that day? Where are all these privileged beings from whom he borrowed energy? For two days the tribunal has known Danton: tomorrow he hopes to sleep in the bosom of glory. Never has he asked for mercy, and you will see him climb the scaffold with the customary serenity of a clear conscience.

[1] Thomas Paine, author of *Common Sense*.

Communist Revolution in the West

SAINT JOAN OF THE STOCKYARDS

According to Lenin, literature and the arts should serve communism. Artists themselves, he believed, should be members of the "politically-conscious vanguard of the entire working class" and their works infused with the spirit of the class struggle, the overthrow of capitalism, and the dictatorship of the proletariat. Claiming that Communist Party control of artistic activity did not limit the artist's freedom but rather freed him from the influences of capitalism and from "bourgeois-anarchist individualism," he argued that although everyone was free to write what he wished to write, the party was also free to dissociate itself from those writers who advocated what it considered anti-communist or anti-party views. He did not, however, indicate how such writers were to publish their works or have them performed in a communist country when the party withdrew its auspices and, with those auspices, its support in money, printing facilities, and theatres.

Lenin's doctrines of literature and art were the foundations of Socialist Realism, which became the official form of literature and criticism in Soviet Russia. Writing had to be realistic and historically concrete; it had to represent revolutionary development and contribute toward educating its audiences in the nature and spirit of socialism. Its themes, which had to be either the socialism that the communists were trying to build (the ideal) or the past from which it would come, were to be expressed in terms that worker-audiences could understand. In actuality, Socialist Realism meant conventional realistic drama with a communist message.

Brecht's theatrical practice, which is in many crucial respects unrealistic, is at odds with Soviet precepts.[1] Himself a Marxist playwright whose works are imbued with Marxism, Brecht believed his plays to be consonant with Socialist Realism, which he defines (in different

---

[1] For an example of Socialist Realism, see *The Long March*.

terms from those of the Russians) as the presentation of social reality from a socialist viewpoint by artistic means rather than its representation by photographic means, and the demonstration of its dialectical laws "in such a way as to promote insight into society's mechanisms and stimulate socialist impulses."

Brecht's plays, which he calls Epic Theatre, are revolutionary in both content and form. The major goals of Epic Theatre are to make the audience actively and critically analyze social behavior and the structure of society, and then act upon the basis of their new understanding. To dramatize a complex social picture, Brecht brings the narrative scope of epic poetry to drama. Employing realistic scenes beside symbolic scenes, serious exhortations beside parody, realistic dialogue, debate, oratory, narrative, direct address to the audience, choral speech, and songs, Brecht brings together multiple strands of action without regard to conventional crises and climaxes. He does not ask the audience to lose themselves in an illusion but rather actively to scrutinize, analyze, and draw conclusions from social phenomena placed on a stage. He tries to accomplish these goals by means of *Verfremdung*—alienation or detachment—which does not mean the removal of emotion but rather the prevention of the illusion of actuality and the avoidance of passive involvement so that the audience may be more critical. Brecht's variety of means helps promote alienation. By interrupting the flow of dramatic action with direct address, songs, placards, films, and the like, he jolts the audience just when it might be hypnotized by stage action. In such plays as *Saint Joan of the Stockyards*, direct address reminds the audience that the events they observe are not reality but are events placed upon a stage. Choral speech and song do not blend imperceptibly with spoken dialogue but, contrasting sharply with it, call attention to themselves as different theatrical modes. Scenery, too, helps promote alienation. With such resources as turntables, lighting boards, slides, and films, the Brechtian stage reveals a complex social environment. By placing realistic properties on what is obviously a stage floor it shows reality but prevents illusion.

Brecht's Marxist plays aim to promote socialist revolution by entertainingly educating their audience toward that end. Fundamentally, they fulfill Lenin's demand that literature and the arts be at the service of socialism, but whereas Lenin's program led to conventional, realistic drama, Brecht created a revolutionary theatrical form. Realistic in essence, it is unrealistic in appearance.

PARTY ORGANIZATION AND PARTY LITERATURE

V. I. Lenin

The new conditions for Social-Democratic work in Russia which have arisen since the October revolution[1] have brought the question of party literature to the fore. The distinction between the illegal and the legal press, that melancholy heritage of the epoch of feudal, autocratic Russia, is beginning to disappear. It is not yet dead, by a long way. The hypocritical government of our Prime Minister is still running amuck, so much so that *Izvestia Soveta Rabochikh Deputatov*[2] is printed "illegally"; but apart from bringing disgrace on the government, apart from striking further moral blows at it, nothing comes of the stupid attempts to "prohibit" that which the government is powerless to thwart.

So long as there was a distinction between the illegal and the legal press, the question of the party and non-party press was decided extremely simply and in an extremely false and abnormal way. The entire illegal press was a party press, being published by organisations and run by groups which in one way or another were linked with groups of practical party workers. The entire legal press was non-party—since parties were banned—but it "gravitated" towards one party or another. Unnatural alliances, strange "bed-fellows" and false cover-devices were inevitable. The forced reserve of those who wished to express party views merged with the immature thinking or mental cowardice of those who had not risen to these views and who were not, in effect, party people.

An accursed period of Aesopian language, literary bondage, slavish speech, and ideological serfdom! The proletariat has put an end to this foul atmosphere which stifled everything living and fresh in Russia. But so far the proletariate has won only half freedom for Russia.

The revolution is not yet completed. While tsarism is *no longer* strong enough to defeat the revolution, the revolution is *not yet* strong

---

[1] A general political strike in October, 1905. This compelled the czar to issue the Manifesto of October 17, 1905, which granted the people civil rights. The Bolsheviks made use of the new freedom of the press to publish their newspapers legally.

[2] *Bulletin of the Soviet of Workers' Deputies.*

From V. I. Lenin, *On Literature and Art* (Moscow: Progress Publishers, 1967). First published in *Novaya Zhizn (New Life)*, No. 12 (November 13, 1905).

enough to defeat tsarism. And we are living in times when everywhere and in everything there operates this unnatural combination of open, forthright, direct and consistent party spirit with an underground, covert, "diplomatic" and dodgy "legality". This unnatural combination makes itself felt even in our newspaper: for all Mr. Guchkov's[3] witticisms about Social-Democratic tyranny forbidding the publication of moderate liberal-bourgeois newspapers, the fact remains that *Proletary*,[4] the Central Organ of the Russian Social-Democratic Labour Party, still remains outside the locked doors of *autocratic*, police-ridden Russia.

Be that as it may, the half-way revolution compels all of us to set to work at once organising the whole thing on new lines. Today literature, even that published "legally", can be nine-tenths party literature. It must become party literature. In contradistinction to bourgeois customs, to the profit-making, commercialised bourgeois press, to bourgeois literary careerism and individualism, "aristocratic anarchism" and drive for profit, the socialist proletariat must put forward the principle of *party literature*, must develop this principle and put it into practice as fully and completely as possible.

What is this principle of party literature? It is not simply that, for the socialist proletariat, literature cannot be a means of enriching individuals or groups; it cannot, in fact, be an individual undertaking, independent of the common cause of the proletariat. Down with non-partisan writers! Down with literary supermen! Literature must become *part* of the common cause of the proletariat, "a cog and a screw" of one single great Social-Democratic mechanism set in motion by the entire politically-conscious vanguard of the entire working class. Literature must become a component of organised, planned and integrated Social-Democratic Party work.

"All comparisons are lame," says a German proverb. So is my comparison of literature with a cog, of a living movement with a mechanism. And I daresay there will ever be hysterical intellectuals to raise a howl about such a comparison, which degrades, deadens, "bureaucratises" the free battle of ideas, freedom of criticism, freedom of literary creation, etc., etc. Such outcries, in point of fact, would be nothing more than an expression of bourgeois-intellectual individualism. There is no question that literature is least of all subject to mechanical adjustment or levelling, to the rule of the majority over the minority. There is no question, either, that in this field greater scope must undoubtedly be allowed for personal initiative, individual inclination,

---

[3] Alexander Ivanovich Guchkov (1862–1936), Russian capitalist.

[4] *Proletarian*, an illegal Bolshevik weekly newspaper, published in Geneva from May 14 to November 12, 1905, under Lenin's editorship.

thought and fantasy, form and content. All this is undeniable; but all this simply shows that the literary side of the proletarian party cause cannot be mechanically identified with its other sides. This, however, does not in the least refute the proposition, alien and strange to the bourgeoisie and bourgeois democracy, that literature must by all means and necessarily become an element of Social-Democratic Party work, inseparably bound up with the other elements. Newspapers must become the organs of the various party organisations, and their writers must by all means become members of these organisations. Publishing and distributing centres, bookshops and reading-rooms, libraries and similar establishments—must all be under party control. The organised socialist proletariat must keep an eye on all this work, supervise it in its entirety, and, from beginning to end, without any exception, infuse into it the life-stream of the living proletarian cause, thereby cutting the ground from under the old, semi-Oblomov,[5] semi-shopkeeper Russian principle: the writer does the writing, the reader does the reading.

We are not suggesting, of course, that this transformation of literary work, which has been defiled by the Asiatic censorship and the European bourgeoisie, can be accomplished all at once. Far be it from us to advocate any kind of standardised system, or a solution by means of a few decrees. Cut-and-dried schemes are least of all applicable here. What is needed is that the whole of our Party, and the entire politically-conscious Social-Democratic proletariat throughout Russia, should become aware of this new problem, specify it clearly and everywhere set about solving it. Emerging from the captivity of the feudal censorship, we have no desire to become, and shall not become, prisoners of bourgeois-shopkeeper literary relations. We want to establish, and we shall establish, a free press, free not simply from the police, but also from capital, from careerism, and what is more, free from bourgeois-anarchist individualism.

These last words may sound paradoxical, or an affront to the reader. What! some intellectual, an ardent champion of liberty, may shout. What, you want to impose collective control on such a delicate, individual matter as literary work! You want workmen to decide questions of science, philosophy, or aesthetics by a majority of votes! You deny the absolute freedom of absolutely individual ideological work!

Calm yourself, gentlemen! First of all, we are discussing party literature and its subordination to party control. Everyone is free to write and say whatever he likes, without any restrictions. But every

---

[5] Chief character of a novel of the same name by I. A. Goncharov. Oblomov, who spends most of his life in his dressing gown, personifies apathy, lethargy, stagnation.

voluntary association (including the party) is also free to expel members who use the name of the party to advocate anti-party views. Freedom of speech and the press must be complete. But then freedom of association must be complete too. I am bound to accord you, in the name of free speech, the full right to shout, lie and write to your heart's content. But you are bound to grant me, in the name of freedom of association, the right to enter into, or withdraw from, association with people advocating this or that view. The party is a voluntary association, which would inevitably break up, first ideologically and then physically, if it did not cleanse itself of people advocating anti-party views. And to define the border-line between party and anti-party there is the party programme, the party's resolutions on tactics and its rules and, lastly, the entire experience of international Social-Democracy, the voluntary international associations of the proletariat, which has constantly brought into its parties individual elements and trends not fully consistent, not completely Marxist and not altogether correct and which, on the other hand, has constantly conducted periodical "cleansings" of its ranks. So it will be with us too, supporters of bourgeois "freedom of criticism", *within* the Party. We are now becoming a mass party all at once, changing abruptly to an open organisation, and it is inevitable that we shall be joined by many who are inconsistent (from the Marxist standpoint), perhaps we shall be joined even by some Christian elements, and even by some mystics. We have sound stomachs and we are rock-like Marxists. We shall digest those inconsistent elements. Freedom of thought and freedom of criticism within the Party will never make us forget about the freedom of organising people into those voluntary associations known as parties.

Secondly, we must say to you bourgeois individualists that your talk about absolute freedom is sheer hypocrisy. There can be no real and effective "freedom" in a society based on the power of money, in a society in which the masses of working people live in poverty and the handful of rich live like parasites. Are you free in relation to your bourgeois publisher, Mr. Writer, in relation to your bourgeois public, which demands that you provide it with pornography in novels and paintings, and prostitution as a "supplement" to "sacred" scenic art? This absolute freedom is a bourgeois or an anarchist phrase (since, as a world outlook, anarchism is bourgeois philosophy turned inside out). One cannot live in society and be free from society. The freedom of the bourgeois writer, artist or actress is simply masked (or hypocritically masked) dependence on the money-bag, on corruption, on prostitution.

And we socialists expose this hypocrisy and rip off the false labels, not in order to arrive at a non-class literature and art (that will be possible only in a socialist extra-class society), but to contrast this hypocritically free literature, which is in reality linked to the bourgeoisie, with a really free one that will be *openly* linked to the proletariat.

It will be a free literature, because the idea of socialism and sympathy with the working people, and not greed or careerism, will bring ever new forces to its ranks. It will be a free literature, because it will serve, not some satiated heroine, not the bored "upper ten thousand" suffering from fatty degeneration, but the millions and tens of millions of working people—the flower of the country, its strength and its future. It will be a free literature, enriching the last word in the revolutionary thought of mankind with the experience and living work of the socialist proletariat, bringing about permanent interaction between the experience of the past (scientific socialism, the completion of the development of socialism from its primitive, utopian forms) and the experience of the present (the present struggle of the worker comrades).

To work, then, comrades! We are faced with a new and difficult task. But it is a noble and grateful one—to organise a broad, multiform and varied literature inseparably linked with the Social-Democratic working-class movement. All Social-Democratic literature must become Party literature. Every newspaper, journal, publishing house, etc., must immediately set about reorganising its work, leading up to a situation in which it will, in one form or another, be integrated into one Party organisation or another. Only then will "Social-Democratic" literature really become worthy of that name, only then will it be able to fulfil its duty and, even within the framework of bourgeois society, break out of bourgeois slavery and merge with the movement of the really advanced and thoroughly revolutionary class.

ON EDUCATION AND THE ARTS

V. I. Lenin

It is necessary that a draft resolution (of the Proletcult[1] Congress) should be drawn up with the utmost urgency, and that it should be endorsed by the Central Committee, in time to have it put to the vote *at this very* session of the Proletcult. On behalf of the Central Committee it should be submitted not later than today, for endorsement both by the Collegium of the People's Commissariat of Education and by the Proletcult Congress, because the Congress is closing today.

Draft Resolution

1) All educational work in the Soviet Republic of workers and peasants, in the field of political education in general and in the field of art in particular, should be imbued with the spirit of the class struggle being waged by the proletariat for the successful achievement of the aims of its dictatorship, i.e., the overthrow of the bourgeoisie, the abolition of classes, and the elimination of all forms of exploitation of man by man.

2) Hence, the proletariat, both through its vanguard—the Communist Party—and through the many types of proletarian organisations in general, should display the utmost activity and play the leading part in all the work of public education.

3) All the experience of modern history and, particularly, the more than half-century-old revolutionary struggle of the proletariat of all countries since the appearance of the *Communist Manifesto* has unquestionably demonstrated that the Marxist world outlook is the only true expression of the interests, the viewpoint, and the culture of the revolutionary proletariat.

4) Marxism has won its historic significance as the ideology of the revolutionary proletariat because, far from rejecting the most valuable achievements of the bourgeois epoch, it has, on the contrary, assimilated and refashioned everything of value in the more than two thousand years of the development of human thought and culture. Only further work on this basis and in this direction, inspired by the prac-

---

[1] Proletarian Cultural Organization.

From V. I. Lenin, *On Literature and Art* (Moscow: Progress Publishers, 1967). Written on October 8, 1920.

tical experience of the proletarian dictoratorship as the final stage in the struggle against every form of exploitation, can be recognised as the development of a genuine proletarian culture.

5) Adhering unswervingly to this stand of principle, the All-Russia Proletcult Congress rejects in the most resolute manner, as theoretically unsound and practically harmful, all attempts to invent one's own particular brand of culture, to remain isolated in self-contained organisations, to draw a line dividing the field of work of the People's Commissariat of Education and the Proletcult, or to set up a Proletcult "autonomy" within establishments under the People's Commissariat of Education and so forth. On the contrary, the Congress enjoins all Proletcult organisations to fully consider themselves in duty bound to act as auxiliary bodies of the network of establishments under the People's Commissariat of Education, and to accomplish their tasks under the general guidance of the Soviet authorities (specifically, of the People's Commissariat of Education) and of the Russian Communist Party, as part of the tasks of the proletarian dictatorship.

THE MODERN THEATRE IS THE EPIC THEATRE

(Selection)

Bertolt Brecht

The modern theatre is the epic theatre. The following table shows certain changes of emphasis as between the dramatic and the epic theatre.[1]

DRAMATIC THEATRE	EPIC THEATRE
plot	*narrative*
implicates the spectator in a stage situation	*turns the spectator into an observer, but*
wears down his capacity for action	*arouses his capacity for action*
provides him with sensations	*forces him to take decisions*
experience	*picture of the world*
the spectator is involved in something	*he is made to face something*
suggestion	*argument*
instinctive feelings are preserved	*brought to the point of recognition*
the spectator is in the thick of it, shares the experience	*the spectator stands outside, studies*
the human being is taken for granted	*the human being is the object of the inquiry*
he is unalterable	*he is alterable and able to alter*
eyes on the finish	*eyes on the course*
one scene makes another	*each scene for itself*
growth	*montage*
linear development	*in curves*
evoutionary determinism	*jumps*
man as a fixed point	*man as a process*
thought determines being	*social being determines thought*
feeling	*reason*

[1] This table does not show absolute antitheses but mere shifts of accent. In a communication of fact, for instance, we may choose whether to stress the element of emotional suggestion or that of plain rational argument. [Translator's note.]

From *Brecht on Theatre*, translated by John Willett. Copyright © 1957, 1963, and 1964 by Suhrkamp Verlag, Frankfurt am Main. This translation and notes © 1964 by John Willett. Reprinted by permission of Hill & Wang, Inc. (American publishers of *Brecht on Theatre*) and Methuen & Co. Ltd. (British publishers). First published in *Versuche 2*, Berlin 1930.

When the epic theatre's methods begin to penetrate the opera the first result is a radical *separation of the elements*. The great struggle for supremacy between words, music and production—which always brings up the question 'which is the pretext for what?': is the music the pretext for the events on the stage, or are these the pretext for the music? etc.—can simply be by-passed by radically separating the elements. So long as the expression 'Gesamtkunstwerk' (or 'integrated work of art') means that the integration is a muddle, so long as the arts are supposed to be 'fused' together, the various elements will all be equally degraded, and each will act as a mere 'feed' to the rest. The process of fusion extends to the spectator, who gets thrown into the melting pot too and becomes a passive (suffering) part of the total work of art. Witchcraft of this sort must of course be fought against. Whatever is intended to produce hypnosis, is likely to induce sordid intoxication, or creates fog, has got to be given up.

Words, music and setting must become more independent of one another.

(a) Music

For the music, the change of emphasis proved to be as follows:

DRAMATIC OPERA	EPIC OPERA
The music dishes up	*The music communicates*
music which heightens the text	*music which sets forth the text*
music which proclaims the text	*music which takes the text for granted*
music which illustrates	*which takes up a position*
music which paints the psychological situation	*which gives the attitude*

Music plays the chief part in our thesis.[2]

(b) Text

We had to make something straightforward and instructive of our fun, if it was not to be irrational and nothing more. The form employed was that of the moral tableau. The tableau is performed by the char-

---

[2] The large number of craftsmen in the average opera orchestra allows of nothing but associative music (one barrage of sound breeding another); and so the orchestral apparatus needs to be cut down to thirty specialists or less. The singer becomes a reporter, whose private feelings must remain a private affair.   [Translator's note.]

acters in the play. The text had to be neither moralizing nor sentimental, but to put morals and sentimentality on view. Equally important was the spoken word and the written word (of the titles). Reading seems to encourage the audience to adopt the most natural attitude towards the work.

(c) Setting

Showing independent works of art as part of a theatrical performance is a new departure. Neher's projections adopt an attitude towards the events on the stage; as when the real glutton sits in front of the glutton whom Neher has drawn. In the same way the stage unreels the events that are fixed on the screen. These projections of Neher's are quite as much an independent component of the opera as are Weill's music and the text. They provide its visual aids.

THEATRE FOR PLEASURE OR
THEATRE FOR INSTRUCTION
(Selection)

Bertolt Brecht

Many people imagine that the term 'epic theatre' is self-contradictory, as the epic and dramatic ways of narrating a story are held, following Aristotle, to be basically distinct. The difference between the two forms was never thought simply to lie in the fact that the one is performed by living beings while the other operates via the written word; epic works such as those of Homer and the medieval singers were at the same time theatrical performances, while dramas like Goethe's *Faust* and Byron's *Manfred* are agreed to have been more effective as books. Thus even by Aristotle's definition the difference between the dramatic and epic forms was attributed to their different methods of construction, whose laws were dealt with by two different branches of aesthetics. The method of construction depended on the different way of presenting the work to the public, sometimes via the stage, sometimes through a book; and independently of that there was the 'dramatic element' in epic works and the 'epic element' in dramatic. The bourgeois novel in the last century developed much that was 'dramatic', by which was meant the strong centralization of the story, a momentum that drew the separate parts into a common relationship. A particular passion of utterance, a certain emphasis on the clash of forces are hallmarks of the 'dramatic'. The epic writer Döblin provided an excellent criterion when he said that with an epic work, as opposed to a dramatic, one can as it were take a pair of scissors and cut it into individual pieces, which remain fully capable of life.

This is no place to explain how the opposition of epic and dramatic lost its rigidity after having long been held to be irreconcilable. Let us just point out that the technical advances alone were enough to permit the stage to incorporate an element of narrative in its dramatic productions. The possibility of projections, the greater adaptability of

From *Brecht on Theatre*, translated by John Willett. Copyright © 1957, 1963, and 1964 by Suhrkamp Verlag, Frankfurt am Main. This translation and notes © 1964 by John Willett. Reprinted by permission of Hill & Wang, Inc. (American publishers of *Brecht on Theatre*) and Methuen & Co. Ltd. (British publishers). Unpublished during Brecht's lifetime, this essay may have been written in 1936 or perhaps earlier.

the stage due to mechanization, the film, all completed the theatre's equipment, and did so at a point where the most important transactions between people could no longer be shown simply by personifying the motive forces or subjecting the characters to invisible metaphysical powers.

To make these transactions intelligible the environment in which the people lived had to be brought to bear in a big and 'significant' way.

This environment had of course been shown in the existing drama, but only as seen from the central figure's point of view, and not as an independent element. It was defined by the hero's reactions to it. It was seen as a storm can be seen when one sees the ships on a sheet of water unfolding their sails, and the sails filling out. In the epic theatre it was to appear standing on its own.

The stage began to tell a story. The narrator was no longer missing, along with the fourth wall. Not only did the background adopt an attitude to the events on the stage—by big screens recalling other simultaneous events elsewhere, by projecting documents which confirmed or contradicted what the characters said, by concrete and intelligible figures to accompany abstract conversations, by figures and sentences to support mimed transactions whose sense was unclear—but the actors too refrained from going over wholly into their role, remaining detached from the character they were playing and clearly inviting criticism of him.

The spectator was no longer in any way allowed to submit to an experience uncritically (and without practical consequences) by means of simple empathy with the characters in a play. The production took the subject-matter and the incidents shown and put them through a process of alienation: the alienation that is necessary to all understanding. When something seems 'the most obvious thing in the world' it means that any attempt to understand the world has been given up .

What is 'natural' must have the force of what is startling. This is the only way to expose the laws of cause and effect. People's activity must simultaneously be so and be capable of being different.

It was all a great change.

The dramatic theatre's spectator says: Yes, I have felt like that too—Just like me—It's only natural—It'll never change—The sufferings of this man appal me, because they are inescapable—That's great art; it all seems the most obvious thing in the world—I weep when they weep, I laugh when they laugh.

The epic theatre's spectator says: I'd never have thought it— That's not the way—That's extraordinary, hardly believable—It's got to stop—The sufferings of this man appal me, because they are unnecessary—That's great art: nothing obvious in it—I laugh when they weep, I weep when they laugh.

The Instructive Theatre

The stage began to be instructive.

Oil, inflation, war, social struggles, the family, religion, wheat, the meat market, all became subjects for theatrical representation. Choruses enlightened the spectator about facts unknown to him. Films showed a montage of events from all over the world. Projections added statistical material. And as the 'background' came to the front of the stage so people's activity was subjected to criticism. Right and wrong courses of action were shown. People were shown who knew what they were doing, and others who did not. The theatre became an affair for philosophers, but only for such philosophers as wished not just to explain the world but also to change it. So we had philosophy, and we had instruction. And where was the amusement in all that? Were they sending us back to school, teaching us to read and write? Were we supposed to pass exams, work for diplomas?

Generally there is felt to be a very sharp distinction between learning and amusing oneself. The first may be useful, but only the second is pleasant. So we have to defend the epic theatre against the suspicion that it is a highly disagreeable, humourless, indeed strenuous affair.

Well: all that can be said is that the contrast between learning and amusing oneself is not laid down by divine rule; it is not one that has always been and must continue to be.

Undoubtedly there is much that is tedious about the kind of learning familiar to us from school, from our professional training, etc. But it must be remembered under what conditions and to what end that takes place.

It is really a commercial transaction. Knowledge is just a commodity. It is acquired in order to be resold. All those who have grown out of going to school have to do their learning virtually in secret, for anyone who admits that he still has something to learn devalues himself as a man whose knowledge is inadequate. Moreover the usefulness of learning is very much limited by factors outside the learner's control. There is unemployment, for instance, against which no knowledge can protect one. There is the division of labour, which makes generalized knowledge unnecessary and impossible. Learning is often among the concerns of those whom no amount of concern will get any forwarder. There is not much knowledge that leads to power, but plenty of knowledge to which only power can lead.

Learning has a very different function for different social strata. There are strata who cannot imagine any improvement in conditions: they find the conditions good enough for them. Whatever happens to oil they will benefit from it. And: they feel the years beginning to tell. There can't be all that many years more. What is the point of learning a lot now? They have said their final word: a grunt. But there are also strata 'waiting their turn' who are discontented with conditions, have a vast interest in the practical side of learning, want at all costs to find out where they stand, and know that they are lost without learning; these are the best and keenest learners. Similar differences apply to countries and peoples. Thus the pleasure of learning depends on all sorts of things; but none the less there is such a thing as pleasurable learning, cheerful and militant learning.

If there were not such amusement to be had from learning the theatre's whole structure would unfit it for teaching.

Theatre remains theatre even when it is instructive theatre, and in so far as it is good theatre it will amuse.

Theatre and Knowledge

But what has knowledge got to do with art? We know that knowledge can be amusing, but not everything that is amusing belongs in the theatre.

I have often been told, when pointing out the invaluable services that modern knowledge and science, if properly applied, can perform for art and specially for the theatre, that art and knowledge are two estimable but wholly distinct fields of human activity. This is a fearful truism, of course, and it is as well to agree quickly that, like most truisms, it is perfectly true. Art and science work in quite different ways: agreed. But, bad as it may sound, I have to admit that I cannot get along as an artist without the use of one or two sciences. This may well arouse serious doubts as to my artistic capacities. People are used to seeing poets as unique and slightly unnatural beings who reveal with a truly godlike assurance things that other people can only recognize after much sweat and toil. It is naturally distasteful to have to admit that one does not belong to this select band. All the same, it must be admitted. It must at the same time be made clear that the scientific occupations just confessed to are not pardonable side interests, pursued on days off after a good week's work. We all know how Goethe was interested in natural history, Schiller in history: as a kind of hobby, it is charitable to assume. I have no wish promptly to accuse these two of having needed these sciences for their poetic activity; I am not trying to shelter behind them; but I must say that I do need the sciences. I have to admit, however, that I look askance at all sorts of people who I know do not operate on the level of scientific understanding: that is to say, who sing as the birds sing, or as people imagine the birds to sing. I don't mean by that that I would reject a charming poem about the taste of fried fish or the delights of a boating party just because the writer had not studied gastronomy or navigation. But in my view the great and complicated things that go on in the world cannot be adequately recognized by people who do not use every possible aid to understanding.

Let us suppose that great passions or great events have to be shown which influence the fate of nations. The lust for power is nowadays held to be such a passion. Given that a poet 'feels' this lust and wants to have someone strive for power, how is he to show the exceedingly complicated machinery within which the struggle for power nowadays takes place? If his hero is a politician, how do politics work? If he is a business man, how does business work? And yet there are writers who find business and politics nothing like so passionately interesting as the individual's lust for power. How are they to acquire the necessary knowledge? They are scarcely likely to learn enough by going round and keeping their eyes open, though even then it is more than they would get by just rolling their eyes in an exalted frenzy. The foundation of a paper like the *Völkischer Beobachter* or a business like Standard Oil is a pretty complicated affair, and such things cannot be conveyed just like that. One important field for the playwright is psychology. It is taken for granted that a poet, if not an ordinary man, must be able without further instruction to discover the motives that lead a man to commit murder; he must be able to give a picture of a murderer's mental state 'from within himself'. It is taken for granted that one only has to look inside oneself in such a case; and then there's always one's imagination. . . . There are various reasons why I can no longer surrender to this agreeable hope of getting a result quite so simply. I can no longer find in myself all those motives which the press or scientific reports show to have been observed in people. Like the average judge when pronouncing sentence, I cannot without further ado conjure up an adequate picture of a murderer's mental state. Modern psychology, from psychoanalysis to behaviourism, acquaints me with facts that lead me to judge the case quite differently, especially if I bear in mind the findings of sociology and do not overlook economics and history. You will say: but that's getting complicated. I have to answer that it *is* complicated. Even if you let yourself be convinced, and agree with me that a large slice of literature is exceedingly primitive, you may still ask with profound concern: won't an evening in such a theatre be a most alarming affair? The answer to that is: no.

Whatever knowledge is embodied in a piece of poetic writing has to be wholly transmuted into poetry. Its utilization fulfils the very pleasure that the poetic element provokes. If it does not at the same time fulfil that which is fulfilled by the scientific element, none the less in an age of great discoveries and inventions one must have a certain inclination to penetrate deeper into things—a desire to make the world controllable—if one is to be sure of enjoying its poetry.

Is the Epic Theatre Some Kind of 'Moral Institution'?

According to Friedrich Schiller the theatre is supposed to be a moral institution. In making this demand it hardly occurred to Schiller that by moralizing from the stage he might drive the audience out of the theatre. Audiences had no objection to moralizing in his day. It was only later that Friedrich Nietzsche attacked him by blowing a moral trumpet. To Nietzsche any concern with morality was a depressing affair; to Schiller it seemed thoroughly enjoyable. He knew of nothing that could give greater amusement and satisfaction than the propagation of ideas. The bourgeoisie was setting about forming the ideas of the nation.

Putting one's house in order, patting oneself on the back, submitting one's account, is something highly agreeable. But describing the collapse of one's house, having pains in the back, paying one's account, is indeed a depressing affair, and that was how Friedrich Nietzsche saw things a century later. He was poorly disposed towards morality, and thus towards the previous Friedrich too.

The epic theatre was likewise often objected to as moralizing too much. Yet in the epic theatre moral arguments only took second place. Its aim was less to moralize than to observe. That is to say it observed, and then the thick end of the wedge followed: the story's moral. Of course we cannot pretend that we started our observations out of a pure passion for observing and without any more practical motive, only to be completely staggered by their results. Undoubtedly there were some painful discrepancies in our environment, circumstances that were barely tolerable, and this not merely on account of moral considerations. It is not only moral considerations that make hunger, cold and oppression hard to bear. Similarly the object of our inquiries was not just to arouse moral objections to such circumstances (even though they could easily be felt—though not by all the audience alike; such objections were seldom for instance felt by those who profited by the circumstances in question) but to discover means for their elimination. We were not in fact speaking in the name of morality but in that of the victims. These truly are two distinct matters, for the victims are often told that they ought to be contented with their lot, for moral reasons. Moralists of this sort see man as existing for morality, not morality for man. At least it should be possible to gather from the above to what degree and in what sense the epic theatre is a moral institution.

ON SOCIALIST REALISM

Bertolt Brecht

1. Socialist Realism means realistically reproducing men's life together by artistic means from a socialist point of view. It is reproduced in such a way as to promote insight into society's mechanisms and stimulate socialist impulses. In the case of Socialist Realism a large part of the pleasure which all art must provoke is pleasure at the possibility of society's mastering man's fate.

2. A Socialist Realist work of art lays bare the dialectical laws of movement of the social mechanism, whose revelation makes the mastering of man's fate easier. It provokes pleasure in their recognition and observation.

3. A Socialist Realist work of art shows characters and events as historical and alterable, and as contradictory. This entails a great change; a serious effort has to be made to find new means of representation.

4. A Socialist Realist work of art is based on a working-class viewpoint and appeals to all men of good will. It shows them the aims and outlook of the working class, which is trying to raise human productivity to an undreamt-of extent by transforming society and abolishing exploitation.

5. The Socialist Realist performance of old classical works is based on the view that mankind has preserved those works which gave artistic expression to advances towards a continually stronger, bolder and more delicate humanity. Such performance accordingly emphasizes those works' progressive ideas.

From *Brecht on Theatre*, translated by John Willett. Copyright © 1957, 1963, and 1964 by Suhrkamp Verlag, Frankfurt am Main. This translation and notes © 1964 by John Willett. Reprinted by permission of Hill & Wang, Inc. (American publishers of *Brecht on Theatre*) and Methuen & Co. Ltd. (British publishers). Unpublished during Brecht's lifetime, these five statements are from a note of September, 1954. The title is not Brecht's but the present editor's.

The Irish Revolution

THE PLOUGH AND THE STARS

For centuries before the Easter Rebellion of 1916, Ireland had been oppressed by English invaders. During the reign of Elizabeth I, for instance, the English devastated Ireland. Oliver Cromwell, sent by England's Puritan government in 1649 to crush an Irish Catholic revolt, massacred thousands of men, sent thousands of Irishwomen to Barbados and Jamaica as slaves, and confiscated thousands of acres of Irish land, with which he rewarded Englishmen.

One hundred and fifty years later, two Irish rebels tried by force of arms to free Ireland from English rule. Though they failed, their examples and their speeches at their trials inspired Irish rebels for more than a century. In 1798, Wolfe Tone, helped by the new French Republic, led the United Irishmen in an unsuccessful revolution against England. In 1803, Robert Emmet also led an unsuccessful revolt. Like Tone, he was captured and found guilty of treason.

Conditions in Ireland deteriorated during the nineteenth century. Though potato crops were destroyed by blight during the so-called Great Famine of 1845–48, Ireland had enough grain and cattle to feed its populace. But business was more compelling to landowners and capitalists, who exported these foods as over 700,000 died and more than 800,000 emigrated during these years. This decimation of Ireland's population continued: 8.3 million in 1845, 6.6 million in 1851, 4.4 million in 1911. In 1858, Irishmen in Ireland and Irish immigrants in the United States created a secret organization dedicated to national independence. Called the Irish Revolutionary Brotherhood (I.R.B.) in Ireland and the Fenian Brotherhood in the U.S., members of both were called Fenians, after the Fianna, the army of the legendary Irish hero Fionn mac Cumhaill (pronounced Finn MacCool). Though a Fenian rising of 1867 failed, the Fenians remained the major Irish revolutionary organization of the latter half of the nineteenth century. In 1905, Arthur Griffith founded Sinn Fein (pronounced Shin Fain, Gaelic for We Ourselves), which aimed for Irish independence and which soon became the popular name for all Irish nationalist groups.

Legal currents as well moved toward independence. After two Home Rule bills failed (1885 and 1893), a third passed the House of Commons in 1912 and was approved by the king in 1914. Because of the outbreak of World War I, however, Home Rule was suspended until hostilities ceased.

Less than a month after the start of World War I, the Supreme Council of the I.R.B. agreed that a rising should occur before the war's end. Two major bodies of troops, whose leaders were either members of the Council or were taken into its confidence, would participate: the Irish Volunteers, formed to defend home rule, and the Citizen Army, founded by the socialist leader James Connolly so that Dublin workers could protect themselves against the police, whom capitalists used as strikebreakers. Connolly agreed to hold his socialist goals in abeyance until after Ireland became independent.

Dramatized in *The Plough and the Stars*, the Easter Rising, also called the Easter Rebellion, the 1916 Rebellion, and Easter Week, began on Monday, April 24, 1916. It ended the following Saturday.

Initially, the rising was scheduled to begin on Easter Sunday, April 23. Arrangements were made for a boatload of German arms and ammunition. Then the rebel leaders changed the date of the rising to Monday, since most of the English officers in Dublin would probably attend the races that day. Unknown to the rebels, their message announcing the change of plan and ordering the arms-bearing ship, the *Aud*, not to arrive before Easter Sunday reached Berlin after the *Aud* had sailed. When she arrived, no one met her.

Eoin MacNeill, Chief of Staff of the Irish Volunteers, who regarded them as a defensive body, had for that reason not been privy to the rebels' plans. When finally he learned of them he issued a countermanding order, for he felt the plans could not succeed. The rebels then informed him of the expected German arms. Realizing how advanced the preparations were, MacNeill resigned, but when he learned that British warships had captured the *Aud* on Good Friday, he was convinced the rebellion was doomed, and to save Irish lives issued another countermanding order. When the I.R.B. Council decided to go ahead, confusion followed. Whereas the insurgents had hoped for a force of 3,000 in Dublin and more than double outside, only 1,200 men showed up in Dublin, a few hundred in the country (outside Dublin, the revolt quickly collapsed).

On Easter Monday, April 24, 1916, at noon, the rebels occupied Dublin's General Post Office, which became their headquarters. Padraic (Patrick) H. Pearse read and posted the proclamation of an Irish Republic, which had little effect on the general public, few of whom joined the insurgents. Instead, as O'Casey records in *The Plough and the Stars* and in the autobiographical novel *Drums Under the Windows*, the poverty-stricken Dubliners, taking advantage of the preoccupation of the Irish Constabulary, looted shops and pubs. On Tuesday, the British brought in artillery and reinforcements, which increased total Crown strength to almost five thousand. That day, a four-page paper, *Irish War News*, made its only appearance. In addition to an anti-English article, it featured announcements by Pearse that enemy casualties outnumbered rebel losses and that Dubliners were on the side of the Republic—inaccuracies which may have been designed for morale purposes and for propaganda (to win over uncommitted Dubliners). On Wednesday, British forces cordoned off the G. P. O. and other major rebel centers. The navy gunboat *Helga* moved up the River Liffey, which runs through Dublin, and shelled Liberty Hall (labor headquarters and home of the Citizen Army), incidentally wrecking the surrounding buildings, heavily populated tenements. On Friday, Major General Sir John G. Maxwell, new Commander-in-Chief of all British forces in Ireland, arrived in Dublin prepared to level the entire city. Heavy bombardment increased. In a communique from the G. P. O., which was beset by fire as well as shells and bullets, Pearse paid homage to the rebels, who "have during the last four days been writing with fire and steel the most glorious chapter in the later history of Ireland." On Saturday, the insurgents' position was impossible. They surrendered unconditionally.

According to Bernard Shaw, "dense ignorance and romantic folly . . . made those unfortunate Sinn Feiners mistake a piece of hopeless mischief for a patriotic stroke for freedom. . . ." Most Dubliners were unsympathetic to the rebels, whom they blamed for having caused the trouble. But with British reprisals, the tide of sympathy shifted. Secret military trials (averaging five minutes) sentenced ninety of the insurgents to death. Of these, fifteen were shot, including Connolly, who was so badly wounded and gangrenous that the firing squad first had to sit him up in a chair. The others' sentences were commuted to varying terms of imprisonment, including life. Within a few weeks, approximately 3,300 men and women (more than participated in the Dublin rising) were arrested; 160 were convicted, 1,862 interned without trial. As Shaw predicted, "It is absolutely impossible to slaughter a man in this position without making him a martyr and a hero, even though the day before he may have been only a minor poet.[1] . . . The shot Irishmen will now take their place beside Emmet. . . ." By their handling of victory, the English military radicalized the Irish people.

But it was a radicalization solely toward nationalism. The Dublin

---

[1] A reference to Padraic H. Pearse.

slums, Shaw accurately pointed out, killed more people each year than rebels and British combined. Regretting that they had not been entirely demolished, he announced with apparent callousness but with real compassion toward Dublin's tenement dwellers, "How I wish I had been in command of the British artillery on that fatal field! How I should have improved my native city!"

WOLFE TONE'S COURT MARTIAL

(1798)

WOLFE TONE I mean not to give the Court any useless trouble, and wish to spare them the idle task of examining witnesses. I admit all the facts alleged and only request leave to read an address, which I have prepared for this occasion.

COLONEL DALY I must warn the prisoner that in acknowledging those facts he admits to his prejudice that he has acted traitorously against his Majesty. Is such his intention?

TONE Stripping this charge of the technicality of its terms, it means, I presume, by the word "traitorously," that I have been found in arms against the soldiers of the King in my native country. I admit this accusation in its most extended sense and request again to explain to the Court the reasons and motives of my conduct.

[*The Court agreed to hear his address.*]

TONE Mr. President and Gentlemen of the Court Martial—I mean not to give you the trouble bringing judicial proof to convict me legally of having acted in hostility to the Government of his Britannic Majesty in Ireland. I admit the fact. From my earliest youth I have regarded the connection between Ireland and Great Britain as the curse of the Irish nation, and felt convinced that while it lasted this country could never be free or happy. My mind has been confirmed in this opinion by the experience of every succeeding year and the conclusions which I have drawn from every fact before my eyes. In consequence, I determined to employ all the powers which my individual efforts could move, in order to separate the two countries.

That Ireland was not able of herself to throw off the yoke, I knew. I therefore sought for aid wherever it was to be found. In honorable poverty I rejected offers which, to a man in my circumstances, might be considered highly advantageous. I remained faithful to what I thought the cause of my country, and sought in the French Republic an ally to rescue three millions of my countrymen from—

[*The Court interrupted the prisoner and remarked that his language was irrelevant to the charge.*]

GENERAL LOFTUS If you have anything to offer in defense or extenuation of that charge the Court will hear you, but they beg that you will confine yourself to that subject.

TONE   I shall, then, confine myself to some points relative to my connection with the French army. Attached to no party in the French Republic—without interest, without money, without intrigue—the openness and integrity of my views raised me to a high and confidential rank in its armies. I obtained the confidence of the Executive Directory, the approbation of my generals, and, I venture to add, the esteem and affection of my brave comrades. When I review these circumstances, I feel a secret and internal consolation which no reverse of fortune, no sentence in the power of this Court to inflict, can ever deprive me of or weaken in any degree. For that purpose I have encountered the chances of war amongst strangers. For that purpose I have repeatedly braved the terrors of the ocean, covered, as I knew it to be, with the triumphant fleets of that power which it was my glory and my duty to oppose. I have sacrificed all my views in life; I have courted poverty; I have left a beloved wife unprotected, and children whom I adored fatherless. After such sacrifices, in a cause which I have always conscientiously considered as the cause of justice and freedom, it is no great effort at this day to add, "the sacrifice of my life."

But I hear it said that this unfortunate country has been a prey to all sorts of horrors. I sincerely lament it. I beg, however, it may be remembered that I have been absent four years from Ireland. To me these sufferings can never be attributed. I designed by fair and open war to procure the separation of two countries. For open war I was prepared, but if instead of that a system of private assassination has taken place, I repeat, while I deplore it, it is not chargeable on me. Atrocities, it seems, have been committed on both sides. I do not less deplore them; I detest them from my heart; and to those who know my character and sentiments, I may safely appeal for the truth of this assertion. With them I need no justification.

In a cause like this, success is everything. Success, in the eyes of the vulgar, fixes its merits. Washington succeeded, and Kosciusko[1] failed.

After a combat nobly sustained, a combat which would have excited the respect and sympathy of a generous enemy, my fate was to become a prisoner. To the eternal disgrace of those who gave the order, I was brought hither in irons like a felon. I mention this for the sake of others. For me, I am indifferent to it. I am aware of the fate which awaits me, and scorn equally the tone of complaint and that of supplication.

---

[1] Tadeusz Kosciusko (1746–1817), Polish patriot who served as an officer in the United States Revolutionary Army.

As to the connection between this country and Great Britain, I repeat: all that has been imputed to me—words, writings, and actions—I here deliberately avow. I have spoken and acted with reflection and on principle, and am ready to meet the consequences. Whatever be the sentence of this Court, I am prepared for it. Its members will surely discharge their duty. I shall take care not to be wanting in mine.

[*The Court asked the prisoner whether he wished to make any further statement before it voted.*]

TONE   I wish to offer a few words relative to one single point, the mode of punishment. In France, our *émigrés*, who stand nearly in the same situation in which I now stand before you, are condemned to be shot. I ask that the Court should adjudge me the death of a soldier and let me be shot by a platoon of grenadiers. I request this indulgence rather in consideration of the uniform which I wear, the uniform of a *chef de brigade*[2] in the French army, than from any personal regard to myself.

[*The Court refused his request and sentenced him to be hanged.*]

[2] Colonel.

ROBERT EMMET'S SPEECH AT HIS
TRIAL FOR TREASON

(1803)

MY LORDS—What have I to say why sentence of death should not be pronounced on me, according to law? I have nothing to say that can alter your predetermination, nor that it will become me to say with any view to the mitigation of that sentence which you are here to pronounce, and I must abide by. But I have that to say which interests me more than life, and which you have labored (as was necessarily your office in the present circumstances of this oppressed country) to destroy. I have much to say why my reputation should be rescued from the load of false accusation and calumny which has been heaped upon it. I do not imagine that, seated where you are, your minds can be so free from impurity as to receive the least impression from what I am going to utter. I have no hopes that I can anchor my character in the breast of a court constituted and trammelled as this is. I only wish, and it is the utmost I expect, that your lordships may suffer it to float down your memories untainted by the foul breath of prejudice, until it finds some more hospitable harbor to shelter it from the storm by which it is at present buffeted. Was I only to suffer death after being adjudged guilty by your tribunal, I should bow in silence, and meet the fate that awaits me without a murmur: but the sentence of law which delivers my body to the executioner will, through the ministry of that law, labor in its own vindication, to consign my character to obloquy—for there must be guilt somewhere: whether in the sentence of the court or in the catastrophe, posterity must determine. A man in my situation, my lords, has not only to encounter the difficulties of fortune, and the force of power over minds which it has corrupted or subjugated, but the difficulties of established prejudice: the man dies, but his memory lives. That mine may not perish, that it may live in the respect of my countrymen, I seize upon this opportunity to vindicate myself from some of the charges alleged against me. When my spirit shall be wafted to a more friendly port; when my shade shall have joined the bands of those martyred heroes who have shed their blood

Irish Eloquence. The Speeches of the Celebrated Irish Orators Philips, Curran and Grattan. To Which Is Added the Powerful Appeal of Robert Emmet, at the Close of His Trial for High Treason. Philadelphia: Key, Mielke & Biddle, 1832.

on the scaffold and in the field, in defence of their country and of virtue, this is my hope; I wish that my memory and name may animate those who survive* me, while I look down with complacency on the destruction of that perfidious government which upholds its domination by blasphemy of the Most High, which displays its power over man as over the beasts of the forest, which sets man upon his brother, and lifts his hand in the name of God against the throat of his fellow who believes or doubts a little more or a little less than the government standard—a government which is steeled to barbarity by the cries of the orphans and the tears of the widows which it has made.

[*Here lord Norbury interrupted Mr. Emmet, saying, that the mean and wicked enthusiasts who felt as he did, were not equal to the accomplishment of their wild designs.*]

I appeal to the immaculate God—I swear by the throne of Heaven, before which I must shortly appear—by the blood of the murdered patriots who have gone before me—that my conduct has been through all this peril and all my purposes, governed only by the convictions which I have uttered, and by no other view, than that of their cure, and the emancipation of my country from the superinhuman oppression under which she has so long and too patiently travailed; and that I confidently and assuredly hope that, wild and chimerical as it may appear, there is still union and strength in Ireland to accomplish this noble enterprise. Of this I speak with the confidence of intimate knowledge, and with the consolation that appertains to that confidence. Think not, my lord, I say this for the petty gratification of giving you a transitory uneasiness; a man who never yet raised his voice to assert a lie will not hazard his character with posterity by asserting a falsehood on a subject so important to his country, and on an occasion like this. Yes, my lords, a man who does not wish to have his epitaph written until his country is liberated will not leave a weapon in the power of envy nor a pretence to impeach the probity which he means to preserve even in the grave to which tyranny consigns him.

[*Here he was again interrupted by the court.*]

Again I say that what I have spoken was not intended for your lordship, whose situation I commiserate rather than envy. My expressions were for my countrymen; if there is a true Irishman present, let my last words cheer him in the hour of his affliction—

[*Here he was again interrupted. Lord Norbury said he did not sit there to hear treason.*]

I have always understood it to be the duty of a judge when a prisoner has been convicted, to pronounce the sentence of the law; I have also understood that judges sometimes think it their duty to hear with patience, and to speak with humanity; to exhort the victim of the laws, and to offer with tender benignity his opinions of the motives by which he was actuated in the crime, of which he had been adjudged guilty. That a judge has thought it his duty so to have done, I have no doubt—but where is the boasted freedom of your institutions? Where is the vaunted impartiality, clemency, and mildness of your courts of justice if an unfortunate prisoner, whom your policy, and not pure justice, is about to deliever into the hands of the executioner, is not suffered to explain his motives sincerely and truly, and to vindicate the principles by which he was actuated?

My lords, it may be a part of the system of angry justice to bow a man's mind by humiliation to the purposed ignominy of the scaffold; but worse to me than the purposed shame, or the scaffold's terrors, would be the shame of such foul and unfounded imputations as have been laid against me in this court. You, my lord, are a judge, I am the supposed culprit; I am a man, you are a man also; by a revolution of power, we might change places, though we never could change characters. If I stand at the bar of this court, and dare not vindicate my character, what a farce is your justice? If I stand at this bar and dare not vindicate my character, how dare you calumniate it? Does the sentence of death which your unhallowed policy inflicts on my body also condemn my tongue to silence and my reputation to reproach? Your executioner may abridge the period of my existence; but while I exist, I shall not forbear to vindicate my character and motives from your aspersions; and as a man to whom fame is dearer than life, I will make the last use of that life in doing justice to that reputation which is to live after me, and which is the only legacy I can leave to those I honor and love, and for whom I am proud to perish. As men, my lord, we must appear at the great day at one common tribunal, and it will then remain for the searcher of all hearts to show a collective universe who was engaged in the most virtuous actions, or actuated by the purest motives—my country's oppressors or—

[*Here he was interrupted, and told to listen to the sentence of the law.*]

My Lord, will a dying man be denied the legal privilege of exculpating himself, in the eyes of the community, of an undeserved reproach thrown upon him during his trial, by charging him with ambition, and attempting to cast away, for a paltry consideration, the liberties of his country? Why did your lordship insult me? Or rather, why insult justice, in demanding of me why sentence of death should not be pronounced? I know, my lord, that form prescribes that you should ask the question; the form also presumes a right of answering. This no doubt may be dispensed with—and so might the whole ceremony of trial, since sentence was already pronounced at the castle, before your jury was empannelled; your lordships are but the priests of the oracle, and I submit; but I insist on the whole of the forms.

[*Here the Court desired him to proceed.*]

I am charged with being an emissary of France! An emissary of France! And for what end? It is alleged that I wished to sell the independence of my country! And for what end? Was this the object of my ambition? And is this the mode by which a tribunal of justice reconciles contradictions? No, I am no emissary; and my ambition was to hold a place among the deliverers of my country—not in power, nor in profit, but in the glory of the achievement! Sell my country's independence to France! And for what? Was it for a change of masters? No! But for ambition! O, my country, was it personal ambition that could influence me, had it been the soul of my actions, could I not by my education and fortune, by the rank and consideration of my family, have placed myself among the proudest of my oppressors? My country was my idol; to it I sacrificed every selfish, every endearing sentiment; and for it, I now offer up my life. O God! No, my lord; I acted as an Irishman, determined on delivering my country from the yoke of a foreign and unrelenting tyranny, and from the more galling yoke of a domestic faction, which is its joint partner and perpetrator in the parricide, for the ignominy of existing with an exterior of splendor and of conscious depravity. It was the wish of my heart to extricate my country from this doubly riveted despotism.

I wished to place her independence beyond the reach of any power on earth; I wished to exalt you to that proud station in the world.

Connexion with France was indeed intended, but only as far as mutual interest would sanction or require. Were they to assume any authority inconsistent with the purest independence, it would be the signal for their destruction. We sought aid, and we sought it, as we had assurances we should obtain it as auxiliaries in war—and allies in peace.

Were the French to come as invaders or enemies, uninvited by the wishes of the people, I should oppose them to the utmost of my strength. Yes, my countrymen, I should advise you to meet them on the beach with a sword in one hand, and a torch in the other; I would meet them with all the destructive fury of war; and I would animate my countrymen to immolate them in their boats before they had contaminated the soil of my country. If they succeeded in landing, and if forced to retire before superior discipline, I would dispute every inch of ground, burn every blade of grass, and the last intrenchment of liberty should be my grave. What I could not do myself, if I should fall, I should leave as a last charge to my countrymen to accomplish, because I should feel conscious that life, any more than death, is unprofitable, when a foreign nation holds my country in subjection.

But it was not as an enemy that the succors of France were to land; I looked indeed for the assistance of France; but I wished to prove to France, and to the world, that Irishmen deserved to be assisted! that they were indignant at slavery, and ready to assert the independence and liberty of their country!

I wished to procure for my country the guarantee which Washington procured for America. To procure an aid which by its example would be as important as its valor, disciplined, gallant, pregnant with science and experience; who would perceive the good, and polish the rough points of our character; they would come to us as strangers, and leave us as friends, after sharing in our perils and elevating our destiny. These were my objects: not to receive new task-masters, but to expel old tyrants; these were my views, and these only became Irishmen. It was for these ends I sought aid from France, because France, even as an enemy, could not be more implacable than the enemy already in the bosom of my country.

[*Here he was interrupted by the court.*]

I have been charged with that importance in the efforts to emancipate my country, as to be considered the keystone of the combination of Irishmen; or, as your lordship expressed it, "the life and blood of conspiracy." You do me honor overmuch. You have given to the subaltern all the credit of a superior. There are men engaged in this conspiracy who are not only superior to me, but even to your own conceptions of yourself, my lord; men, before the splendor of whose genius and virtues, I should bow with respectful deference, and who would think themselves dishonored to be called your friend—who would not disgrace themselves by shaking your bloodstained hand—

[*Here he was interrupted.*]

What, my lord, shall you tell me, on the passage to that scaffold, which that tyranny, of which you are only the intermediary executioner, has erected for my murder, that I am accountable for all the blood that has, and will be shed in this struggle of the oppressed against the oppressor? Shall you tell me this—and must I be so very a slave as not to repel it?

I do not fear to approach the omnipotent Judge, to answer for the conduct of my whole life; and am I to be appalled and falsified by a mere remnant of mortality here? By you too, who, if it were possible to collect all the innocent blood that you have shed in your unhallowed ministry, in one great reservoir, your lordship might swim in it.

[*Here the Judge interfered.*]

Let no man dare, when I am dead, to charge me with dishonor. Let no man attaint my memory by believing that I could have engaged in any cause but that of my country's liberty and independence, or that I could have become the pliant minion of power in the oppression or the miseries of my countrymen. The proclamation of the provisional government speaks for our views; no inference can be tortured from it to countenance barbarity or debasement at home, or subjection, humiliation, or treachery from abroad. I would not have submitted to a foreign oppressor, for the same reason that I would resist the foreign and domestic oppressor. In the dignity of freedom I would have fought upon the threshold of my country, and its enemy should enter only by passing over my lifeless corpse. Am I, who lived but for my country, and who have subjected myself to the dangers of the jealous and watchful oppressor, and the bondage of the grave, only to give my countrymen their rights, and my country her independence, and am I to be loaded with calumny, and not suffered to resent or repel it? No, God forbid!

If the spirits of the illustrious dead participate in the concerns and cares of those who are dear to them in this transitory life—O ever dear and venerated shade of my departed father, look down with scrutiny upon the conduct of your suffering son; and see if I have even for a moment deviated from those principles of morality and patriotism which it was your care to instil into my youthful mind and for which I am now to offer up my life.

My lords, you are impatient for the sacrifice. The blood which you seek is not congealed by the artificial terrors which surround your victim; it circulates warmly and unruffled, through the channels which God created for noble purposes, but which you are bent to destroy, for purposes so grievous, that they cry to heaven. Be yet patient! I have but a few words more to say. I am going to my cold and silent grave. My lamp of life is nearly extinguished. My race is run. The grave opens to receive me, and I sink into its bosom! I have but one request to ask at my departure from this world—it is the charity of its silence! Let no man write my epitaph: for as no man who knows my motives dare now vindicate them, let not prejudice or ignorance asperse them. Let them and me repose in obscurity and peace, and my tomb remain uninscribed, until other times, and other men, can do justice to my character. When my country takes her place among the nations of the earth, then, and not till then, let my epitaph be written. I have done.

DECLARATION OF THE IRISH REPUBLIC

(April 24, 1916)

POBLACHT NA H EIREANN[1]

THE PROVISIONAL GOVERNMENT

OF THE IRISH REPUBLIC

TO THE PEOPLE OF IRELAND

IRISHMEN AND IRISHWOMEN: In the name of God and of the dead generations from which she receives her old tradition of nationhood. Ireland, through us, summons her children to her flag and strikes for her freedom.

Having organised and trained her manhood through her secret revolutionary organisation, the Irish Republican Brotherhood, and through her open military organisations, the Irish Volunteers and the Irish Citizen Army, having patiently perfected her discipline, having resolutely waited for the right moment to reveal itself, she now seizes that moment, and, supported by her exiled children in America and by gallant allies in Europe, but relying in the first on her own strength, she strikes in full confidence of victory.

We declare the right of the people of Ireland to the ownership of Ireland, and to the unfettered control of Irish destinies, to be sovereign and indefeasible. The long usurpation of that right by a foreign people and government has not extinguished the right, nor can it ever be extinguished except by the destruction of the Irish people. In every generation the Irish people have asserted their right to national freedom and sovereignty; six times during the past three hundred years they have asserted it in arms. Standing on that fundamental right and again asserting it in arms in the face of the world, we hereby proclaim the Irish Republic as a Sovereign Independent State, and we pledge our lives of our comrades-in-arms to the cause of its freedom, of its welfare, and of its exaltation among the nations.

The Irish Republic is entitled to, and hereby claims, the allegiance of every Irishman and Irishwoman. The Republic guarantees religious and civil liberty, equal rights and equal opportunities to all its citizens, and declares its resolve to pursue the happiness and prosperity of the whole nation and of all its parts, cherishing all the children of the nation equally, and oblivious of the differences carefully fostered

[1] (Gaelic) Republic of Ireland.

84

by an alien government, which have divided a minority from the majority in the past.

Until our arms have brought the opportune moment for the establishment of a permanent National Government, representative of the whole people of Ireland and elected by the suffrages of all her men and women, the Provisional Government, hereby constituted, will administer the civil and military affairs of the Republic in trust for the people.

We place the cause of the Irish Republic under the protection of the Most High God, Whose blessing we invoke upon our arms, and we pray that no one who serves that cause will dishonour it by cowardice, inhumanity, or rapine. In this supreme hour the Irish nation must, by its valour and discipline and by the readiness of its children to sacrifice themselves for the common good, prove itself worthy of the august destiny to which it is called.

Signed on Behalf of the Provisional Government,
Thomas J. Clarke

Sean MacDiarmada	Thomas MacDonagh
P. H. Pearse	Eamonn Ceannt
James Connolly	Joseph Plunkett

IRISH WAR NEWS

Vol. I, No. 1.

Dublin, Tuesday, April 25, 1916

(Selections)

"If the Germans Conquered England"

In the London "New Statesman" for April 1st, an article is published—"If the Germans Conquered England"—which has the appearance of a very clever piece of satire written by an Irishman. The writer draws a picture of England under German rule, almost every detail of which exactly fits the case of Ireland at the present day. Some of the sentences are so exquisitely appropriate that it is impossible to believe that the writer had not Ireland in mind when he wrote them. For instance:

"England would be constantly irritated by the lofty moral utterances of German statesmen who would assert—quite sincerely, no doubt—that England was free, freer indeed than she had ever been before. Prussian freedom, they would explain, was the only real freedom, and therefore England was free. They would point to the flourishing railways and farms and colleges. They would possibly point to the contingent of M.P.'s,[1] which was permitted, in spite of its deplorable disorderliness, to sit in a permanent minority in the Reichstag. And not only would the Englishman have to listen to a constant flow of speeches of this sort, he would find a respectable official Press secretly bought over by the Government to say the same kind of things over and over, every day of the week. He would find, too, that his children were coming home from school with new ideas of history . . . They would ask him if it was true that until the Germans came England had been an unruly country, constantly engaged in civil war. . . . The object of every schoolbook would be to make the English child grow up in the notion that the history of his country was a thing to forget, and that the one bright spot in it was the fact that it had been conquered by cultured Germany."

"If there was a revolt, German statesmen would deliver grave speeches about 'disloyalty,' 'ingratitude,' 'reckless agitators who would ruin their country's prosperity.' . . . Prussian soldiers would be encamped in every barracks—the English conscripts having been sent out of the

---

[1] Members of Parliament.

country to be trained in Germany, or to fight the Chinese—in order to come to the aid of German morality, should English sedition come to blows with it."

"England would be exhorted to abandon her own genius in order to imitate the genius of her conquerors, to forget her own history for a larger history, to give up her own language for a 'universal' language—in other words, to destroy her household gods one by one, and put in their place alien gods. Such would be a nation of slaves, even though every slave in the country had a chicken in his pot and a golden dish to serve it on."

Put "Ireland" in the place of "England" in these extracts and "England" in the place of "Germany," and it will be admitted that the humiliating state of national subjection in which we live and the cunning methods of spiritual conquest practised on us by England have seldom been better described. If the article was not written by an Irishman in a bitterly satiric mood, it shows how well Englishmen understand how the treatment they have been accustomed to apply to other nations would feel, applied to themselves. But my own opinion certainly is that every sentence I have quoted stamps the article as the production of a very able Sinn Feiner.

STOP PRESS!
THE IRISH REPUBLIC

(Irish) "War News" is published today because a momentous thing has happened. The Irish Republic has been declared in Dublin, and a Provisional Government has been appointed to administer its affairs. The following have been named in the Provisional Government: Thomas J. Clarke, Sean MacDiarmada, P. H. Pearse, James Connolly, Thomas MacDonagh, Eamonn Ceannt, Joseph Plunkett.

The Irish Republic was proclaimed by a poster, which was prominently displayed in Dublin.

9:30 a.m. this morning the following statement was made by Commandant General, P. H. Pearse:

The Irish Republic was proclaimed in Dublin on Easter Monday, 24th April, at 12 noon. Simultaneously with the issue of the proclamation of the Provisional Government the Dublin Division of the Army of the Republic, including the Irish Volunteers, Citizen Army, Hibernian Rifles, and other bodies, occupied dominating points in the city. The G.P.O. was seized at 12 noon, the Castle was attacked at the same moment, and shortly afterwards the Four Courts were occupied. The Irish troops hold the City Hall and dominate the Castle. Attacks were immediately commenced by the British forces and were everywhere repulsed. At the moment of writing this report (9:30 a.m., Tuesday), the Republican forces hold all their positions and the British forces have nowhere broken through. There has been heavy and continuous fighting for nearly 24 hours, the casualties of the enemy being much more numerous than those on the Republican side. The Republican forces everywhere are fighting with splendid gallantry. The populace of Dublin are plainly with the Republic, and the officers and men are everywhere cheered as they march through the streets. The whole centre of the city is in the hands of the Republic, whose flag flies from the G.P.O.

Commandant General P. H. Pearse is commander in chief of the Army of the Republic and is President of the Provisional Government. Commandant General James Connolly is commanding the Dublin districts. Communication with the country is largely cut, but reports to hand show that the country is rising, and bodies of men from Kildare and Fingall have already reported in Dublin.

HOMAGE TO THE REBELS

Padraic H. Pearse

Headquarters. Army of the Irish Republic.
General Post Office

Dublin.
28th April 1916. 9:30, a.m.

The Forces of the Irish Republic, which was proclaimed in Dublin on Easter Monday, 24th April, have been in possession of the central part of the Capital, since 12 noon on that day. Up to yesterday afternoon, Headquarters was in touch with all the main outlying positions, and despite furious and almost continuous assaults by the British Forces all those positions were then still being held, and the Commandants in charge were confident of their ability to hold them for a long time.

During the course of yesterday afternoon and evening, the enemy succeeded in cutting our communications with our other positions in the City, and Headquarters is to-day isolated.

The enemy has burnt down whole blocks of houses, apparently with the object of giving themselves a clear field for the play of Artillery and Field guns against us. We have been bombarded during the evening and night by Shrapnel and Machine Gun fire, but without material damage to our position, which is of great strength.

We are busy completing arrangements for the final defence of Headquarters, and are determined to hold it while the buildings last.

I desire now, lest I may not have an opportunity later, to pay homage to the gallantry of the Soldiers of Irish Freedom who have during the last four days been writing with fire and steel the most glorious chapter in the later history of Ireland. Justice can never be done to their heroism, to their discipline, to their gay and unconquerable spirit in the midst of peril and death.

Let me, who have led them into this, speak, in my own, and in my fellow-Commanders' names, and in the name of Ireland present and to come, their praise, and ask those who come after them to remember them.

For four days they have fought and toiled, almost without cessation, almost without sleep; and in the intervals of fighting, they have sung songs of the freedom of Ireland. No man has complained, no man has asked "why?" Each individual has spent himself, happy to pour out his strength for Ireland and for freedom. If they do not win this fight, they will at least have deserved to win it. But win it they will, although they may win it in death. Already they have won a great thing. They have redeemed Dublin from many shames and made her name splendid among the names of Cities.

If I were to mention names of individuals, my list would be a long one.

I will name only that of Commandant General James Connolly, Commanding the Dublin division. He lies wounded, but is still the guiding brain of our resistance.

If we accomplish no more than we have accomplished, I am satisfied. I am satisfied that we have saved Ireland's honour. I am satisfied that we should have accomplished more, that we should have accomplished the task of enthroning, as well as proclaiming, the Irish Republic as a Sovereign State, had our arrangements for a simultaneous rising of the whole country, with a combined plan as sound as the Dublin plan has been proved to be, been allowed to go through on Easter Sunday. Of the fatal countermanding order which prevented those plans from being carried out, I shall not speak further. Both Eoin MacNeill and we have acted in the best interests of Ireland.

For my part, as to anything I have done in this, I am not afraid to face either the judgment of God, or the judgment of posterity.

> *(Signed) P. H. Pearse, Commandant General Commander in Chief the Army of the Irish Republic and President of the Provisional Government.*

THE AGREEMENT TO AN
UNCONDITIONAL SURRENDER

In order to prevent the further slaughter of Dublin citizens, and in the hope of saving the lives of our followers now surrounded and hopelessly outnumbered, the members of the Provisional Government present at Headquarters have agreed to an unconditional surrender, and the Commandants of the various districts in the City and Country will order their commands to lay down arms.

P. H. Pearse
29th April 1916
3.45 p.m.

DRUMS UNDER THE WINDOWS

(Selection)

Sean O'Casey

The Easter vigil was nearly over. Thousands were crumbling tobacco in the palms of their hands, preparing for the first smoke in seven long Lenten weeks of abstinence; the time had passed for forcing oneself (if you were lucky) to swallow sharply tasting potted herrings, leathery strips of salted ling, and tea without milk. Steak and onions, bacon and cabbage, with pig's cheek as a variation, would again glorify the white-scrubbed kitchen tables of Dublin workers. Dancing for the young; the rollicking call into Eden would again swing into life to the tune of *Hoosh the Cat from under the Table* or *Lift the Roof Higher*; older ones, thinking of their children, would be getting ready for a trip to Portmarnock's Velvet Strand, or Malahide's silver one; and those who weren't would be poring over the names of horses booked to run at Fairyhouse on Easter Monday. The danger aglow in an All-Ireland Parade of the Volunteers had passed. It had been whispered, only whispered, mind you, that it had been planned by a few of remember-for-ever boys to suddenly change the parade from a quiet walk into an armed revolt. A near thing. Only for God's gillie, Eoin Mac Neill, Chief of Stuff, and Bulmer Hobson, God's gillie's gillie, the Volunteer Sacredary, neither of whom had been told about the plan, but who caught the wisp of a whisper, the deadly dreama would have been on top of the people. But these two sent out couriers in trains, on horseback, on bicycles, in donkeycarts, and on roller-skates, running, galloping, and puffing all over the country, to countermind the whole thing, and so muted the silver trumpets that had lifted themselves up to call to the great race that was to come. So the country stretched itself before the fire, examined the form of the horses, filled its pipe, and watched the pig's cheek simmering on the fire for the morrow's dinner, thanking God that the long threatening hadn't come at last.

And on Easter Monday, off they went to the races, to their velvet strands, or got out their pretty frocks for the night dancing, all in a state of grace after the Easter devotions, full up of the blessed *joie deo feevre*; part of the country coming to the city to see the Museum, the Four Courts, the Custom House, and the Pro-Cathedral; while up one street Roger Casement, surrounded by armed detectives, was being taken to a boat chartered to land him at the nearest point to Tyburn; and down another street Bulmer Hobson, in the midst of armed I.R.B. men, was being taken to where he could do no good. All was quiet as a none breathless in madoration. Then down the centre of O'Connell Street, silent but for the tramp of their feet, came hundreds of armed Volunteers and Irish Citizen Army, led by Pearse, Connolly, and Tom Clarke, to halt, wheel, and face the General Post Office.

—There go the go-boys! muttered an old man, half to himself and half to an elderly, thin lady beside him who had stopped to help him stare at the Volunteers. Well, Mac Neill put a stop to their gallop! What th' hell are th' up to now? They seem to be bent on disturbin' th' whoremony of the sacred day. Goin' in, eh? Wha' for, I wondher? Can't be wantin' postage stamps. Can't be to get th' right time, for there's a clock in th' window. What'r they doin', ma'am? I dunno. Somethin' brewin'? Ma'am, there's always somethin' brewin'. I'm seventy, an' I've never known an hour that I didn't hear tell of somethin' brewin'. Be God, they're takin' th' clock outa th' window! That's odd, now. Looka, they're smashin' out th' windows with their rifles! There's a shower o' glass—right over th' passers-by! That's goin' beyond th' beyond. Tha's, tha's just hooliganism. We bether be gettin' outa here—th' police'll be here any minute! Didn' I tell you before, ma'am, I dunno! They're shovin' out the Post Office workers; pointin' their guns at them. We bether be gettin' outa here while we're safe. Houl' on a second—here's someone out to read a paper. What's he sayin'? I dunno. How th' hell can you expect a fella to hear from here? Oh! pushin' th' people off th' streets, now. Eh? G'on home, is it? An' who are you t'ordher me about? Takin' over th' city? D'ye tell me that? Well, you're not goin' to take over me! I'm a peaceful man out on a peaceful sthroll on a peaceful day, an' I stand be me constitutional rights. Gunfire here soon? Arrah, from where? From where, ma'am? I dunno, I'm tellin' you! He says he's speakin' in th' name of th' Irish Republic, so now you're as wise as I am meself. The police'll soon explain matthers. Don't be talkin', looka what's comin' up O'Connell Street! A company o' throttin' lancers —full regalia with carbines, lances, an' all! Comin' to clear th' Post Office. Don't be pushin' me ribs in, ma'am! Hear th' jingle of them! This looks like business. Here we see, ma'am, the Irish Republic endin' quicker'n it began. Jasus, Mary, an' Joseph! th' fools are firin' on them! Here, get outa th' way, ma'am, an' let a man move! Near knocked you down? Why th' hell are you clingin' on me tail for, then? Didn' I tell you hours ago that it was dangerous dawdlin' here? D'ye hear that volley! Looka th' police runnin' for their lives! Here, let's get outa this; we've dilly-dallied too long where we've no real business to be.

—Oh, looka them breakin' into the shops! Isn't that provokin', ma'am? After all, th' boys are out for somethin' higher. Looka this fella comin' along with a gramophone. Eh, sonny boy, where'd you get that? Didja hear that answer? Go an' find out! Uncivilised lot. Looka these comin' with a piano, no less! Didja here that? Give them a shove! Cheek, wha'? Look, they're bringin' out handcarts an' prams. A sad day for Dublin's fair name. What's that fella in beard an' knickerbockers doin'? Pastin' up bills. Willya read that—callin' on the citizens to do nothin' to dishonour the boys. Why doesn't he mind his own business? Sheehy-Skeffington? Never heard of him. One o' Ireland's noblest sons? Is it on for coddin' me y'are? If he was less noble an' less unselfish, I'd ha' heard a lot of him? Maybe; but he's not goin' to be let dictate to me. It's none o' his business if I want to rifle, rob, an' plundher. Looka! There he goes now, with two others, in a web o' soldiers! That doesn't look like he was noble. What was that, now, went whizzin' by me? A bullet? You're jokin'! I can tell them, if they harm me, there'll be more about it!

The tinkle of breaking glass wandered down the whole street, and people were pushing and pulling each other, till through broken windows all the treasures of India, Arabia, and Samarkand were open before them. Sean watched them as they pulled boxes down on top of themselves, flung clothing all over the place; tried to pull new garments over their old ones; while one woman, stripped naked, was trying on camisole after camisole, ending with calm touches that smoothed out the light-blue one that satisfied her at last. All who were underdressed before were overdressed now, and for the first time in their frosty lives the heat of good warm things encircled them.

He heard the humming zipzz of bullets flying a little way over-head, and guessed someone was firing to frighten the looters; so he dodged into the doorway of a shop to put a protection between him and them. A solidly built man came trotting along carrying a large jar by the handle against his right thigh, while from his left hung a pair of vividly yellow boots. A sharp ping sounded, and the jar separated into halves, letting a golden stream of liquor honour the road. The man stopped, and gazed at the jagged neck of the jar left in his hand.

—Jasus! he said, not a dhrop of it left—the wasteful bastards!

Sean squirmed round an angle of the doorway to get a look into the shop. Through the great jagged hole in the window he saw the inside was a litter of tossed clothing, caps, shoes, collars, and ties on which people were trampling, and over which they were jostling each other; ignoring the value of what lay on the floor or what was spread over the counter, for the hidden value of what lay neatly folded in the still unopened boxes. One man, alone, was rooting among a heap of caps on the floor, feverishly planting one after the other on his head, and flinging to the far end of the shop those which didn't seem to fit. Another, trying by main force to pull a delicate-looking pair of tweed trousers over a pair of big thick boots, was cursing loudly when he discovered they wouldn't go, and cursing louder still when he found he couldn't get them off again. A third was holding his old coat tightly between his legs while he excitedly thrust raggedly shirted arms through the sleeves of a brand-new one; while yet another was calling out that if anyone came across a seven-size in socks, they might let him know. And there, too, was the old man, leaning on the counter directing with his stick a younger man on a ladder, busy searching among the boxes on the higher shelves.

—What's in that one to your left? he shouted to the man on the ladder; to your left, man! Shirts? What kinda shirts? Ordinary cotton ones? Aw, don't waste time clawin' them things! They can be picked up anywhere. That box to your right—to your right! Good God, man! D'ye not know your right from your left? De Luxe written on them? Throw them down, thrown them down! Where'r you pushin', ma'am? This isn't a spring sale. You'll have to keep ordher if you want to do business here. Wha'? How th' hell do I know where to direct you to the ladies' department! One, two, three, four, five, six, an' one for Sunday—they'll be about enough for the time bein'. Have a look for a box marked pyjamas—I always had a notion of wantin' to feel how they felt on a fella. What's that? What do they want th' ambulance for? A woman's been shot? Wha', just outside? Who done it? A sniper, or somebody? God Almighty, where's our boasted law an' ordher!

Sean watched their wonderful activity, and couldn't desecrate their disorder with dishonour. All these are they who go to Mass every Sunday and holy day of obligation; whose noses are ground down by the clergy on the grindstone of eternal destiny; who go in mortal fear of the threat of a priest, he thought; but now he was glad to see they hadn't lost their taste for things material. In spite of the clergy's fifing and drumming about venial and mortal sin, they were stretching out their hands for food, for raiment, for colour, and for life. If the lilies of the field, that neither toiled nor spun, could be lovely, how much more that these whose lives were a ceaseless labour should be lovely too? The time would come when they would no longer need to take their kingdom of heaven by violence, for they would build it themselves, and warmth, adornment, and satisfaction in the midst of fair sounds and bright colours would be their own.

When the shooting seemed to have got less, Sean slid cautiously out of his shelter and, keeping close to the walls of shop and house, made his way home. Darkness had fallen, and his near-sighted eyes could see but a few feet in front of them. Coming to the bridge across the canal at Spencer Dock, his semi-consciousness heard a calm, tired voice say somewhere, Halt! Who goes there? A few steps farther, and the voice, tired no longer, terse and threatening, said again, Who goes there! In the hesitating shock of seeing nothing, he managed to say, Friend, and a moment after, passed by the dim form of a soldier with the rifle at the ready, who passed him by with the advice of, Answer quicker, next time, friend. A narrow squeak, that! A few seconds more of hesitation and he'd have been high among the stars. Watch your steps, Sean. A little farther on, his breast almost touched a bayonet as another voice said, Who goes there? Murmuring, Friend, the bayonet was lowered, and a soldier's voice said, Pass on, friend. They were dotted along the road up to the corner of the street that held his home. Pouring in by the North Wall, and no-one here to stop them. Poor ould Ireland!

He halted at the doorway thrust through with the knowledge that it was dangerous for him to be abroad at night. His eyes were blank in the darkness. He thought of the things that had happened, and wondered how it would all end. It was a deserted city now, but for those who fought each other. The pubs had emptied, the trams had jingled back to their sheds, the shops were shut. Lansdowne Road, Rathmines, and Rathgar gathered up their fine clothes and ran home; the janitors of the Bank of Ireland came rushing out to slam-to the great iron gates with a clang, turning the thick lips of the lock with hurried hands, and the sentries rushed into the guardroom; those coming home from Fairyhouse had been stopped by British barricades, and choruses of How th' hell am I goin' to get home ascended to God and His blessed saints. And Sean, standing in the doorway of his house, gazed back towards the centre of the city and saw a great plume of flame rising high into the sky: the first passion-flower had blossomed.

The next day, early, not allowed to cross the canal, Sean took a longer back way over the railways, and got to the nearer fringe of the city where talk was furious, and wild guesses were made of what was happening.

—Th' attack on the Castle's failed, and Sean Connolly, the modest and noble, had died murmuring that he died for Ireland. And you can't even climb through O'Connell Street, the dead are piled that high in it. An' th' Sinn Feiners have taken th' Bank of Ireland!

—What!

—Occupied it; overpowered the senthries, shot them before, shot them behind, and flung their riddled bodies at the foot of King Billy's statue.

—No? God, what're we comin' to! With th' Bank of Ireland gone, we'll all be ruined. How're we goin' to get our old-age pensions; an' ring-papers won't be worth a damn!

—An'—listen, man alive—an', an' th' figures of Liberty, Fortitude, an' Justice that stood on th' top of the ayste side of the Bank is sthrewn over th' wide world. Smithereens they are now; rubble; dust.

—No! An' th' others, Hibernia, Fidelity, an' somthin'—what happened to them?

—Them! Aw, them was took down an' brought in for safety till betther times came. Just in time.

—But wait till I tell yous: a fella standin' on the Park Magazine Hill says he could see plain an army of Germans marchin' forward dead on th' horizon. No I don't mean frontier—I said horizon. Which horizon? Dtch dtch! There's only one horizon, man, an' it's th' place where th' sky an' earth meet together. You hope it's thrue? Well, I don't; it's bad enough now between our own and the English; but what would it be between the three of them? Only the lark in the clear air 'ud be safe then, an' he'd have to fly higher than usual.

Sean was behind his mother when she gawked out of the window in the back room, seeking to see something of what was happening.

—There's some soldiers in th' church tower, she said, the last word blending with a crackling roar, while the two of them staggered about the room, choked and blinded from a cloud of powdered mortar thick as a white thundercloud.

—I'm shot, Jack, she whimpered; but feeling her all over, he found she wasn't; and he hurried her into the other room where she lay down, panting, on the old horsehair sofa. He gave her a drink of water, then coaxed her down to a neighbour below who set about making a cup of tea for her. As he was going back to see what had happened, a number of soldiers, in charge of an officer and sergeant, came in and went upstairs with him, leaving two men to guard the outside door. The officer stood beside Sean, a revolver in his hand, while the sergeant searched the back room. After some time, the sergeant came out and whispered to the officer.

—Come downstairs with me, said the officer to Sean.

They placed him stiff against the wall of the house, outside, while the sergeant searched him, taking off his old boots to have a look inside, a soldier kneeling on one knee before him, butt of rifle to the knee, the bayonet but a foot away from Sean's chest. They were searching for an automatic, they told him, and he wondered how one could fit into either of his boots. A violent explosion in the waste land beyond the wall bordering the railway sent a storm of stones, tufts of grass, and bunches of poppies skyhigh, showers of them falling around

Sean and his searchers. Another, and then, a second later, a vicious ping on the wall beside him, sent Sean word that some sniper was having a shot at the soldiers around him. The officer slid down the street into a shop, and the soldiers, bending low, followed him, leaving Sean stretched out against the wall, alone, watched by neighbours who were peeping from their doorways in the houses lower down the street. He took his outstretched arms from the wall, turned in, and mounted the stairs to his home. While by the wall, he had felt that his end was near, and had had a stiff time trying to hold on to his pride and dignity. Now he was shaking, and tense with fright. Either the badly aimed shells fired from the gunboat *Helga* or the sniper's bullet may have saved his life. For a long time he had tried to keep out of danger, and as often had found himself in the thick of it. Three times, at work, he had had narrow escapes: once when a bucket had been whipped from a swinging hand by a train passing by at fifty miles an hour; once when a scaffold had collapsed, and he had come down with it, escaping with a bad shock and many sore bruises; and once on a high roof, cleaning glass, a fellow-worker in a hurry to show the foreman how alert he was, stepped on a plank, leading over the glass before him; the plank had snapped, the glass had given way, and the poor devil had fallen forty or fifty feet, to be smashed to pieces on a concrete floor below. And today, he and his mother had had a stream of machine-gun bullets sweeping between their two heads, making a hash of the wall behind them. How often during the riots of drunken policemen had he escaped a batoning? More often than he wished to remember. He didn't like this sort of thing at all. As he grew in grace and wisdom, he was growing less and less of a hero. Like the fine and upright Alderman Tom Kelly, he wanted to die in bed surrounded by medicine bottles.

Good God! looka th' mess the back room was in! The one old palliasse they had had been ripped open with a bayonet, and the dirty feathers had been scattered about. Their one mattress, too, had been torn the same way, and the straw, mixed with the feathers, littered the floor. And all this on top of his aching, trembling legs, and oozing neck. Had he been made of less sterner stuff, he'd have sat on the edge of the ruined bed to weep. But he must sway his thoughts away from an inclination to tears to hard resistance, and an icy acceptance of what was beyond his power to avoid.

He lighted some sticks, put some water into a small saucepan, and made himself a cup of tea. In the old dresser he found a small lump of a loaf, and cut himself a slice; no more, for the neighbours might send back his mother any minute and she'd need her share. But he ate all the bread there, for he wanted all he could get to modify with new strength the energy lost through his oozing neck, his aching legs, and troubled mind. He was sipping the tea when in came a sergeant and two Tommies, and his heart sank again.

—'Ere, you, said the sergeant, motioning towards the Tommies, go with 'em; the church; 'urry! Why? Never mind the why. They 'as their orders—that's enough for you.

—Whose orders—the Lord Lieutenant's?

—Naw! Company officer's. 'Urry!

Sean sighed, and slipped a volume of Keats into a pocket, put on his cap, and went with them to the church. In the porch a young officer sat by a small table, a notebook before him, pencil in hand. Name? Address? Age? Occupation? Sean saw the officer bend a searching look at him when he said, Unemployed. Another search. What's this, eh? Oh, a book! Poetry—harmless enough. Why don't you join the army? No interest in armies—not even the Salvation Army. Civil answers, my man, will serve you better. Into the church with him.

Soldiers were asleep, asprawl, in the baptistery; others snored lying on the tiles of the chancel; and an armed sentry stood at the east end and west end of the church. Piles of haversacks, belts, boots, and rifles were heaped on, and around, the Communion Table. But two other prisoners were there, each widely separated from the other. It was strange to be this way in a church where he had so often sat as a worshipper, in which he found his first genuine, educated friend— the Rector. How angry he would be if he knew the soldiers were making themselves at home in the House of God! Do This in Remembrance Of Me were the words forming a semicircle above the Holy Table.

That whole evening, and throughout the night, he sat wearily on the hard bench, finding out that things even of beauty weren't joys for ever. He could but give now the faint smile like a star shining through autumn mists. It was a wry smile, but it wasn't a tear. Even here, even now, even so, perhaps he was one with those

> *Who love their fellows even to the death,*
> *Who feel the giant agony of the world,*
> *And more, like slaves to poor humanity,*
> *Labour for mortal good.*

The deadly whiteness of the lilies was here upon him; but not the deadly whiteness of the snow: not yet, though sunken from the healthy breath of morn, and far from the fiery noon and eve's one star.

He had to put every thought of anxiety about his mother away from him. Sit here; say nothing—that was all he could do. What use would he be at home, anyway? We were all helled by the enemy. The neighbours would keep her on her feet till he came back, and they took counsel together. In spite of his pride, his bowels yearned for a share of the Maconochie stew some of the soldiers were eating.

The next evening, all the lusty men of the locality were marshalled, about a hundred of them, Sean joining in, and were marched under guard (anyone trying to bolt was to be shot dead) down a desolate road to a great granary. Into the dreary building they filed, one by one; up a long flight of dark stone steps, to a narrow doorway, where each, as he came forward, was told to jump through into the darkness and take a chance of what was at the bottom. Sean dropped through, finding that he landed many feet below on a great heap of maize that sent up a cloud of fine dust, near choking him. When his eyes got accustomed to it, he saw a narrow beam of light trickling in through some badly-shuttered windows, and realised he was in a huge grain store, the maize never less than five feet deep so that it was a burden to walk from one spot to another, for each leg sank down to the thigh, and had to be dragged up before another step could be taken. It took him a long time to get to a window, and crouch there, watching the sky over the city through a crack in the shutters. A burning molten glow shone in the sky beyond, and it looked as if the whole city was blazing. One ear caught the talk of a group of men near by who were playing cards. He couldn't read Keats here, for the light was too bad for his eyes. More light, were the last words of Goethe, and it looked as if they would be his last words too.

—I dunno how it'll end, said one of the card-players; the German submarines are sweepin' up th' Liffey like salmon, an' when they let loose it's goodbye England. My thrick, there, eh!

—I heard, said another player, that th' Dublin Mountains is black with them—coal-scuttle helmets an' all—Your deal, Ned.

—Th' Sinn Feiners has taken to an unknown destination that fella who ordhered the Volunteers in th' counthry to stay incognito wherever they were—what's his name? Oh, I've said it a hundherd times. What's this it is?

—Is it Father O'Flynn? asked a mocking voice in a corner.

—No mockery, Skinner Doyle; this isn't a time for jokin'. Eh, houl' on there—see th' ace o' hearts!

Then they heard them, and all the heads turned to where Sean was crouching at the window; for in the fussy brattle of ceaseless musketry fire, all now listened to the slow, dignified, deadly boom of the big guns.

—Christ help them now! said Skinner Doyle.

Next day, he heard his name called from the hole at the end

of the store where the sentry stood. Wading through the corn, he was told to leap up, and leaping, was caught by a corporal who helped him to scramble to the floor above. He was to go home for a meal, accompanied by a soldier, for while the rest were permitted to disperse home for an hour, they were suspicious of him because his room was the one that received the fire from those searching out a sniper. He was covered with the dust of the corn, and though he had pulled up the collar of his coat to protect the wound in his neck, he felt the dust of the grain tearing against its rawness, and felt anxious about it. But he had to be patient, so he trudged home, silent, by the side of the soldier. When he sat down, and, in reply to the soldier's question, said there was nothing in the house with which to make a meal,

—Wot, nothink? asked the soldier, shocked. Isn't there somewheres as you can get some grub?

—Yes, said Sean; a huckster's round the corner, but I've no money to pay for it.

—'E'll give it, 'e'll 'ave to; you come with me, said the Tommy; Gawd blimey, a man 'as to eat!

So round to Murphy's went the Saxon and the Gael, for food. Murphy was a man who, by paying a hundred pounds for a dispensation, had married his dead wife's sister, so that the property might be kept in the family; and Sean thought how much comfort and security for a long time such a sum would bring to his mother and to him. The soldier's sharp request to give this prisoner feller some grub got Sean a loaf, tea and sugar, milk in a bottle, rashers, and a pound of bully beef. On the way back, Sean got his mother, and they had a royal meal, the soldier joining them in a cup of scald.

In the sky the flames were soaring higher, till the heavens looked like a great ruby hanging from God's ear. It was tingeing the buildings with a scarlet glow, while the saints stretched their ears to catch the tenour of the Irish prayers going up, for each paternoster and Ave Maria mingled with the biting snarl from the Howth guns, and the answering roar from Saxon rifle, machine-gun, and cannon, that were weaving a closer cordon of fire round the Sinn Feiners, the fire creeping towards the group of innocents blessed with arms in their hands for the first time. Now it was above them, licking away the roof from over their heads, and they were too weary to go on trying to put it out. Their haggard faces were chipped into bleeding jaggedness by splinters flying from shattered stones and brick; the wounded were in a corner making their moan to themselves, while a few men and women were risking their lives to get the seriously hurt away to some hospital, wending through falling walls, fire and brimstone, and gauntlets of burning buildings. The grey-green Volunteer uniform now no longer looked neat; they were ragged, and powdered thick with the pulverised mortar clouding from the walls. The fighters now looked like automatons moving unsteadily about, encased tightly in a fog of dust and acrid ashes. They were silent, unshaven, maybe muttering an act of contrition for things done before they went to war; wan-eyed, they persuaded their drooping lids to lift again, for drowsiness might mean a sudden and silent death to them. Those handiest with a rifle kept firing into the flames coming closer; a few, hoarse and parched, still tried to control the flames with tiny buckets of water, their leaders, before a wall of flame, standing dignified among them, already garlanded for death; gay outwardly, and satisfied, their inner wakefulness wondering how they'd fare when the world faded. They had helped God to rouse up Ireland: let the whole people answer for them now! For them now, tired and worn, there was but a long, long sleep; a thin ribbon of flame from a line of levelled muskets, and then a long sleep. For evermore, Ireland's Easter lilies would have a crimson streak through them.

The thyme had turned to rue. And through the ring of fire and smoke, passing by the flying bullets, went the brown-robed Capuchins, bending over the wounded, unable to do much, but standing by their people and the danger. Father Aloysius, with a white apron on a broom-stick, hurries to the British barricade to ask for a surgeon, but an elegant Colonel Taylor turns his back on him and leaves him there alone with the Tommies and with God; and later on an equally elegant Captain does all a man can do to help the minister with humane thoughts and a courteous address. And Cathleen ni Houlihan,[1] in her bare feet, is singing for her pride that had almost gone is come back again. In tattered gown, and hair uncombed, she sings, shaking the ashes from her hair, and smoothing out the bigger creases in her dress; she is

> *Singing of men that in battle array,*
> *Ready in heart and ready in hand,*
> *March with banner and bugle and fife*
> *To the death, for their native land.*

A rare time for death in Ireland; and in the battle's prologue many a common man, woman, and child had said goodbye to work and love and play; and many more in an hour or so would receive a terse message that life no longer needed them. There they are, lying so quiet—a child surprised in the doorway; an old man stretched in the street; a young man near a lamp-post which he had clutched when the bullet struck him, and down which he had slid when he died,

[1] Personification of Ireland.

his curiously white face containing wide eyes staring upwards, as if asking the sky why this had happened, a stiff arm still half-encircling the lamp standard; a young lassie in holiday attire, lying on her face, maybe hurrying home when she heard the uproar, but going too slow, for on the brilliant white blouse a purple patch of death was spreading over the middle of the back; an old woman on the floor of her tenement room, alone, her blood seeping through the ceiling below; all of the goodly company of the dead who died for Ireland. Jesu, have pity! Quiet, comrades, quiet. It was necessary that you should die for Ireland, too. You didn't want to die. I know, I know. You signed no proclamation; you invaded no building; you pulled no trigger; I know, I know. But Ireland needed you all the same. Many will die like that before Ireland can go free. They must put up with it. You will be unknown for ever; you died without a word of praise; you will be buried without even a shadowy ceremony; no bugle will call your name; no gunshot will let loose brave echoes over your grave; you will not be numbered among the accepted slain. But listen, comrades, listen: Whitman will be there to meet you; he will marshal you into the march-past with the greater dead; on the cornet he will give you a shrill salute. Listen—there it goes! Forward! March!

Here comes Padruig[2] Pearse down the silent street, two elegant British officers waiting for him. He comes steadily, in no hurry; unafraid, to where two elegant British officers are waiting to meet him. His men have been beaten; the cordon of flame has burnt out their last fading hope. *The struggle is over; our boys are defeated; and Ireland's surrounded with silence and gloom:* the old ballad is singing in his ears. He wears a topcoat, for the Easter sun has gone west, and a nipping breeze blows. It is the wind of death blowing keenly on his brave man's pure face. His eyes droop, for he hasn't slept for days. He has lain down, but not to sleep. Soon he will sleep long and well. He feels this is no defeat; that to stand up in an armed fight against subjection is a victory for Ireland. So he stands silently, and listens to the elegant British officer demanding unconditional surrender. The fools, the fools! So he agrees, and hands over his sword; bows, and returns to marshal his men for a general surrender. Soon Whitman will be shaking his hand, and reciting,

> *Vivas to those who have failed!*
> *And to all generals who lost engagements, and all overcome heroes!*
> *And the numberless unknown heroes equal to the greatest heroes known!*

[2] A variant spelling of Padraic (Gaelic for Patrick).

The sky had gone black and the rain was falling; cold rain, with the sting of vanishing winter in it. Along the silent, empty street small groups of men come marching. They are tired, tattered, and sleepy, hungry shadows of the neat, trim, and steady Volunteers who had marched the opposite way a week ago. Crowds behind the soldiers cheered when they saw the proud but woebegone men come marching through the blackened lanes of smouldering buildings. They marched silent; no whistle or lilt came from any parched lip or dry throat: the time was past for song. The hot, bitter vapour from charred wood, leather, and cloth seared their nostrils; and cinders, smoking red in the centre, strewing the street, crunched under their passing feet. Down they came, covered with hundreds of rifles, with machine-guns trained on them, thousands of soldiers staring at them piling their poor arms in a heap; the Tommies wondering and bewildered that such a pitiable pile of metal should try to overthrow the might and power of England's armed forces.

NEGLECTED MORALS OF THE IRISH RISING

(Selections)

Bernard Shaw

It is greatly to be regretted that so very little of Dublin has been demolished. The General Post Office was a monument, fortunately not imperishable, of how extremely dull eighteenth-century pseudo-classic architecture can be. Its demolition does not matter. What does matter is that all the Liffey slums have not been demolished. Their death and disease rates have every year provided waste, destruction, crime, drink, and avoidable homicide on a scale which makes the fusillades of the Sinn Feiners and the looting of their camp-followers hardly worth turning the head to notice. It was from these slums that the auxiliaries poured forth for whose thefts and outrages the Volunteers will be held responsible, though their guilt lies at all our doors. Let us grieve, not over the fragment of Dublin city that is knocked down, but over at least three-quarters of what has been preserved. How I wish I had been in command of the British artillery on that fatal field! How I should have improved my native city!

. . . .

Whose fault is the dense ignorance and romantic folly which made these unfortunate Sinn Feiners mistake a piece of hopeless mischief for a patriotic stroke for freedom such as Shelley sang and Byron took arms for? Were they taught citizenship in their schools? Were their votes bought with anything but balderdash? Granted that their heads, like their newspapers, were stuffed with ultra-insular patriotic conceit, is this a time at which England can with any countenance throw a stone at them on that score? Has not the glorification of patriotism, of reckless defiance, of superior numbers and resources, of readiness to kill and be killed for the old flag, of implacable hatred of the enemy and the invader, of the sacred rights of small nations to self-government and freedom, been thundered at them for more than a year by British writers who talk and feel as if England were still the England of

From Bernard Shaw, *The Matter with Ireland*, edited by David H. Greene and Dan H. Laurence. Copyright © 1962 by the Public Trustee as Executor of the Estate of George Bernard Shaw. Reprinted by permission of The Society of Authors, for the Bernard Shaw Estate. (This article was first published in *The New Statesman*, May 6, 1916.—ed.)

Alfred, and Socialism, the only alternative to Sinn Fein, were sedition and blasphemy? Is it not a little unreasonable of us to clamor for the blood of men who have simply taken us at our word and competed for our hero-worship with the Belgians and the Serbians, who have also devoted their Sackville-streets to fire and slaughter in a struggle at impossible odds with giant empires?

I can speak my mind freely on this matter, for I have attacked the romantic Separatism of Ireland with every device of invective and irony and dialectic at my command. As it happens, my last onslaught on Sinn Fein reached Ireland, through the columns of The Irish Times, two days before the insurrection. It was too late; and, in any case, the Volunteers had plenty of assurances from the most vociferous English patriots that I am not a person to be attended to. But exasperating as the mischief and folly and ignorance of the rising are to my practical sense, I must not deny, now that it is crushed, that these men were patriotic according to their own lights, brave according to our lights, public in their aims, and honorable in their Republican political ideal. I notice, also, that the newspapers which describe them as personally contemptible contradict their correspondents by pictures which exhibit them as well-set-up, soldierly men.

THE EASTER WEEK EXECUTIONS

(Selection)

Bernard Shaw

You say that "so far as the leaders are concerned no voice has been raised in this country against the infliction of the punishment which has so speedily overtaken them." As the Government shot the prisoners first and told the public about it afterwards, there was no opportunity for effective protest. But it must not be assumed that those who merely shrugged their shoulders when it was useless to remonstrate accept for one moment the view that what happened was the execution of a gang of criminals.

My own view—which I should not intrude on you had you not concluded that it does not exist—is that the men who were shot in cold blood after their capture or surrender were prisoners of war, and that it was, therefore, entirely incorrect to slaughter them. The relation of Ireland to Dublin Castle is in this respect precisely that of the Balkan States to Turkey, of Belgium or the city of Lille to the Kaiser, and of the United States to Great Britain.

Until Dublin Castle is superseded by a National Parliament and Ireland voluntarily incorporated with the British Empire, as Canada, Australasia, and South Africa have been incorporated, an Irishman resorting to arms to achieve the independence of his country is doing only what Englishmen will do if it be their misfortune to be invaded and conquered by the Germans in the course of the present war.

Further, such an Irishman is as much in order morally in accepting assistance from the Germans in his struggle with England as England is in accepting the assistance of Russia in her struggle with Germany. The fact that he knows that his enemies will not respect his rights if they catch him, and that he must therefore fight with a rope round his neck, increases his risk, but adds in the same measure to his glory in the eyes of his compatriots and of the disinterested admirers of patriotism throughout the world.

From Bernard Shaw, *The Matter with Ireland,* edited by David H. Greene and Dan H. Laurence. Copyright © 1962 by the Public Trustee as Executor of the Estate of George Bernard Shaw. Reprinted by permission of The Society of Authors, for the Bernard Shaw Estate. [This letter to *The Daily News* (London) appeared on May 10, 1916—ed.]

It is absolutely impossible to slaughter a man in this position without making him a martyr and a hero, even though the day before the rising he may have been only a minor poet. The shot Irishmen will now take their places beside Emmet and the Manchester martyrs.[1] in Ireland, and besides the heroes of Poland and Serbia and Belgium in Europe; and nothing in heaven or on earth can prevent it.

[1] Three Fenians who were hanged in Manchester for killing a policeman.

The
Chinese
Communist
Revolution

THE LONG MARCH

Regarded in Red China as important aspects of the revolutionary movement, literature and art are obliged to follow the Communist Party line, which changes when political circumstances change. In Red China, a work of art must be judged by both political and aesthetic criteria. Although Mao Tse-tung admits that "Works of art which lack artistic quality have no force, however progressive they are politically," he emphasizes that the political criterion is the more important. "The revolutionary struggle on the ideological and artistic fronts," he says, "must be subordinated to the political struggle because only through politics can the needs of the class and the masses find expression in concentrated form." The Party dictates the goals and tactics of the political struggle.

The aim of literature and art, says Chairman Mao, "must . . . be to serve the masses of the people." Literature and art must "eulogize the proletariat, the Communist Party, New Democracy, and socialism" and condemn as reactionary and counterrevolutionary the forces working against them. Since the audience of revolutionary art is the people, it must be understood and appreciated by the masses of the people, and not merely by a few intellectuals.

But forms of artistic expression change. Should new methods be stifled because they are not immediately understood and appreciated by the masses of the people? Admitting that "Often correct and good things have first been regarded not as fragrant flowers but as poisonous weeds," and that therefore "Different forms and styles in art should develop freely," Mao endorsed the slogan "Let a hundred flowers blossom, let a hundred schools of thought contend" as "the policy for promoting the progress of the arts and the sciences and a flourishing socialist culture in our land." Despite the slogan, freedom of artistic expression in Red China was only apparent, not real. Although a hundred flowers might be allowed to blossom, said Mao, criteria were necessary to distinguish flowers from poisonous weeds. Of the six distinguishing criteria he formulated, he cited two as "most important": "They should be beneficial, and not harmful, to socialist transformation and socialist con-struction" and "They should help to strengthen, and not discard or weaken, the leadership of the Communist Party." As for the hundred schools of thought, he made explicit what was implicit in these criteria: "What should our policy be towards non-Marxist ideas? As far as unmistakable counterrevolutionaries and saboteurs of the socialist cause are concerned, the matter is easy: we simply deprive them of their freedom of speech." These policies, whose result is Socialist Realism, dominate all theatrical expression in mainland China today.

An appropriate subject for a Red Chinese play is the historic "Long March" of the Red Army from October 1934 to October 1935. Over-coming vast difficulties—including weather, dangerous terrain, and attacks by the forces of Chiang Kai-shek, with whom the communists were engaged in civil war—the Red Army marched over eight thousand miles from southeast China to northern China, where they fought the Japanese invaders. A singular physical achievement, the march was also an impressive political and propaganda event, for it brought the prin-ciples and presence of the Red Army to a large part of the nation.

TALKS AT THE YENAN FORUM
ON LITERATURE AND ART

Mao Tse-tung

Introduction

May 2, 1942

Comrades! You have been invited to this forum today to exchange
ideas and examine the relationship between work in the literary and
artistic fields and revolutionary work in general. Our aim is to ensure
that revolutionary literature and art follow the correct path of development and provide better help to other revolutionary work in facilitating
the overthrow of our national enemy and the accomplishment of the
task of national liberation.

In our struggle for the liberation of the Chinese people there are
various fronts, among which there are the fronts of the pen and of the
gun, the cultural and the military fronts. To defeat the enemy we must
rely primarily on the army with guns. But this army alone is not enough;
we must also have a cultural army, which is absolutely indispensable
for uniting our own ranks and defeating the enemy. Since the May 4th
Movement[1] such a cultural army has taken shape in China, and it has

[1] The May 4th Movement was an anti-imperialist and anti-feudal revolutionary movement which began on May 4, 1919. In the first half of that year, the
victors of World War I, *i.e.*, Britain, France, the United States, Japan, Italy and
other imperialist countries, met in Paris to divide the spoils and decide that Japan
should take over all the privileges previously enjoyed by Germany in Shantung
Province, China. The students of Peking were the first to show determined opposition
to this scheme, holding rallies and demonstrations on May 4. The Northern warlord
government arrested more than thirty students in an effort to suppress this opposition. In protest, the students of Peking went on strike and large numbers of students
in other parts of the country responded. On June 3 the Northern warlord government started arresting students in Peking en masse, and within two days about a
thousand were taken into custody. This aroused still greater indignation throughout
the country. From June 5 onwards, the workers of Shanghai and many other cities
went on strike and the merchants in these places shut their shops. Thus, what was
at first a patriotic movement consisting mainly of intellectuals rapidly developed
into a national patriotic movement embracing the proletariat, the urban petty
bourgeoisie and the bourgeoisie. And along with the growth of this patriotic movement, the new cultural movement which had begun before May 4 as a movement

From *Mao Tse-tung on Literature and Art* (Peking: Foreign Languages Press, 1967).

helped the Chinese revolution, gradually reduced the domain of China's feudal culture and of the comprador culture which serves imperialist aggression, and weakened their influence. To oppose the new culture the Chinese reactionaries can now only "pit quantity against quality." In other words, reactionaries have money, and though they can produce nothing good, they can go all out and produce in quantity. Literature and art have been an important and successful part of the cultural front since the May 4th Movement. During the ten years' civil war, the revolutionary literature and art movement grew greatly. That movement and the revolutionary war both headed in the same general direction, but these two fraternal armies were not linked together in their practical work because the reactionaries had cut them off from each other. It is very good that since the outbreak of the War of Resistance Against Japan, more and more revolutionary writers and artists have been coming to Yenan and our other anti-Japanese base areas. But it does not necessarily follow that, having come to the base areas, they have already integrated themselves completely with the masses of the people here. The two must be completely integrated if we are to push ahead with our revolutionary work. The purpose of our meeting today is precisely to ensure that literature and art fit well into the whole revolutionary machine as a component part, that they operate as powerful weapons for uniting and educating the people and for attacking and destroying the enemy, and that they help the people fight the enemy with one heart and one mind. What are the problems that must be solved to achieve this objective? I think they are the problems of the class stand of the writers and artists, their attitude, their audience, their work and their study.

The problem of class stand. Our stand is that of the proletariat and of the masses. For members of the Communist Party, this means keeping to the stand of the Party, keeping to Party spirit and Party policy. Are there any of our literary and art workers who are still mistaken or not clear in their understanding of this problem? I think there are. Many of our comrades have frequently departed from the correct stand.

The problem of attitude. From one's stand there follow specific attitudes towards specific matters. For instance, is one to extol or to expose? This is a question of attitude. Which attitude is wanted? I would say both. The question is, whom are you dealing with? There are

against feudalism and for the promotion of science and democracy, grew into a vigorous and powerful revolutionary cultural movement whose main current was the propagation of Marxism-Leninism. [All notes to Mao's *Talks* . . . by translator (anonymous).]

three kinds of persons, the enemy, our allies in the united front and our own people; the last are the masses and their vanguard. We need to adopt a different attitude towards each of the three. With regard to the enemy, that is, Japanese imperialism and all the other enemies of the people, the task of revolutionary writers and artists is to expose their duplicity and cruelty and at the same time to point out the inevitability of their defeat, so as to encourage the anti-Japanese army and people to fight staunchly with one heart and one mind for their overthrow. With regard to our different allies in the united front, our attitude should be one of both alliance and criticism, and there should be different kinds of alliance and different kinds of criticism. We support them in their resistance to Japan and praise them for any achievement. But if they are not active in the War of Resistance, we should criticize them. If anyone opposes the Communist Party and the people and keeps moving down the path of reaction, we will firmly oppose him. As for the masses of the people, their toil and their struggle, their army and their Party, we should certainly praise them. The people, too, have their shortcomings. Among the proletariat many retain petty-bourgeois ideas, while both the peasants and the urban petty bourgeoisie have backward ideas; these are burdens hampering them in their struggle. We should be patient and spend a long time in educating them and helping them to get these loads off their backs and combat their own shortcomings and errors, so that they can advance with great strides. They have remoulded themselves in struggle or are doing so, and our literature and art should depict this process. As long as they do not persist in their errors, we should not dwell on their negative side and consequently make the mistake of ridiculing them or, worse still, of being hostile to them. Our writings should help them to unite, to make progress, to press ahead with one heart and one mind, to discard what is backward and develop what is revolutionary, and should certainly not do the opposite.

The problem of audience, *i.e.*, the people for whom our works of literature and art are produced. In the Shensi-Kansu-Ningsia Border Region[2] and the anti-Japanese base areas of northern and central China, this problem differs from that in the Kuomintang areas, and differs still more from that in Shanghai before the War of Resistance. In the Shanghai

[2] The Shensi-Kansu-Ningsia Border Region was the revolutionary base area which was gradually built up after 1931 through revolutionary guerrilla warfare in northern Shensi. When the Central Red Army arrived in northern Shensi after the Long March, it became the seat of the Central Committee of the Chinese Communist Party and the central base area of the revolution.

period, the audience for works of revolutionary literature and art consisted mainly of a section of the students, office workers and shop assistants. After the outbreak of the War of Resistance the audience in the Kuomintang areas became somewhat wider, but it still consisted mainly of the same kind of people because the government there prevented the workers, peasants and soldiers from having access to revolutionary literature and art. In our base areas the situation is entirely different. Here the audience for works of literature and art consists of workers, peasants, soldiers and revolutionary cadres. There are students in the base areas, too, but they are different from students of the old type; they are either former or future cadres. The cadres of all types, fighters in the army, workers in the factories and peasants in the villages all want to read books and newspapers once they become literate, and those who are illiterate want to see plays and operas, look at drawings and paintings, sing songs and hear music; they are the audience for our works of literature and art. Take the cadres alone. Do not think they are few; they far outnumber the readers of any book published in the Kuomintang areas. There, an edition usually runs to only 2,000 copies, and even three editions add up to only 6,000; but as for the cadres in the base areas, in Yenan alone there are more than 10,000 who read books. Many of them, moreover, are tempered revolutionaries of long standing, who have come from all parts of the country and will go out to work in different places, so it is very important to do educational work among them. Our literary and art workers must do a good job in this respect.

Since the audience for our literature and art consists of workers, peasants and soldiers and of their cadres, the problem arises of understanding them and knowing them well. A great deal of work has to be done in order to understand them and know them well, to understand and know well all the different kinds of people and phenomena in the Party and government organizations, in the villages and factories and in the Eighth Route and New Fourth Armies. Our writers and artists have their literary and art work to do, but their primary task is to understand people and know them well. In this regard, how have matters stood with our writers and artists? I would say they have been lacking in knowledge and understanding; they have been like "a hero with no place to display his prowess." What does lacking in knowledge mean? Not knowing people well. The writers and artists do not have a good knowledge either of those whom they describe or of their audience; indeed they may hardly know them at all. They do not know the workers or peasants or soldiers well, and do not know the cadres well either. What does lacking in understanding mean? Not understanding the language, that is, not being familiar with the rich, lively language of the masses. Since many writers and artists stand aloof from the masses and lead empty lives, naturally they are unfamiliar with the language of the people. Accordingly, their works are not only insipid in language but often contain nondescript expressions of their own coining which run counter to popular usage. Many comrades like to talk about "a mass style." But what does it really mean? It means that the thoughts and feelings of our writers and artists should be fused with those of the masses of workers, peasants and soldiers. To achieve this fusion, they should conscientiously learn the language of the masses. How can you talk of literary and artistic creation if you find the very language of the masses largely incomprehensible? By "a hero with no place to display his prowess," we mean that your collection of great truths is not appreciated by the masses. The more you put on the airs of a veteran before the masses and play the "hero," the more you try to peddle such stuff to the masses, the less likely they are to accept it. If you want the masses to understand you, if you want to be one with the masses, you must make up your mind to undergo a long and even painful process of tempering. Here I might mention the experience of how my own feelings changed. I began life as a student and at school acquired the ways of a student; I then used to feel it undignified to do even a little manual labour, such as carrying my own luggage in the presence of my fellow students, who were incapable of carrying anything, either on their shoulders or in their hands. At that time I felt that intellectuals were the only clean people in the world, while in comparison workers and peasants were dirty. I did not mind wearing the clothes of other intellectuals, believing them clean, but I would not put on clothes belonging to a worker or peasant, believing them dirty. But after I became a revolutionary and lived with workers and peasants and with soldiers of the revolutionary army, I gradually came to know them well, and they gradually came to know me well too. It was then, and only then, that I fundamentally changed the bourgeois and petty-bourgeois feelings implanted in me in the bourgeois schools. I came to feel that compared with the workers and peasants the unremoulded intellectuals were not clean and that, in the last analysis, the workers and peasants were the cleanest people and, even though their hands were soiled and their feet smeared with cow-dung, they were really cleaner than the bourgeois and petty-bourgeois intellectuals. That is what is meant by a change in feelings, a change from one class to another. If our writers and artists who come from the intelligentsia want their works to be well received by the masses, they must change and remould their thinking and their feelings. Without such a change, without such remoulding, they can do nothing well and will be misfits.

The last problem is study, by which I mean the study of Marxism-Leninism and of society. Anyone who considers himself a revolutionary Marxist writer, and especially any writer who is a member of the Communist Party, must have a knowledge of Marxism-Leninism. At present, however, some comrades are lacking in the basic concepts of Marxism. For instance, it is a basic Marxist concept that being determines consciousness, that the objective realities of class struggle and national struggle determine our thoughts and feelings. But some of our comrades turn this upside down and maintain that everything ought to start from "love." Now as for love, in a class society there can be only class love; but these comrades are seeking a love transcending classes, love in the abstract and also freedom in the abstract, truth in the abstract, human nature in the abstract, etc. This shows that they have been very deeply influenced by the bourgeoisie. They should thoroughly rid themselves of this influence and modestly study Marxism-Leninism. It is right for writers and artists to study literary and artistic creation, but the science of Marxism-Leninism must be studied by all revolutionaries, writers and artists not excepted. Writers and artists should study society, that is to say, should study the various classes in society, their mutual relations and respective conditions, their physiognomy and their psychology. Only when we grasp all this clearly can we have a literature and art that is rich in content and correct in orientation.

I am merely raising these problems today by way of introduction; I hope all of you will express your views on these and other relevant problems.

Conclusion

May 23, 1942

Comrades! Our forum has had three meetings this month. In the pursuit of truth we have carried on spirited debates in which scores of Party and non-Party comrades have spoken, laying bare the issues and making them more concrete. This, I believe, will very much benefit the whole literary and artistic movement.

In discussing a problem, we should start from reality and not from definitions. We would be following a wrong method if we first looked up definitions of literature and art in textbooks and then used them to determine the guiding principles for the present-day literary and artistic movement and to judge the different opinions and controversies that arise today. We are Marxists, and Marxism teaches that in our approach to a problem we should start from objective facts, not from abstract definitions, and that we should derive our guiding principles, policies and measures from an analysis of these facts. We should do the same in our present discussion of literary and artistic work.

What are the facts at present? The facts are: the War of Resistance Against Japan which China has been fighting for five years: the world-wide anti-fascist war; the vacillations of China's big landlord class and big bourgeoisie in the War of Resistance and their policy of high-handed oppression of the people; the revolutionary movement in literature and art since the May 4th Movement—its great contributions to the revolution during the last twenty-three years and its many shortcomings; the anti-Japanese democratic base areas of the Eighth Route and New Fourth Armies and the integration of large numbers of writers and artists with these armies and with the workers and peasants in these areas; the difference in both environment and tasks between the writers and artists in the base areas and those in the Kuomintang areas; and the controversial issues concerning literature and art which have arisen in Yenan and the other anti-Japanese base areas. These are the actual, undeniable facts in the light of which we have to consider our problems.

What then is the crux of the matter? In my opinion, it consists fundamentally of the problems of working for the masses and how to work for the masses. Unless these two problems are solved, or solved properly, our writers and artists will be ill-adapted to their environment and their tasks and will come up against a series of difficulties from without and within. My concluding remarks will centre on these two problems and also touch upon some related ones.

I

The first problem is: literature and art for whom?

This problem was solved long ago by Marxists, especially by Lenin. As far back as 1905 Lenin pointed out emphatically that our literature and art should "serve . . . the millions and tens of millions of working people."[3] For comrades engaged in literary and artistic work

[3] See V. I. Lenin, "Party Organisation and Party Literature" [above, p. 117], in which he described the characteristics of proletarian literature as follows:
  It will be a free literature, because the idea of socialism and sympathy with the working people, and not greed or careerism, will bring ever new forces to its ranks. It will be a free literature, because it will serve, not some satiated heroine, not the bored "upper ten thousand" suffering from fatty degeneration, but the millions and tens of millions of working people—the flower of the country, its strength and its future. It will be a free literature, enriching the last word in the revolutionary thought of mankind with the experience and living work of the socialist proletariat, bringing about permanent interaction between the ex-

in the anti-Japanese base areas it might seem that this problem is already solved and needs no further discussion. Actually, that is not the case. Many comrades have not found a clear solution. Consequently their sentiments, their works, their actions and their views on the guiding principles for literature and art have inevitably been more or less at variance with the needs of the masses and of the practical struggle. Of course, among the numerous men of culture, writers, artists and other literary and artistic workers engaged in the great struggle for liberation together with the Communist Party and the Eighth Route and New Fourth Armies, a few may be careerists who are with us only temporarily, but the overwhelming majority are working energetically for the common cause. By relying on these comrades, we have achieved a great deal in our literature, drama, music and fine arts. Many of these writers and artists have begun their work since the outbreak of the War of Resistance; many others did much revolutionary work before the war, endured many hardships and influenced broad masses of the people by their activities and works. Why do we say, then, that even among these comrades there are some who have not reached a clear solution of the problem of whom literature and art are for? Is it conceivable that there are still some who maintain that revolutionary literature and art are not for the masses of the people but for the exploiters and oppressors?

Indeed literature and art exist which are for the exploiters and oppressors. Literature and art for the landlord class are feudal literature and art. Such were the literature and art of the ruling class in China's feudal era. To this day such literature and art still have considerable influence in China. Literature and art for the bourgeoisie are bourgeois literature and art. People like Liang Shih-chiu,[4] whom Lu Hsun criticized, talk about literature and art as transcending classes, but in fact they uphold bourgeois literature and art and oppose proletarian literature and art. Then literature and art exist which serve the imperialists—for example, the works of Chou Tso-jen, Chang Tzu-ping[5] and their like—which we call traitor literature and art. With us, literature and art are for the people, not for any of the above groups. We have said that China's new culture at

perience of the past (scientific socialism, the completion of the development of socialism from its primitive, utopian forms) and the experience of the present (the present struggle of the worker comrades).

[4] Liang Shih-chiu, a member of the counter-revolutionary National Socialist Party, for a long time propagated reactionary American bourgeois ideas on literature and art. He stubbornly opposed the revolution and reviled revolutionary literature and art.

[5] Chou Tso-jen and Chang Tzu-ping capitulated to the Japanese aggressors after the Japanese occupied Peking and Shanghai in 1937.

the present stage is an anti-imperialist, anti-feudal culture of the masses of the people under the leadership of the proletariat. Today, anything that is truly of the masses must necessarily be led by the proletariat. Whatever is under the leadership of the bourgeoisie cannot possibly be of the masses. Naturally, the same applies to the new literature and art which are part of the new culture. We should take over the rich legacy and the good traditions in literature and art that have been handed down from past ages in China and foreign countries, but the aim must still be to serve the masses of the people. Nor do we refuse to utilize the literary and artistic forms of the past, but in our hands these old forms, remoulded and infused with new content, also become something revolutionary in the service of the people.

Who, then, are the masses of the people? The broadest sections of the people, constituting more than 90 per cent of our total population, are the workers, peasants, soldiers and urban petty bourgeoisie. Therefore, our literature and art are first for the workers, the class that leads the revolution. Secondly, they are for the peasants, the most numerous and most steadfast of our allies in the revolution. Thirdly, they are for the armed workers and peasants, namely, the Eighth Route and New Fourth Armies and the other armed units of the people, which are the main forces of the revolutionary war. Fourthly, they are for the labouring masses of the urban petty bourgeoisie and for the petty-bourgeois intellectuals, both of whom are also our allies in the revolution and capable of long-term co-operation with us. These four kinds of people constitute the overwhelming majority of the Chinese nation, the broadest masses of the people.

Our literature and art should be for the four kinds of people we have enumerated. To serve them, we must take the class stand of the proletariat and not that of the petty bourgeoisie. Today, writers who cling to an individualist, petty-bourgeois stand cannot truly serve the masses of revolutionary workers, peasants and soldiers. Their interest is mainly focused on the small number of petty-bourgeois intellectuals. This is the crucial reason why some of our comrades cannot correctly solve the problem of "for whom?" In saying this I am not referring to theory. In theory, or in words, no one in our ranks regards the masses of workers, peasants and soldiers as less important than the petty-bourgeois intellectuals. I am referring to practice, to action. In practice, in action, do they regard petty-bourgeois intellectuals as more important than workers, peasants and soldiers? I think they do. Many comrades concern themselves with studying the petty-bourgeois intellectuals and analysing their psychology, and they concentrate on portraying these intellectuals and excusing or defending their shortcomings, instead of guiding the intellectuals to join with them in getting closer to the masses of workers, peasants and soldiers, taking part in the practical struggles of the masses, portraying and educating the masses. Coming from the petty bourgeoisie and being themselves intellectuals, many comrades seek friends only among intellectuals and concentrate on studying and describing them. Such study and description are proper if done from a proletarian position. But that is not what they do, or not what they do fully. They take the petty-bourgeois stand and produce works that are the self-expression of the petty bourgeoisie, as can be seen in quite a number of literary and artistic products. Often they show heartfelt sympathy for intellectuals of petty-bourgeois origin, to the extent of sympathizing with or even praising their shortcomings. On the other hand, these comrades seldom come into contact with the masses of workers, peasants and soldiers, do not understand or study them, do not have intimate friends among them and are not good at portraying them; when they do depict them, the clothes are the clothes of working people but the faces are those of petty-bourgeois intellectuals. In certain respects they are fond of the workers, peasants and soldiers and the cadres stemming from them; but there are times when they do not like them and there are some respects in which they do not like them: they do not like their feelings or their manner or their nascent literature and art (the wall newspapers, murals, folk songs, folk tales, etc.). At times they are fond of these things too, but that is when they are hunting for novelty, for something with which to embellish their own works, or even for certain backward features. At other times they openly despise these things and are partial to what belongs to the petty-bourgeois intellectuals or even to the bourgeoisie. These comrades have their feet planted on the side of the petty-bourgeois intellectuals; or, to put it more elegantly, their innermost soul is still a kingdom of the petty-bourgeois intelligentsia. Thus they have not yet solved, or not yet clearly solved, the problem of "for whom?" This applies not only to newcomers to Yenan; even among comrades who have been to the front and worked for a number of years in our base areas and in the Eighth Route and New Fourth Armies, many have not completely solved this problem. It requires a long period of time, at least eight or ten years, to solve it thoroughly. But however long it takes, solve it we must and solve it unequivocally and thoroughly. Our literary and art workers must accomplish this task and shift their stand; they must gradually move their feet over to the side of the workers, peasants and soldiers, to the side of the proletariat, through the process of going into their very midst and into the thick of practical struggles and through the process of studying Marxism and society. Only in this way can we have a literature and art that are truly for the workers, peasants and soldiers, a truly proletarian literature and art.

This question of "for whom?" is fundamental; it is a question of principle. The controversies and divergences, the opposition and disunity arising among some comrades in the past were not on this fundamental question of principle but on secondary questions, or even on issues involving no principle. On this question of principle, however, there has been hardly any divergence between the two contending sides and they have shown almost complete agreement; to some extent, both tend to look down upon the workers, peasants and soldiers and divorce themselves from the masses. I say "to some extent" because, generally speaking, these comrades do not look down upon the workers, peasants and soldiers or divorce themselves from the masses in the same way as the Kuomintang does. Nevertheless, the tendency is there. Unless this fundamental problem is solved, many other problems will not be easy to solve. Take, for instance, the sectarianism in literary and art circles. This too is a question of principle, but sectarianism can only be eradicated by putting forward and faithfully applying the slogans, "For the workers and peasants!," "For the Eighth Route and New Fourth Armies!" and "Go among the masses!" Otherwise the problem of sectarianism can never be solved. Lu Hsun once said:

> A common aim is the prerequisite for a united front. . . . The fact that our front is not united shows that we have not been able to unify our aims, and that some people are working only for small groups or indeed only for themselves. If we all aim at serving the masses of workers and peasants, our front will of course be united.[6]

The problem existed then in Shanghai; now it exists in Chungking too. In such places the problem can hardly be solved thoroughly, because the rulers oppress the revolutionary writers and artists and deny them the freedom to go out among the masses of workers, peasants and soldiers. Here with us the situation is entirely different. We encourage revolutionary writers and artists to be active in forming intimate contacts with the workers, peasants and soldiers, giving them complete freedom to go among the masses and to create a genuinely revolutionary literature and art. Therefore, here among us the problem is nearing solution. But nearing solution is not the same as a complete and thorough solution. We must study Marxism and study society, as we have been

---

[6] Lu Hsun, "My View on the League of Left-Wing Writers."

saying, precisely in order to achieve a complete and thorough solution. By Marxism we mean living Marxism which plays an effective role in the life and struggle of the masses, not Marxism in words. With Marxism in words transformed into Marxism in real life, there will be no more sectarianism. Not only will the problem of sectarianism be solved, but many other problems as well.

II

Having settled the problem of whom to serve, we come to the next problem, how to serve. To put it in the words of some of our comrades: should we devote ourselves to raising standards, or should we devote ourselves to popularization?

In the past, some comrades, to a certain or even a serious extent, belittled and neglected popularization and laid undue stress on raising standards. Stress should be laid on raising standards, but to do so one-sidedly and exclusively, to do so excessively, is a mistake. The lack of a clear solution to the problem of "for whom?", which I referred to earlier, also manifests itself in this connection. As these comrades are not clear on the problem of "for whom?", they have no correct criteria for the "raising of standards" and the "popularization" they speak of, and are naturally still less able to find the correct relationship between the two. Since our literature and art are basically for the workers, peasants and soldiers, "popularization" means to popularize among the workers, peasants and soldiers, and "raising standards" means to advance from their present level. What should we popularize among them? Popularize what is needed and can be readily accepted by the feudal landlord class? Popularize what is needed and can be readily accepted by the bourgeoisie? Popularize what is needed and can be readily accepted by the petty-bourgeois intellectuals? No, none of these will do. We must popularize only what is needed and can be readily accepted by the workers, peasants and soldiers themselves. Consequently, prior to the task of educating the workers, peasants and soldiers, there is the task of learning from them. This is even more true of raising standards. There must be a basis from which to raise. Take a bucket of water, for instance; where is it to be raised from if not from the ground? From mid-air? From what basis, then, are literature and art to be raised? From the basis of the feudal classes? From the basis of the bourgeoisie? From the basis of the petty-bourgeois intellectuals? No, not from any of these; only from the basis of the masses of workers, peasants and soldiers. Nor does this mean raising the workers, peasants and soldiers to the "heights" of the feudal classes, the bourgeoisie or the petty-bourgeois intellectuals;

it means raising the level of literature and art in the direction in which the workers, peasants and soldiers are themselves advancing, in the direction in which the proletariat is advancing. Here again the task of learning from the workers, peasants and soldiers comes in. Only by starting from the workers, peasants and soldiers can we have a correct understanding of popularization and of the raising of standards and find the proper relationship between the two.

In the last analysis, what is the source of all literature and art? Works of literature and art, as ideological forms, are products of the reflection in the human brain of the life of a given society. Revolutionary literature and art are the products of the reflection of the life of the people in the brains of revolutionary writers and artists. The life of the people is always a mine of the raw materials for literature and art, materials in their natural form, materials that are crude, but most vital, rich and fundamental; they make all literature and art seem pallid by comparison; they provide literature and art with an inexhaustible source, their only source. They are the only source for there can be no other. Some may ask, is there not another source in books, in the literature and art of ancient times and of foreign countries? In fact, the literary and artistic works of the past are not a source but a stream; they were created by our predecessors and the foreigners out of the literary and artistic raw materials they found in the life of the people of their time and place. We must take over all the fine things in our literary and artistic heritage, critically assimilate whatever is beneficial, and use them as examples when we create works out of the literary and artistic raw materials in the life of the people of our own time and place. It makes a difference whether or not we have such examples, the difference betwen crudeness and refinement, between roughness and polish, between a low and a high level, and between slower and faster work. Therefore, we must on no account reject the legacies of the ancients and the foreigners or refuse to learn from them, even though they are the works of the feudal or bourgeois classes. But taking over legacies and using them as examples must never replace our own creative work; nothing can do that. Uncritical transplantation or copying from the ancients and the foreigners is the most sterile and harmful dogmatism in literature and art. China's revolutionary writers and artists, writers and artists of promise, must go among the masses; they must for a long period of time unreservedly and wholeheartedly go among the masses of workers, peasants and soldiers, go into the heat of the struggle, go to the only source, the broadest and richest source, in order to observe, experience, study and analyse all the different kinds of people, all the classes, all the masses, all the vivid patterns of life and struggle, all the raw materials of literature and art. Only then can they proceed to creative work. Otherwise, you will have nothing to work with and you will be nothing but a phoney writer or artist, the kind that Lu Hsun in his will so earnestly cautioned his son never to become.[7]

Although man's social life is the only source of literature and art and is incomparably livelier and richer in content, the people are not satisfied with life alone and demand literature and art as well. Why? Because, while both are beautiful, life as reflected in works of literature and art can and ought to be on a higher plane, more intense, more concentrated, more typical, nearer the ideal, and therefore more universal than actual everyday life. Revolutionary literature and art should create a variety of characters out of real life and help the masses to propel history forward. For example, there is suffering from hunger, cold and oppression of the one hand, and exploitation and oppression of man by man on the other. These facts exist everywhere and people look upon them as commonplace. Writers and artists concentrate such everyday phenomena, typify the contradictions and struggles within them and produce works which awaken the masses, fire them with enthusiasm and impel them to unite and struggle to transform their environment. Without such literature and art, this task could not be fulfilled, or at least not so effectively and speedily.

What is meant by popularizing and by raising standards in works of literature and art? What is the relationship between these two tasks? Popular works are simpler and plainer, and therefore more readily accepted by the broad masses of the people today. Works of a higher quality, being more polished, are more difficult to produce and in general do not circulate so easily and quickly among the masses at present. The problem facing the workers, peasants and soldiers is this: they are now engaged in a bitter and bloody struggle with the enemy but are illiterate and uneducated as a result of long years of rule by the feudal and bourgeois classes, and therefore they are eagerly demanding enlightenment, education and works of literature and art which meet their urgent needs and which are easy to absorb, in order to heighten their enthusiasms in struggle and confidence in victory, strengthen their unity and fight the enemy with one heart and one mind. For them the prime need is not "more flowers on the brocade" but "fuel in snowy weather." In present conditions, therefore, popularization is the more pressing task. It is wrong to belittle or neglect popularization.

Nevertheless, no hard and fast line can be drawn between popularization and the raising of standards. Not only is it possible to

[7] See Lu Hsun's essay, "Death."

popularize some works of higher quality even now, but the cultural level of the broad masses is steadily rising. If popularization remains at the same level for ever, with the same stuff being supplied month after month and year after year, always the same "Little Cowherd"[8] and the same "man, hand, mouth, knife, sow, goat,"[9] will not the educators and those being educated be six of one and half a dozen of the other? What would be the sense of such popularization? The people demand popularization and, following that, higher standards; they demand higher standards month by month and year by year. Here popularization means popularizing for the people and raising of standards means raising the level for the people. And such raising is not from mid-air, or behind closed doors, but is actually based on popularization. It is determined by and at the same time guides popularization. In China as a whole the development of the revolution and of revolutionary culture is uneven and their spread is gradual. While in one place there is popularization and then raising of standards on the basis of popularization, in other places popularization has not even begun. Hence good experience in popularization leading to higher standards in one locality can be applied in other localities and serve to guide popularization and the raising of standards there, saving many twists and turns along the road. Internationally, the good experience of foreign countries, and especially Soviet experience, can also serve to guide us. With us, therefore, the rising of standards is based on popularization, while popularization is guided by the raising of standards. Precisely for this reason, so far from being an obstacle to the raising of standards, the work of popularization we are speaking of supplies the basis for the work of raising standards which we are now doing on a limited scale, and prepares the necessary conditions for us to raise standards in the future on a much broader scale.

Besides such raising of standards as meets the needs of the masses directly, there is the kind which meets their needs indirectly, that is, the kind which is needed by the cadres. The cadres are the advanced elements of the masses and generally have received more education; literature and art of a higher level are entirely necessary for them. To ignore this would be a mistake. Whatever is done for the cadres is also entirely for the masses, because it is only through the cadres that

[8] The "Little Cowherd" is a popular Chinese folk operetta with only two people acting in it, a cowherd and a village girl, who sing a question and answer duet. In the early days of the War of Resistance Against Japan, this form was used, with new words, for anti-Japanese propaganda and for a time found great favour with the public.

[9] The Chinese characters for these six words are written simply, with only a few strokes, and were usually included in the first lessons in old primers.

we can educate and guide the masses. If we go against this aim, if what we give the cadres cannot help them educate and guide the masses, our work of raising standards will be like shooting at random and will depart from the fundamental principle of serving the masses of the people.

To sum up: through the creative labour of revolutionary writers and artists, the raw materials found in the life of the people are shaped into the ideological form of literature and art serving the masses of the people. Included here are the more advanced literature and art as developed on the basis of elementary literature and art and as required by those sections of the masses whose level has been raised, or, more immediately, by the cadres among the masses. Also included here are elementary literature and art which, conversely, are guided by more advanced literature and art and are needed primarily by the over-whelming majority of the masses at present. Whether more advanced or elementary, all our literature and art are for the masses of the people, and in the first place for the workers, peasants and soldiers; they are created for the workers, peasants and soldiers and are for their use.

Now that we have settled to the problem of the relationship be-tween the raising of standards and popularization, that of the relationship between the specialists and the popularizers can also be settled. Our specialists are not only for the cadres, but also, and indeed chiefly, for the masses. Our specialists in literature should pay attention to the wall newspapers of the masses and to the reportage written in the army and the villages. Our specialists in drama should pay attention to the small troupes in the army and the villages. Our specialists in music should pay attention to the songs of the masses. Our specialists in the fine arts should pay attention to the fine arts of the masses. All these comrades should make close contact with comrades engaged in the work of popularizing literature and art among the masses. On the one hand, they should help and guide the popularizers, and on the other, they should learn from these comrades and, through them, draw nourishment from the masses to replen-ish and enrich themselves so that their specialities do not become "ivory towers," detached from the masses and from reality and devoid of content or life. We should esteem the specialists, for they are very valuable to our cause. But we should tell them that no revolutionary writer or artist can do any meaningful work unless he is closely linked with the masses, gives expression to their thoughts and feelings and serves them as a loyal spokesman. Only by speaking for the masses can he educate them and only by being their pupil can he be their teacher. If he regards himself as their master, as an aristocrat who lords it over the "lower orders," then, no matter how talented he may be, he will not be needed by the masses and his work will have no future.

Is this attitude of ours utilitarian? Materialists do not oppose utilitarianism in general but the utilitarianism of the feudal, bourgeois and petty-bourgeois classes; they oppose those hypocrites who attack utilitarianism in words but in deeds embrace the most selfish and short-sighted utilitarianism. There is no "ism" in the world that transcends utilitarian considerations; in class society there can be only the utilitarianism of this or that class. We are proletarian revolutionary utilitarians and take as our point of departure the unity of the present and future interests of the broadest masses, who constitute over 90 per cent of the population; hence we are revolutionary utilitarians aiming for the broadest and the most long-range objectives, not narrow utilitarians concerned only with the partial and the immediate. If, for instance, you reproach the masses for their utilitarianism and yet for your own utility, or that of a narrow clique, force on the market and propagandize among the masses a work which pleases only the few but is useless or even harmful to the majority, then you are not only insulting the masses but also revealing your own lack of self-knowledge. A thing is good only when it brings real benefit to the masses of the people. Your work may be as good as "The Spring Snow," but if for the time being it caters only to the few and the masses are still singing the "Song of the Rustic Poor,"[10] you will get nowhere by simply scolding them instead of trying to raise their level. The question now is to bring about a unity between "The Spring Snow" and the "Song of the Rustic Poor," between higher standards and popularization. Without such a unity, the highest art of any expert cannot help being utilitarian in the narrowest sense; you may call this art "pure and lofty" but that is merely your own name for it which the masses will not endorse.

Once we have solved the problems of fundamental policy, of serving the workers, peasants and soldiers and of how to serve them, such other problems as whether to write about the bright or the dark side of life and the problem of unity will also be solved. If everyone agrees on the fundamental policy, it should be adhered to by all our workers, all our schools, publications and organizations in the field of literature and art and in all our literary and artistic activities. It is wrong to depart from this policy and anything at variance with it must be duly corrected.

[10] "The Spring Snow" and the "Song of the Rustic Poor" were songs of the Kingdom of Chu in the 3rd century B.C. The music of the first was on a higher level than that of the second. As the story is told in "Sung Yu's Reply to the King of Chu" in Prince Chao Ming's *Anthology of Prose and Poetry*, when someone sang "The Spring Snow" in the Chu capital, only a few dozen people joined in, but when the "Song of the Rustic Poor" was sung, thousands did so.

III

Since our literature and art are for the masses of the people, we can proceed to discuss a problem of inner-party relations, *i.e.*, the relation between the Party's work in literature and art and the Party's work as a whole, and in addition a problem of the Party's external relations, *i.e.*, the relation between the Party's work in literature and art and the work of non-Party people in this field, a problem of the united front in literary and art circles.

Let us consider the first problem. In the world today all culture, all literature and art belong to definite classes and are geared to definite political lines. There is in fact no such thing as art for art's sake, art that stands above classes or art that is detached from or independent of politics. Proletarian literature and art are part of the whole proletarian revolutionary cause; they are, as Lenin said, cogs and wheels[11] in the whole revolutionary machine. Therefore, Party work in literature and art occupies a definite and assigned position in Party revolutionary work as a whole and is subordinated to the revolutionary tasks set by the Party in a given revolutionary period. Opposition to this arrangement is certain to lead to dualism or pluralism, and in essence amounts to "politics—Marxist, art —bourgeois," as with Trotsky. We do not favour overstressing the importance of literature and art, but neither do we favour underestimating their importance. Literature and art are subordinate to politics, but in their turn exert a great influence on politics. Revolutionary literature and art are part of the whole revolutionary cause, they are cogs and wheels in it, and though in comparison with certain other and more important parts they may be less significant and less urgent and may occupy a secondary position, nevertheless, they are indispensable cogs and wheels in the whole machine, an indispensable part of the entire revolutionary cause. If we had no literature and art even in the broadest and most ordinary sense, we could not carry on the revolutionary movement and win victory. Failure to recognize this is wrong. Furthermore, when we say that literature and art are subordinate to politics, we mean class politics, the politics of the masses, not the politics of a few so-called statesmen. Politics, whether revolutionary or counter-revolutionary, is the struggle of class against class, not the activity of a few individuals. The revolutionary struggle on the ideological and artistic fronts must be subordinate to the political struggle because only through politics

---

[11] See V. I. Lenin, "Party Organisation and Party Literature" [above, p. 117]:   "Literature must become *part* of the common cause of the proletariat, 'a cog and a screw' of one single great Social-Democratic mechanism set in motion by the entire politically-conscious vanguard of the entire working class."

can the needs of the class and the masses find expression in concentrated form. Revolutionary statesmen, the political specialists who know the science or art of revolutionary politics, are simply the leaders of millions upon millions of statesmen—the masses. Their task is to collect the opinions of these mass statesmen, sift and refine them, and return them to the masses, who then take them and put them in to practice. They are therefore not the kind of aristocratic "statesmen" who work behind closed doors and fancy they have a monopoly of wisdom. Herein lies the difference in principle between proletarian statesmen and decadent bourgeois statesmen. This is precisely why there can be complete unity between the political character of our literary and artistic works and their truthfulness. It would be wrong to fail to realize this and to debase the politics and the statesmen of the proletariat.

Let us consider next the question of the united front in the world of literature and art. Since literature and art are subordinate to politics and since the fundamental problem in China's politics today is resistance to Japan, our Party writers and artists must in the first place unite on this issue of resistance to Japan with all non-Party writers and artists (ranging from Party sympathizers and petty-bourgeois writers and artists to all those writers and artists of the bourgeois and landlord classes who are in favour of resistance to Japan). Secondly, we should unite with them on the issue of democracy. On this issue there is a section of anti-Japanese writers and artists who do not agree with us, so the range of unity will unavoidably be somewhat more limited. Thirdly, we should unite with them on issues peculiar to the literary and artistic world, questions of method and style in literature and art; here again, as we are for socialist realism and some people do not agree, the range of unity will be narrower still. While on one issue there is unity, on another there is struggle, there is criticism. The issues are at once separate and interrelated, so that even on the very ones which give rise to unity, such as resistance to Japan, there are at the same time struggle and criticism. In a united front, "all unity and no struggle" and "all struggle and no unity" are both wrong policies—as with the Right capitulationism and tailism, or the "Left" exclusivism and sectarianism, practised by some comrades in the past. This is as true in literature and art as in politics.

The petty-bourgeois writers and artists constitute an important force among the forces of the united front in literary and art circles in China. There are many shortcomings in both their thinking and their works, but, comparatively speaking, they are inclined towards the revolution and are close to the working people. Therefore, it is an especially important task to help them overcome their shortcomings and to win them over to the front which serves the working people.

IV

Literary and art criticism is one of the principal methods of struggle in the world of literature and art. It should be developed and, as comrades have rightly pointed out, our past work in this respect has been quite inadequate. Literary and art criticism is a complex question which requires a great deal of special study. Here I shall concentrate only on the basic problem of criteria in criticism. I shall also comment briefly on a few specific problems raised by some comrades and on certain incorrect views.

In literary and art criticism there are two criteria, the political and the artistic. According to the political criterion, everything is good that is helpful to unity and resistance to Japan, that encourages the masses to be of one heart and one mind, that opposes retrogression and promotes progress; on the other hand, everything is bad that is detrimental to unity and resistance to Japan, foments dissension and discord among the masses and opposes progress and drags people back. How can we tell the good from the bad—by the motive (the subjective intention) or by the effect (social practice)? Idealists stress motive and ignore effect, while mechanical materialists stress effect and ignore motive. In contradistinction to both, we dialectical materialists insist on the unity of motive and effect. The motive of serving the masses is inseparably linked with the effect of winning their approval; the two must be united. The motive of serving the individual or a small clique is not good, nor is it good to have the motive of serving the masses without the effect of winning their approval and benefiting them. In examining the subjective intention of a writer or artist, that is, whether his motive is correct and good, we do not judge by his declarations but by the effect of his actions (mainly his works) on the masses in society. The criterion for judging subjective intention or motive is social practice and its effect. We want no sectarianism in our literary and art criticism and, subject to the general principle of unity for resistance to Japan, we should tolerate literary and art works with a variety of political attitudes. But at the same time, in our criticism we must adhere firmly to principle and severely criticize and repudiate all works of literature and art expressing views in opposition to the nation, to science, to the masses and to the Communist Party, because these so-called works of literature and art proceed from the motive and produce the effect of undermining unity for resistance to Japan. According to the artistic criterion, all works of a higher artistic quality are good or comparatively good, while those of a lower artistic quality are bad or comparatively bad. Here, too, of course, social effect must be taken into account. There is hardly a writer or artist who does not consider his own work beautiful, and our criticism ought to permit the free competition of all varieties of works of art; but it is also entirely necessary to subject these works to correct criticism according to the criteria of the science of aesthetics, so that art of a lower level can be gradually raised to a higher and art which does not meet the demands of the struggle of the broad masses can be transformed into art that does.

There is the political criterion and there is the artistic criterion; what is the relationship between the two? Politics cannot be equated with art, nor can a general world outlook be equated with a method of artistic creation and criticism. We deny not only that there is an abstract and absolutely unchangeable political criterion, but also that there is an abstract and absolutely unchangeable artistic criterion; each class in every class society has its own political and artistic criteria. But all classes in all class societies invariably put the political criterion first and the artistic criterion second. The bourgeoisie always shuts out proletarian literature and art, however great their artistic merit. The proletariat must similarly distinguish among the literary and art works of past ages and determine its attitude towards them only after examining their attitude to the people and whether or not they had any progressive significance historically. Some works which politically are downright reactionary may have a certain artistic quality. The more reactionary their content and the higher their artistic quality, the more poisonous they are to the people, and the more necessary it is to reject them. A common characteristic of the literature and art of all exploiting classes in their period of decline is the contradiction between their reactionary political content and their artistic form. What we demand is the unity of politics and art, the unity of content and form, the unity of revolutionary political content and the highest possible perfection of artistic form. Works of art which lack artistic quality have no force, however progressive they are politically. Therefore, we oppose both the tendency to produce works of art with a wrong political viewpoint and the tendency towards the "poster and slogan style" which is correct in political viewpoint but lacking in artistic power. On questions of literature and art we must carry on a struggle on two fronts.

Both these tendencies can be found in the thinking of many comrades. A good number of comrades tend to neglect artistic technique; it is therefore necessary to give attention to the raising of artistic standards. But as I see it, the political side is more of a problem at present. Some comrades lack elementary political knowledge and consequently have all sorts of muddled ideas. Let me cite a few examples from Yenan.

"The theory of human nature." Is there such a thing as human nature? Of course there is. But there is only human nature in the concrete, no human nature is the abstract. In class society there is only human nature of a class character; there is no human nature above classes. We uphold the human nature of the proletariat and of the masses of the people, while the landlord and bourgeois classes uphold the human nature of their own classes, only they do not say so but make it out to be the only human nature in existence. The human nature boosted by certain petty-bourgeois intellectuals is also divorced from or opposed to the masses; what they call human nature is in essence nothing but bourgeois individualism, and so, in their eyes, proletarian human nature is contrary to human nature. "The theory of human nature" which some people in Yenan advocate as the basis of their so-called theory of literature and art puts the matter in just this way and is wholly wrong.

"The fundamental point of departure for literature and art is love, love of humanity." Now love may serve as a point of departure, but there is a more basic one. Love as an idea is a product of objective practice. Fundamentally, we do not start from ideas but from objective practice. Our writers and artists who come from the ranks of the intellectuals love the proletariat because society has made them feel that they and the proletariat share a common fate. We hate Japanese imperialism because Japanese imperialism oppresses us. There is absolutely no such thing in the world as love or hatred without reason or cause. As for the so-called love of humanity, there has been no such all-inclusive love since humanity was divided into classes. All the ruling classes of the past were fond of advocating it, and so were many so-called sages and wise men, but nobody has ever really practised it, because it is impossible in class society. There will be genuine love of humanity—after classes are eliminated all over the world. Classes have split society into many antagonistic groupings; there will be love of all humanity when classes are eliminated, but not now. We cannot love enemies, we cannot love social evils, our aim is to destroy them. This is common sense; can it be that some of our writers and artists still do not understand this?

"Literary and artistic works have always laid equal stress on the bright and the dark, half and half." This statement contains many muddled ideas. It is not true that literature and art have always done this. Many petty-bourgeois writers have never discovered the bright side. Their works only expose the dark and are known as the "literature of exposure." Some of their works simply specialize in preaching pessimism and world-weariness. On the other hand, Soviet literature in the period of socialist construction portrays mainly the bright. It, too, describes shortcomings in work and portrays negative characters, but this only serves as a contrast to bring out the brightness of the whole picture and is not on a so-called half-and-half basis. The writers and artists of the bourgeoisie in its period of reaction depict the revolutionary masses as mobs and themselves as saints, thus reversing the bright and the dark. Only truly revolutionary writers and artists can correctly solve the problem of whether to extol or to expose. All the dark forces harming the masses of the people must be exposed and all the revolutionary struggles of the masses of the people must be extolled; this is the fundamental task of revolutionary writers and artists.

"The task of literature and art has always been to expose." This assertion, like the previous one, arises from ignorance of the science of history. Literature and art, as we have shown, have never been devoted solely to exposure. For revolutionary writers and artists the targets for exposure can never be the masses, but only the aggressors, exploiters and oppressors and the evil influence they have on the people. The masses too have shortcomings, which should be overcome by criticism and self-criticism within the people's own ranks, and such criticism and self-criticism is also one of the most important tasks of literature and art. But this should not be regarded as any sort of "exposure of the people." As for the people, the question is basically one of education and of raising their level. Only counter-revolutionary writers and artists describe the people as "born fools" and the revolutionary masses as "tyrannical mobs."

"This is still the period of the satirical essay, and Lu Hsun's style of writing is still needed." Living under the rule of the dark forces and deprived of freedom of speech, Lu Hsun used burning satire and freezing irony, cast in the form of essays, to do battle; and he was entirely right. We, too, must hold up to sharp ridicule the fascists, the Chinese reactionaries and everything that harms the people; but in the Shensi-Kansu-Ningsia Border Region and the anti-Japanese base areas behind the enemy lines, where democracy and freedom are granted in full to the revolutionary writers and artists and withheld only from the counter-revolutionaries, the style of the essay should not simply be like Lu Hsun's. Here we can shout at the top of our voices and have no need for veiled and roundabout expressions, which are hard for the people to understand. When dealing with the people and not with their enemies, Lu Hsun never ridiculed or attacked the revolutionary people and the revolutionary Party in his "satirical essay period," and these essays were entirely different in manner from those directed against the enemy. To criticize the people's shortcomings is necessary, as we have already said, but in doing so we must truly take the stand of the people and speak out of whole-hearted eagerness to protect and educate them. To treat comrades like enemies is to go over to the stand of the enemy. Are we then to abolish satire? No. Satire is always necessary. But there are several kinds of satire, each with a different attitude, satire to deal with our enemies, satire to deal with our allies and satire to deal with our own ranks. We are not opposed to satire in general; what we must abolish is the abuse of satire.

"I am not given to praise and eulogy. The works of people who eulogize what is bright are not necessarily great and the works of those who depict the dark are not necessarily paltry." If you are a bourgeois writer or artist, you will eulogize not the proletariat but the bourgeoisie, and if you are a proletarian writer or artist, you will eulogize not the bourgeoisie but the proletariat and working people: it must be one or the other. The works of the eulogists of the bourgeoisie are not necessarily great, nor are the works of those who show that the bourgeoisie is dark necessarily paltry; the works of the eulogists of the proletariat are not necessarily not great, but the works of those who depict the so-called "darkness" of the proletariat are bound to be paltry—are these not facts of history as regards literature and art? Why should we not eulogize the people, the creators of the history of mankind? Why should we not eulogize the proletariat, the Communist Party, New Democracy and socialism? There is a type of person who has no enthusiasm for the people's cause and looks coldly from the side-lines at the struggles and victories of the proletariat and its vanguard; what he is interested in, and will never weary of eulogizing, is himself, plus perhaps a few figures in his small coterie. Of course, such petty-bourgeois individualists are unwilling to eulogize the deeds and virtues of the revolutionary people or heighten their courage in struggle and their confidence in victory. Persons of this type are merely termites in the revolutionary ranks; of course, the revolutionary people have no need for these "singers."

"It is not a question of stand; my class stand is correct, my intentions are good and I understand all right, but I am not good at expressing myself and so the effect turns out bad." I have already spoken about the dialectical materialist view of motive and effect. Now I want to ask, is not the question of effect one of stand? A person who acts solely by motive and does not inquire what effect his action will have is like a doctor who merely writes prescriptions but does not care how many patients die of them. Or take a political party which merely makes declarations but does not care whether they are carried out. It may well be asked, is this a correct stand? And is the intention here good? Of course, mistakes may occur even though the effect has been taken into account beforehand, but is the intention good when one continues in the same old rut after facts have proved that the effect is bad? In judging a party or a doctor, we must look at practice, at the effect. The same applies in judging a writer. A person with truly good intentions must take the effect into account, sum up experience and study the methods or, in creative work, study the technique of expression. A person with truly good intentions must criticize the shortcomings and mistakes in his own work with the utmost candour and resolve to correct them. This is precisely why Communists employ the method of self-criticism. This alone is the correct stand. Only in this process of serious and responsible practice is it possible gradually to understand what the correct stand is and gradually obtain a good grasp of it. If one does not move in this direction in practice, if there is simply the complacent assertion that one "understands all rights," then in fact one has not understood at all.

"To call on us to study Marxism is to repeat the mistake of the dialectical materialist creative method, which will harm the creative mood." To study Marxism means to apply the dialectical materialist and historical materialist viewpoint in our observation of the world, of society and of literature and art; it does not mean writing philosophical lectures into our works of literature and art. Marxism embraces but cannot replace realism in literary and artistic creation, just as it embraces but cannot replace the atomic and electronic theories in physics. Empty, dry dogmatic formulas do indeed destroy the creative mood; not only that, they first destroy Marxism. Dogmatic "Marxism" is not Marxism, it is anti-Marxism. Then does not Marxism destroy the creative mood? Yes, it does. It definitely destroys creative moods that are feudal, bourgeois, petty-bourgeois, liberalistic, individualist, nihilist, art-for-art's sake, aristocratic, decadent or pessimistic, and every other creative mood that is alien to the masses of the people and to the proletariat. So far as proletarian writers and artists are concerned, should not these kinds of creative moods be destroyed? I think they should, they should be utterly destroyed. And while they are being destroyed, something new can be constructed.

V

The problems discussed here exist in our literary and art circles in Yenan. What does that show? It shows that wrong styles of work still exist to a serious extent in our literary and art circles and that there are still many defects among our comrades, such as idealism, dogmatism, empty illusions, empty talk, contempt for practice and aloofness from the masses, all of which call for an effective and serious campaign of rectification.

We have many comrades who are still not very clear on the difference between the proletariat and the petty bourgeoisie. There are many Party members who have joined the Communist Party organizationally but have not yet joined the Party wholly or at all ideologically. Those who have not joined the Party ideologically still carry a great deal of the muck of the exploiting classes in their heads, and have no idea at all of what proletarian ideology, or communism, or the Party is. "Proletarian ideology?" they think. "The same old stuff!" Little do they know that it is no easy matter to acquire this stuff. Some will never have the slightest Communist flavour about them as long as they live and can only end up by leaving the Party. Therefore, though the majority in our Party and in our ranks are clean and honest, we must in all seriousness put things in order both ideologically and organizationally if we are to develop the revolutionary movement more effectively and bring it to speedier success. To put things in order organizationally requires our first doing so ideologically, our launching a struggle of proletarian ideology against non-proletarian ideology. An ideological struggle is already under way in literary and art circles in Yenan, and it is most necessary. Intellectuals of petty-bourgeois origin always stubbornly try in all sorts of ways, including literary and artistic ways, to project themselves and spread their views, and they want the Party and the world to be remoulded in their own image. In the circumstances it is our duty to jolt these "comrades" and tell them sharply, "That won't work! The proletariat cannot accommodate itself to you; to yield to you would actually be to yield to the big landlord class and the big bourgeoisie and to run the risk of undermining our Party and our country." Whom then must we yield to? We can mould the Party and the world only in the image of the proletarian vanguard. We hope our comrades in literary and art circles will realize the seriousness of this great debate and join actively in this struggle, so that every comrade may become sound and our entire ranks may become truly united and consolidated ideologically and organizationally.

Because of confusion in their thinking, many of our comrades are not quite able to draw a real distinction between our revolutionary base areas and the Kuomintang areas and they make many mistakes as a consequence. A good number of comrades have come here from the garrets of Shanghai, and in coming from those garrets to the revolutionary base areas, they have passed not only from one kind of place to another but from one historical epoch to another. One society is semi-feudal, semi-colonial, under the rule of the big landlords and big bourgeoisie, the other is a revolutionary new-democratic society under the leadership of the proletariat. To come to the revolutionary bases means to enter an epoch unprecedented in the thousands of years of Chinese history, an epoch in which the masses of the people wield state power. Here the people around us and the audience for our propaganda are totally different. The past epoch is gone, never to return. Therefore, we must integrate ourselves with the new masses without any hesitation. If, living among the new masses, some comrades, as I said before, are still "lacking in knowledge and understanding" and remain "heroes with no place to display their prowess," then difficulties will arise for them, and not only when they go out to the villages; right here in Yenan difficulties will arise for them. Some comrades may think, "Well, I had better continue writing for the readers in the Great Rear Area;[12] it is a job I know well and has 'national significance'." This idea is entirely wrong. The Great Rear Area is also changing. Readers there expect authors in the revolutionary base areas to tell about the new people and the new world and not to bore them with the same old tales. Therefore, the more a work is written for the masses in the revolutionary base areas, the more national significance will it have. Fadeyev in *The Debacle*[13] only told the story of a small guerrilla unit and had no intention of pandering to the palate of readers in the old world; yet the book has exerted world-wide influence. At any rate in China its influence is very great, as you know. China is moving forward, not back, and it is the revolutionary base areas, not any of the backward, retrogressive areas, that are leading China forward. This is a fundamental issue that, above all, comrades must come to understand in the rectification movement.

Since integration into the new epoch of the masses is essential, it is necessary thoroughly to solve the problem of the relationship between the individual and the masses. This couplet from a poem by Lu Hsun should be our motto:

[12] The Great Rear Area was the name given during the War of Resistance to the vast areas under Kuomintang control in southwestern and northwestern China which were not occupied by the Japanese invaders, as distinguished from the "small rear area", the anti-Japanese base areas behind the enemy lines under the leadership of the Communist Party.

[13] *The Debacle* by the famous Soviet writer Alexander Fadeyev was published in 1927 and translated into Chinese by Lu Hsun. The novel describes the struggle of a partisan detachment of workers, peasants and revolutionary intellectuals in Siberia against the counter-revolutionary brigands during the Soviet civil war.

> *Fierce-browed, I coolly defy a thousand pointing fingers,*
> *Head-bowed, like a willing ox I serve the children.*[14]

The "thousand pointing fingers" are our enemies, and we will never yield to them, no matter how ferocious. The "children" here symbolize the proletariat and the masses. All Communists, all revolutionaries, all revolutionary literary and art workers should learn from the example of Lu Hsun and be "oxen" for the proletariat and the masses, bending their backs to the task until their dying day. Intellectuals who want to integrate themselves with the masses, who want to serve the masses, must go through a process in which they and the masses come to know each other well. This process may, and certainly will, involve much pain and friction, but if you have the determination, you will be able to fulfil these requirements.

Today I have discussed only some of the problems of fundamental orientation for our literature and art movement; many specific problems remain which will require further study. I am confident that comrades here are determined to move in the direction indicated. I believe that in the course of the rectification movement and in the long period of study and work to come, you will surely be able to bring about a transformation in yourselves and in your works, to create many fine works which will be warmly welcomed by the masses of the people, and to advance the literature and art movement in the revolutionary base areas and throughout China to a glorious new stage.

[14] This couplet is from Lu Hsun's "In Mockery of Myself."

ON "LET A HUNDRED FLOWERS BLOSSOM, LET A HUNDRED SCHOOLS OF THOUGHT CONTEND"

Mao Tse-tung

"Let a hundred flowers blossom, let a hundred schools of thought contend" and "long-term coexistence and mutual supervision"—how did these slogans come to be put forward? They were put forward in the light of China's specific conditions, on the basis of the recognition that various kinds of contradictions still exist in socialist society, and in response to the country's urgent need to speed up its economic and cultural development. Letting a hundred flowers blossom and a hundred schools of thought contend is the policy for promoting the progress of the arts and the sciences and a flourishing socialist culture in our land. Different forms and styles in art should develop freely and different schools in science should contend freely. We think that it is harmful to the growth of art and science if administrative measures are used to impose one particular style of art or school of thought and to ban another. Questions of right and wrong in the arts and sciences should be settled through free discussion in artistic and scientific circles and through practical work in these fields. They should not be settled in summary fashion. A period of trial is often needed to determine whether something is right or wrong. Throughout history, new and correct things have often failed at the outset to win recognition from the majority of people and have had to develop by twists and turns in struggle. Often correct and good things have first been regarded not as fragrant flowers but as poisonous weeds. Copernicus' theory of the solar system and Darwin's theory of evolution were once dismissed as erroneous and had to win through over bitter opposition. Chinese history offers many similar examples. In a socialist society, conditions for the growth of the new are radically different from and far superior to those in the old society. Nevertheless, it still often happens that new, rising forces are held back and rational proposals constricted. Moreover, the growth of new things may be hindered in the absence of deliberate suppression simply through lack of discernment. It is therefore necessary to be

From *Mao Tse-tung on Literature and Art* (Peking: Foreign Languages Press, 1967). First published February, 1957.

careful about questions of right and wrong in the arts and sciences, to encourage free discussion and avoid hasty conclusions. We believe that such an attitude can help to ensure a relatively smooth development of the arts and sciences.

Marxism, too, has developed through struggle. At the beginning, Marxism was subjected to all kinds of attack and regarded as a poisonous weed. It is still being attacked and is still regarded as a poisonous weed in many parts of the world. In the socialist countries, it enjoys a different position. But non-Marxist and, moreover, anti-Marxist ideologies exist even in these countries. In China, although in the main socialist transformation has been completed with respect to the system of ownership, and although the large-scale and turbulent class struggles of the masses characteristic of the previous revolutionary periods have in the main come to an end, there are still remnants of the overthrown landlord and comprador classes, there is still a bourgeoisie, and the remoulding of the petty bourgeoisie has only just started. The class struggle is by no means over. The class struggle between the proletariat and the bourgeoisie, the class struggle between the different political forces, and the class struggle in the ideological field between the proletariat and the bourgeoisie will continue to be long and tortuous and at times will even become very acute. The proletariat seeks to transform the world according to its own world outlook, and so does the bourgeoisie. In this respect, the question of which will win out, socialism or capitalism, is still not really settled. Marxists are still a minority among the entire population as well as among the intellectuals. Therefore, Marxism must still develop through struggle. Marxism can develop only through struggle, and not only is this true of the past and the present, it is necessarily true of the future as well. What is correct invariably develops in the course of struggle with what is wrong. The true, the good and the beautiful always exist by contrast with the false, the evil and the ugly, and grow in struggle with the latter. As soon as a wrong thing is rejected and a particular truth accepted by mankind, new truths begin their struggle with new errors. Such struggles will never end. This is the law of development of truth and, naturally, of Marxism as well.

It will take a fairly long period of time to decide the issue in the ideological struggle between socialism and capitalism in our country. The reason is that the influence of the bourgeoisie and of the intellectuals who come from the old society will remain in our country for a long time to come, and so will their class ideology. If this is not sufficiently understood, or is not understood at all, the gravest mistakes will be made and the necessity of waging the struggle in the ideological field will be ignored. Ideological struggle is not like other forms of struggle. The only method to be used in this struggle is that of painstaking reasoning and not crude coercion. Today, socialism is in an advantageous position in the ideological struggle. The main power of the state is in the hands of the working people led by the proletariat. The Communist Party is strong and its prestige stands high. Although there are defects and mistakes in our work, every fair-minded person can see that we are loyal to the people, that we are both determined and able to build up our motherland together with them, and that we have already achieved great successes and will achieve still greater ones. The vast majority of the bourgeoisie and intellectuals who come from the old society are patriotic and are willing to serve their flourishing socialist motherland; they know they will be helpless and have no bright future to look forward to if they turn away from the socialist cause and from the working people led by the Communist Party.

People may ask, since Marxism is accepted as the guiding ideology by the majority of the people in our country, can it be criticized? Certainly it can. Marxism is scientific truth and fears no criticism. If it did, and if it could be overthrown by criticism, it would be worthless. In fact, aren't the idealists criticizing Marxism every day and in every way? Aren't those who harbour bourgeois and petty-bourgeois ideas and do not wish to change—aren't they also criticizing Marxism in every way? Marxists should not be afraid of criticism from any quarter. Quite the contrary, they need to temper and develop themselves and win new positions in the teeth of criticism and in the storm and stress of struggle. Fighting against wrong ideas is like being vaccinated—a man develops greater immunity from disease as a result of vaccination. Plants raised in hot-houses are unlikely to be sturdy. Carrying out the policy of letting a hundred flowers blossom and a hundred schools of throught contend will not weaken but strengthen the leading position of Marxism in the ideological field.

What should our policy be towards non-Marxist ideas? As far as unmistakable counter-revolutionaries and saboteurs of the socialist cause are concerned, the matter is easy: we simply deprive them of their freedom of speech. But incorrect ideas among the people are quite a different matter. Will it do to ban such ideas and deny them any opportunity for expression? Certainly not. It is not only futile but very harmful to use summary methods in dealing with ideological questions among the people, with questions concerned with man's mental world. You may ban the expression of wrong ideas, but the ideas will still be there. On the other hand, if correct ideas are pampered in hothouses without being exposed to the elements or immunized from disease, they will not win out against erroneous ones. Therefore, it is only by employing the method of discussion, criticism and reasoning that we can really foster correct ideas and overcome wrong ones, and that we can really settle issues.

Inevitably, the bourgeoisie and petty bourgeoisie will give expression to their own ideologies. Inevitably, they will stubbornly express themselves on political and ideological questions by every possible means. You cannot expect them to do otherwise. We should not use the method of suppression and prevent them from expressing themselves, but should allow them to do so and at the same time argue with them and direct appropriate criticism at them. We must undoubtedly criticize wrong ideas of every description. It certainly would not be right to refrain from criticism, look on while wrong ideas spread unchecked and allow them to monopolize the field. Mistakes must be criticized and poisonous weeds fought wherever they crop up. However, such criticism should not be dogmatic, and the metaphysical method should not be used, but efforts should be made to apply the dialectical method. What is needed is scientific analysis and convincing argument. Dogmatic criticism settles nothing. We are against poisonous weeds of any kind, but we must carefully distinguish between what is really a poisonous weed and what is really a fragrant flower. Together with the masses of the people, we must learn to differentiate carefully between the two and to use correct methods to fight the poisonous weeds.

At the same time as we criticize dogmatism, we must direct our attention to criticizing revisionism. Revisionism, or Right opportunism, is a bourgeois trend of thought that is even more dangerous than dogmatism. The revisionists, the Right opportunists, pay lip-service to Marxism; they too attack "dogmatism." But what they are really attacking is the quintessence of Marxism. They oppose or distort materialism and dialectics, oppose or try to weaken the people's democratic dictatorship and the leading role of the Communist Party, and oppose or try to weaken socialist transformation and socialist construction. After the basic victory of the socialist revolution in our country, there are still a number of people who vainly hope to restore the capitalist system and fight the working class on every front, including the ideological one. And their right-hand men in this struggle are the revisionists.

At first glance, the two slogans—let a hundred flowers blossom and let a hundred schools of thought contend—have no class character; the proletariat can turn them to account, and so can the bourgeoisie or other people. But different classes, strata and social groups each have their own views on what are fragrant flowers and what are poisonous weeds. What then, from the point of view of the broad masses of the people, should be the criteria today for distinguishing fragrant flowers from poisonous weeds? In the political life of our people, how should right be distinguished from wrong in one's words and actions? On the basis of the principles of our Constitution, the will of the overwhelming majority of our·people and the common political positions which have been proclaimed on various occasions by our political parties and groups, we consider that, broadly speaking, the criteria should be as follows:

> *(1) Words and actions should help to unite, and not divide, the people of our various nationalities.*
> *(2) They should be beneficial, and not harmful, to socialist transformation and socialist construction.*
> *(3) They should help to consolidate, and not undermine or weaken, the people's democratic dictatorship.*
> *(4) They should help to consolidate, and not undermine or weaken, democratic centralism.*
> *(5) They should help to strengthen, and not discard or weaken, the leadership of the Communist Party.*
> *(6) They should be beneficial, and not harmful, to international socialist unity and the unity of the peace-loving people of the world.*

Of these six criteria, the most important are the socialist path and the leadership of the Party. These criteria are put forward not to hinder but to foster the free discussion of questions among the people. Those who disapprove of these criteria can still put forward their own views and argue their case. However, since the majority of the people have clear-cut criteria to go by, criticism and self-criticism can be conducted along proper lines, and the criteria can be applied to people's words and actions to determine whether they are right or wrong, whether they are fragrant flowers or poisonous weeds. These are political criteria. Naturally, in judging the validity of scientific theories or assessing the aesthetic value of works of art, additional pertinent criteria are needed. But these six political criteria are applicable to all activities in the arts and the sciences. In a socialist country like ours, can there possibly be any useful scientific or artistic activity which runs counter to these political criteria?

The views set out above are based on China's specific historical conditions. Conditions vary in different socialist countries and with different Communist Parties. Therefore, we do not maintain that other countries and Parties should or must follow the Chinese way.

ON THE LONG MARCH
Mao Tse-tung

Speaking of the Long March, one may ask, "What is its significance?" We answer that the Long March is the first of its kind in the annals of history, that it is a manifesto, a propaganda force, a seeding-machine. Since Pan Ku divided the heavens from the earth and the Three Sovereigns and Five Emperors[1] reigned, has history ever witnessed a long march such as ours? For twelve months we were under daily reconaissance and bombing from the skies by scores of planes, while on land we were encircled and pursued, obstructed and intercepted by a huge force of several hundred thousand men, and we encountered untold difficulties and dangers on the way; yet by using our two legs we swept across a distance of more than twenty-five thousand *li* through the length and breadth of eleven provinces. Let us ask, has history ever known a long march to equal ours? No, never. The Long March is a manifesto. It has proclaimed to the world that the Red Army is an army of heroes, while the imperialists and their running dogs, Chiang Kai-shek and his like, are impotent. It has proclaimed their utter failure to encircle, pursue, obstruct and intercept us. The Long March is also a propaganda force. It has announced to some 200 million people in eleven provinces that the road of the Red Army is their only road to liberation. Without the Long March, how could the broad masses have learned so quickly about the existence of the great truth which the Red Army embodies? The Long March is also a seeding-machine. In the eleven provinces it has sown many seeds which will sprout, leaf, blossom, and bear fruit, and will yield a harvest in the future. In a word, the Long March has ended with victory for us and defeat for the enemy. Who brought the Long March to victory? The Communist Party. Without the Communist Party, a long march of this kind would have been inconceivable. The Chinese Communist Party, its leadership, its cadres and its members fear no difficulties or hardships. Whoever ques-

---

[1] Pan Ku, according to Chinese mythology, was the creator of the world and the first ruler of mankind. The Three Sovereigns and Five Emperors were legendary rulers in ancient China. [All notes to Mao's "On The Long March" by translator (anonymous).]

From Mao Tse-tung, *On Tactics Against Japanese Imperialism* (Peking: Foreign Languages Press, 1965). The selection is from a report given by Mao Tse-tung on December 27, 1935.

tions our ability to lead the revolutionary war will fall into the morass of opportunism. A new situation arose as soon as the Long March was over. In the battle of Chihlochen the Central Red Army and the Northwestern Red Army, fighting in fraternal solidarity, shattered the traitor Chiang Kai-shek's campaign of "encirclement and suppression" against the Shensi-Kansu border area and thus laid the cornerstone for the task undertaken by the Central Committee of the Party, the task of setting up the national headquarters of the revolution in northwestern China.

This being the situation with regard to the main body of the Red Army, what about the guerrilla warfare in the southern provinces? Our guerrilla forces there have suffered some setbacks but have not been wiped out. In many places, they are reasserting themselves, growing and expanding.[2]

In the Kuomintang areas, the workers' struggle is now moving beyond the factory walls, and from being an economic struggle is becoming a political struggle. A heroic working-class struggle against the Japanese and the traitors is now in intense ferment and, judging by the situation, it will erupt before long.

The peasants' struggle has never ceased. Harassed by aggression from abroad, by difficulties at home and by natural disasters, the peasants have unleashed widespread struggles in the form of guerrilla warfare, mass uprisings and famine riots. The anti-Japanese guerrilla warfare now going on in the northeastern provinces and eastern Hopei[3] is their reply to the attacks of Japanese imperialism.

The student movement has already grown considerably and will certainly go on doing so. But this movement can sustain itself and break through the martial law imposed by the traitors and the policy of disruption and massacre practised by the police, the secret service agents, the scoundrels in the educational world and the fascists only if it is co-ordinated with the struggles of the workers, peasants and soldiers.

We have already dealt with the vacillation of the national bourgeoisie, the rich peasants and small landlords and the possibility that they may actually participate in the anti-Japanese struggle.

The minority nationalities, and especially the people of Inner Mongolia who are directly menaced by Japanese imperialism, are now rising up in struggle. As time goes on, their struggle will merge with

---

[2] When the main forces of the Red Army in southern China shifted position during 1934–35, they left behind some units to operate as guerrillas.

[3] The anti-Japanese guerrilla war in eastern Hopei refers to the peasant uprising against Japan there in May 1935.

that of the people in northern China and with the operations of the Red Army in the Northwest.

All this indicates that the revolutionary situation is now changing from a localized into a nation-wide one and that it is gradually changing from a state of unevenness to a certain degree of evenness. We are on the eve of a great change. The task of the Party is to form a revolutionary national united front by combining the activities of the Red Army with all the activities of the workers, the peasants, the students, the petty bourgeoisie and the national bourgeoisie throughout the country.

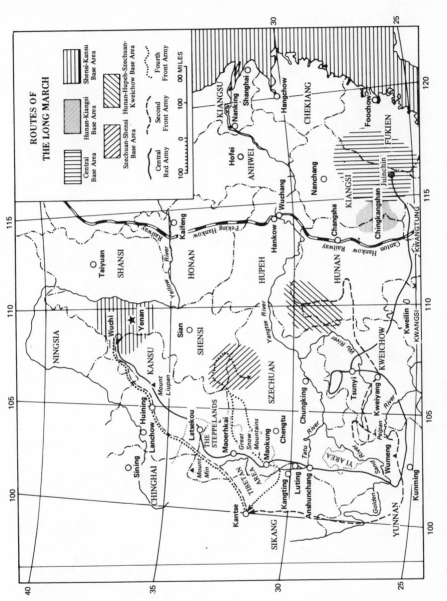

From Chen Chi-tung, *The Long March* (Peking: Foreign Languages Press, 1956).

Third
World
Revolution

CANDAULES, COMMISSIONER

A myth of revolution and sex in the kingdom of Lydia, in Asia Minor, the story of Candaules, Gyges, and Nyssia—apparently historical figures of the eighth century, B.C.—is told by Plato in his *Republic* and Herodotus in his *History*. To Plato, the myth suggests little essential difference between the just and unjust man, for with power to become invisible, no just man would remain just. In his account, Gyges— wearing a ring that makes him invisible—seduces Nyssia and seizes Candaules' kingdom, both on his own initiative. The magic ring does not figure in Herodotus' narrative of the overthrow of a kingdom; Candaules shows his naked wife to Gyges, who is hidden, and Nyssia, who accidentally catches sight of him, proposes that he kill her husband and take his place. From Plato, *Candaules, Commissioner* derives the device of the magic ring, from Herodotus the husband's display of his wife's nakedness. The play transforms the question of who instigated the overthrow of Candaules' kingdom—the opportunist Gyges (according to Plato); Nyssia, who in Herodotus gives Gyges the choice of death or herself and the kingdom; or Candaules himself (also in Herodotus), whose insistence on showing his wife to Gyges touches off the process that leads to his murder—into an exploration of the underlying and immediate causes of revolution.

In the French production at the Ecole Normale Supérieure, as the director and author reveal, the actor playing Gyges followed an essentially Platonic line. This Gyges planned the revolution from the start. Though a Maoist rather than a Fabian socialist, he—like Fabius (the Roman general who defeated Hannibal), the man after whom the Fabians are named—waited patiently for the appropriate moment and then, when his neurotic master and mistress provided it, struck hard and decisively. Gyges' revolutionary ardor was counterpointed by the decadence of the *ancien régime*, as represented by Candaules and Nyssia. In this production—entitled *Le nouveau Candaule* (The New Candaules)—the neuroses of the impotent voyeur Candaules and the self-hating Nyssia, who may purposely have incited the revolution and

149

willed her own destruction, were crucial in providing the right moment for Gyges to strike. To the acting company, the director states, "Gyges was not taken in by Candaules, but from the beginning was waiting for an opportunity to free himself." Although the director disagreed with this interpretation, the actor playing Gyges, according to the author, seems to have had his way. In this production, which aimed to radicalize the audience, the play became "a primer for revolutionaries." Evidently, the entire atmosphere surrounding the production—which took place among veterans of the French student uprising of 1968—was revolutionary. As the author said in a letter shortly after he saw this production, there were "revolutionary slogans everywhere, Mao's sayings on the walls and in the dressing room at the play . . . statements about the class struggle. . . . And the actor who played Gyges really put some 'fire' into the last burning scene—so much so that he began to frighten the actor playing Candaules."

In the Stanford Repertory Theatre production, the emphasis was not on the rise of the third world but on the decline of the west. The play became "a critique of the American Dream, in which Gyges almost believed." Following Herodotus, this production stressed as the causes of revolution the master and mistress, whose neuroses revealed to their young servant the hollowness of the life he had been trying to emulate and led him to a realization of his position among his own people. In this production, Gyges did not even throw the bomb; it was Nyssia's deranged mind that suggested he did. At Stanford, the production might have been subtitled, "The Making of a Revolutionary," as Gyges reluctantly moved from one role to another. The colonial regime fell not so much through the strength of its assailants as through the weakness of its defenders.

In *Candaules, Commissioner*, the Greek myth is rendered in terms of racist attitudes, imperialism and colonialism, and civil war. The play suggests the Vietnamese war, which is also marked by these characteristics and which, like the Ambassador's party, features battle-watching in a fashionable Saigon restaurant (and on television sets in the U.S.); which has similar characteristics regarding the counting of casualties; and whose proponents make use of slogans similar to the cant phrases of Candaules. Nevertheless, though *Candaules, Commissioner* suggests this conflict, it is not primarily "about" it. Like the myth on which it is based, the play transcends particular events.

THE REPUBLIC

(Selection from Book II)

Plato

Now, that those who practise justice do so involuntarily and
because they have not the power to be unjust will best appear if we
imagine something of this kind: having given both to the just and
the unjust power to do what they will, let us watch and see whither
desire will lead them; then we shall discover in the very act the just
and unjust man to be proceeding along the same road, following their
good, and are only diverted into the path of justice by the force of law.
The liberty which we are supposing may be most completely given to
them in the form of such a power as is said to have been possessed
by Gyges the ancestor of Croesus the Lydian. According to the tradition, Gyges was a shepherd in the service of the king of Lydia; there
was a great storm, and an earthquake made an opening in the earth at
the place where he was feeding his flock. Amazed at the sight, he
descended into the opening, where, among other marvels, he beheld a
hollow brazen horse, having doors, at which he stooping and looking
in saw a dead body of stature, as appeared to him, more than human,
and having nothing on but a gold ring; this he took from the finger
of the dead and reascended. Now, the shepherds met together, according to custom that they might send their monthly report about the
flocks to the king; into their assembly he came having the ring on his
finger, and as he was sitting among them he chanced to turn the collet
of the ring inside his hand, when instantly he became invisible to the
rest of the company and they began to speak of him as if he were
no longer present. He was astonished at this, and again touching
the ring he turned the collet outwards and reappeared; he made several
trials of the ring, and always with the same result—when he turned
the collet inwards he became invisible, when outwards he reappeared.
Whereupon he contrived to be chosen one of the messengers who were
sent to the court; where as soon as he arrived he seduced the queen,
and with her help conspired against the king and slew him, and took
the kingdom. Suppose now that there were two such magic rings, and
the just put on one of them and the unjust the other; no man can be

From *The Dialogues of Plato*, translated by Benjamin Jowett. Oxford University
Press, 1871.

imagined to be of such an iron nature that he would stand fast in justice. No man would keep his hands off what was not his own when he could safely take what he liked out of the market, or go into houses and lie with any one at his pleasure, or kill or release from prison whom he would, and in all respects be like a god among men. Then the actions of the just would be as the actions of the unjust; they would both come at last to the same point. And this we may truly affirm to be a great proof that a man is just, not willingly or because he thinks that justice is any good to him individually, but of necessity, for wherever any one thinks that he can safely be unjust there he is unjust. For all men believe in their hearts that injustice is far more profitable to the individual than justice, and he who argues as I have been supposing will say that they are right. If you could imagine any one obtaining this power of becoming invisible, and never doing any wrong or touching what was another's, he would be thought by the lookers-on to be a most wretched idiot, although they would praise him to one another's faces, and keep up appearances with one another from a fear that they too might suffer injustice.

HISTORY

(Selection from Book I)

Herodotus

The sovereignty of Lydia, which had belonged to the Heraclides, passed into the family of Croesus, who were called the Mermnadae, in the manner which I will now relate. There was a certain king of Sardis, Candaules by name, whom the Greeks called Myrsilus.[1] He was a descendant of Alcaeus, son of Hercules. The first king of this dynasty was Agron, son of Ninus, grandson of Belus, and great-grandson of Alcaeus; Candaules, son of Myrsus, was the last. The kings who reigned before Agron sprang from Lydus, son of Atys, from whom the people of the land, called previously Meonians, received the name of Lydians. The Heraclides, descended from Hercules and the slave girl of Jardanus, having been entrusted by these princes with the management of affairs, obtained the kingdom by an oracle. Their rule endured for two and twenty generations of men, a space of five hundred and five years; during the whole of which period, from Agron to Candaules, the crown descended in the direct line from father to son.

Now it happened that this Candaules was in love with his own wife; and not only so, but thought her the fairest woman in the whole world. This fancy had strange consequences. There was in his body-guard a man whom he specially favored, Gyges, the son of Dascylus. All affairs of greatest moment were entrusted by Candaules to this person, and to him he was wont to extol the surpassing beauty of his wife. So matters went on for a while. At length, one day, Candaules, who was fated to end ill, thus addressed his follower: "I see thou dost not credit what I tell thee of my lady's loveliness; but come now, since men's ears are less credulous than their eyes, contrive some means whereby thou mayst behold her naked." At this the other loudly exclaimed, saying, "What most unwise speech is this, master, which thou hast uttered? Wouldst thou have me behold my mistress when she is naked? Bethink thee that a woman, with her clothes, puts off her bashfulness. Our fathers, in time past, distinguished right and wrong plainly enough, and it is our wisdom to submit to be taught by them.

[1] Son of Myrsus.

From *History of Herodotus*, translated by George Rawlinson. London: John Murray, 1862.

153

There is an old saying, 'Let each look on his own.' I hold thy wife for the fairest of all womankind. Only, I beseech thee, ask me not to do wickedly."

Gyges thus endeavored to decline the king's proposal, trembling lest some dreadful evil should befall him through it. But the king replied to him, "Courage, friend; suspect me not of the design to prove thee by this discourse; nor dread thy mistress, lest mischief befall thee at her hands. Be sure I will so manage that she shall not even know that thou hast looked upon her. I will place thee behind the open door of the chamber in which we sleep. When I enter to go to rest she will follow me. There stands a chair close to the entrance, on which she will lay her clothes one by one as she takes them off. Thou wilt be able thus at thy leisure to peruse her person. Then, when she is moving from the chair toward the bed, and her back is turned on thee, be it thy care that she see thee not as thou passest through the doorway."

Gyges, unable to escape, could but declare his readiness. Then Candaules, when bedtime came, led Gyges into his sleeping chamber, and a moment after the queen followed. She entered, and laid her garments on the chair, and Gyges gazed on her. After a while she moved toward the bed, and her back being then turned, he glided stealthily from the apartment. As he was passing out, however, she saw him, and instantly divining what had happened, she neither screamed as her shame impelled her, nor even appeared to have noticed aught, purposing to take vengeance upon the husband who had so affronted her. For among the Lydians, and indeed among the barbarians generally, it is reckoned a deep disgrace, even to a man, to be seen naked.

No sound or sign of intelligence escaped her at the time. But in the morning, as soon as day broke, she hastened to choose from among her retinue, such as she knew to be most faithful to her, and preparing them for what was to ensue, summoned Gyges into her presence. Now it had often happened before that the queen had desired to confer with him, and he was accustomed to come to her at her call. He therefore obeyed the summons, not suspecting that she knew aught of what had occurred. Then she addressed these words to him: "Take thy choice, Gyges, of two courses which are open to thee. Slay Candaules, and thereby become my lord, and obtain the Lydian throne, or die this moment in his room. So wilt thou not again, obeying all behests of thy master, behold what is not lawful for thee. It must needs be, that either he perish by whose counsel this thing was done, or thou, who sawest me naked, and so didst break our usages." At these words Gyges stood awhile in mute astonishment; recovering after a time, he earnestly besought the queen that she would not compel him to so hard a choice. But finding he implored in vain, and that necessity was indeed laid on him to kill or be killed, he made choice of life for himself, and replied by this inquiry: "If it must be so, and thou compellest me against my will to put my lord to death, come, let me hear how thou wilt have me set on him." "Let him be attacked," she answered, "on that spot where I was by him shown naked to you, and let the assault be made when he is asleep."

All was then prepared for the attack, and when night fell, Gyges, seeing that he had no retreat or escape, but must absolutely either slay Candaules, or himself be slain, followed his mistress into the sleeping room. She placed a dagger in his hand, and hid him carefully behind the self-same door. Then Gyges, when the king was fallen asleep, entered privily into the chamber and struck him dead. Thus did the wife and kingdom of Candaules pass into the possession of Gyges, of whom Archilochus the Parian, who lived about the same time, made mention in a poem written in Iambic trimeter verse.[2]

Gyges was afterwards confirmed in the possession of the throne by an answer of the Delphic oracle. Enraged at the murder of their king, the people flew to arms, but after a while the partisans of Gyges came to terms with them, and it was agreed that if the Delphic oracle declared him king of the Lydians, he should reign; if otherwise, he should yield the throne to the Heraclides. As the oracle was given in his favor he became king. The Pythoness,[3] however, added that, in the fifth generation from Gyges, vengeance should come for the Heraclides; a prophecy of which neither the Lydians nor their princes took any account till it was fulfilled. Such was the way in which the Mermnadae deposed the Heraclides, and themselves obtained the sovereignty.

---

[2] There is extant a fragment of a line of Archilochus which mentions Gyges. In *The Rhetoric*, Book III, Chapter 7, Aristotle mentions that in a satire Archilochus has Charon say, "Not for the wealth of Gyges."

[3] The priestess of Apollo at Delphi.

QUOTATIONS FROM CHAIRMAN MAO TSE-TUNG

(Selections)

Imperialism will not last long because it always does evil things. It persists in grooming and supporting reactionaries in all countries who are against the people, it has forcibly seized many colonies and semi-colonies and many military bases, and it threatens the peace with atomic war. Thus, forced by imperialism to do so, more than 90 per cent of the people of the world are rising or will rise up in struggle against it. Yet imperialism is still alive, still running amuck in Asia, Africa and Latin America. In the West imperialism is still oppressing the people at home. This situation must change. It is the task of the people of the whole world to put an end to the aggression and oppression perpetrated by imperialism, and chiefly by U. S. imperialism.

Interview with a Hsinhua News Agency correspondent (September 29, 1958).

A revolution is not a dinner party, or writing an essay, or painting a picture, or doing embroidery; it cannot be so refined, so leisurely and gentle, so temperate, kind, courteous, restrained and magnanimous. A revolution is an insurrection, an act of violence by which one class overthrows another.

"Report on an Investigation of the Peasant Movement in Hunan" (March, 1927).

Revolutions and revolutionary wars are inevitable in class society, and without them it is impossible to accomplish any leap in social development and to overthrow the reactionary ruling classes and therefore impossible for the people to win political power.

"On Contradiction" (August, 1937).

Every Communist must grasp the truth, "Political power grows out of the barrel of a gun."

"Problems of War and Strategy" (November 6, 1938).

From *Quotations from Chairman Mao Tse-tung* (Peking: Foreign Languages Press, 1968).

THE AUTHOR LOOKS AT REVOLUTION

Daniel C. Gerould

I wrote *Candaules, Commissioner* in the winter of 1964–1965—in retrospect, a happy time of illusion when it appeared that Barry Goldwater's overwhelming defeat by Lyndon B. Johnson would permit the forces of liberalism to liquidate the war in Vietnam (still only a minor nightmare at that period) and bring about greater social and racial justice at home. By the time the play was starting to get known and be performed several years later, it was already more up-to-date than when it was first written. The battle-watching at the Ambassador's, I saw from reading the newspapers, was being imitated in Saigon by the customers at a fashionable rooftop restaurant. And during the production at Stanford in the last week of January, 1968, all the details of the palace revolution that gets out of hand in Scene 4 were given new actuality by news reports of an impending coup in South Vietnam which made the audience think that the play was following current events closely, rather than vice versa.

In a number of unexpected ways, *Candaules* has been pursued by history and constantly re-interpreted by it. Not only the Gulf of Tonkin, the bombing of North Vietnam, and events in Saigon, but also the black revolution, student uprisings, the third world, and anti-imperialism have all come into the picture.

Perhaps because the play is based on an ancient Greek legend (from which it gets its characters and story) and grows out of my own personal experiences of another time and place for its emotional outlook, *Candaules* is not only about Vietnam but about the eternal master-slave relationship and applies to any of the innumerable revolutions that it produces. The sources of the play lie in Herodotus' history of the Persian wars and in my memories as an American soldier in Southeast Asia in 1951–1953. Then in 1964 reading and brooding about Vietnam revived my reminiscences about the Persian wars and the Korean War. In the midst of our latest efforts to make backward Asians as free and happy as we are, I recalled a story in Herodotus' *History* (an early account of the struggle between the civilized western world and the barbarians from the east) which had always fascinated me:

the erotic tale about Candaules, king of ancient Lydia, who insisted on showing his beautiful wife Nyssia stark naked to his bodyguard Gyges and then lost his life and empire because of his folly.

For the mentality of the benevolent imperialist, I drew on my days as a private first class in an army education center in Okinawa—a peaceful enough spot to spend the Korean War, among decent, well-meaning Americans who thought they were doing good, bringing civilization and speaking pidgin English to their servants. Being a lowly functionary in a colonial occupation force, I was both servant and master, and I was thus able to experience the effects of good will toward one's inferiors from both sides.

Our determination to improve the natives' lot in Vietnam brought all this back to me. I saw myself again being chauffered over dusty, bumpy, dirt roads by an Oriental driver; I would try to strike up a friendly, "democratic" conversation as I sat in the back seat and stared at the back of his head.

The Greek legend, my own experiences, and contemporary history started to fuse. There was Candaules, High Commissioner of Economic Assistance to Lydia—a small Asian country where a civil war had been raging for seventeen years—riding over the winding roads and expounding to his native chauffeur Gyges on the superior way of life he and western civilization were bringing in the form of paved roads, a higher standard of living, and opportunities for advancement in domestic service. Such paternalism led naturally to Candaules' desire to share a glimpse of his beautiful wife's bare flesh with his servant, who must of course desire to possess everything his master has. This new Candaules is a well-intentioned, humane bureaucrat, an expert in the rice economy, interested in feeding people, and a part of the whole liberal machinery that wages wars.

Once I conceived of Candaules as a government official and Gyges as his native driver, their relative positions in the diplomatic limousine in the opening scene or prologue defined their relationship, and their clothes—the diplomat's formal dress and the chauffeur's uniform—not only established their conscious theatrical roles but also began the emphasis on dress and undress, of which Nyssia is the focus.

The trip through the outskirts of Sardis in the limousine also brings into the play a fourth character who never actually appears but who is essential to the dynamics of its development: the people or chorus. Candaules and Gyges drive past a cafe where people are eating ice cream by the edge of a hole made by a terrorist bomb, they see a crowd of "happy peasants" waving flags, they hear a group of war orphans thumping on the fenders of the car, and they are finally stopped by an angry mob who beat on the car windows menacingly and peer in at the commissioner.

Riot and revolution are a constant threat; Candaules and Nyssia are afraid of what the people may do and are always aware of their threatening presence. Gyges is the visible representative of the unseen hordes. To both Candaules and Nyssia he is the "typical Lydian," the embodiment of their hopes and fears. Their anxious comments, patronizing or contemptuous, create an invisible chorus of ragged victims of the war who finally revolt. Although I saw no necessity for showing them on the stage, two productions (The Stanford Repertory Theatre and L'Aquarium) used blackrobed property men to make sounds and gestures for the crowd.

In the last scene a full-scale revolution topples the colonial empire. Nyssia and Candaules report on the progress of the disorders. The explosion of a plastic bomb at a children's movie (according to Nyssia, thrown by Gyges at her instigation) leads to a wave of arrests and the rounding up of students in special detention camps. This repressive action in turn sets off rioting in the streets, causing more police brutality and violence. Candaules claims that his country engineered a coup in order to get rid of the ruling clique and replace it with another more easily manageable; due to the bombing, the uprising has gone out of control and spread throughout the entire structure of society.

Love of order, punctuality, and property constitute Candaules' understanding of justice; even as he is about to be burned alive, he cannot grasp why Gyges or his wife should not feel gratitude for his desire to make them happy. Candaules sees the world only though the lenses of his official, abstract ideology. A victim of this sterility, Nyssia is consumed with hatred for her husband and for herself. Gyges—Plato's shepherd with his magic ring—remains enigmatic. The worst he can wish Nyssia and Candaules is that they should have to till the soil—have contact with his reality which their clothes and shoes and luxury screens from their sight.

At the Stanford Repertory Theatre, directed by Bill Sharp, *Candaules* was interpreted as a critique of the American Dream, in which Gyges almost believed. Played by Norbert Davidson, a young black actor and playwright, Gyges was a naïve and innocent servant, caught between his master's patronizing liberalism and his mistress' compulsive fear and guilt. Between them, Candaules and Nyssia offer the two responses of the white intellectual to those whose skin is dark: rational promises of a better future, and, on a deeper level, a desire for self-abasement and punishment.

They fight among themselves for possession of Gyges' soul, and he is passively molded by their competition. Racked by indecision and conflicting loyalties, his slave mentality makes him the inheritor of a portion of his superior's ideology. This Gyges clearly did not throw the bomb, nor could he ever; it is only Nyssia's sick imagination which suggests the idea. Gyges reacts with astonishment to her revelation and only reluctantly cooperates in the burning of Candaules. The bankruptcy of the illusions and dreams of the middle-aged couple has a shattering effect on Gyges, but only at the very end of the play did it force him to act and then very unwillingly, as he assumed the mantle of his master whom he still could not help but imitate.

At the Ecole Normale Supérieure among the veterans of the Paris student uprising of May 1968, *Candaules* was interpreted as a primer for revolutionaries. Gyges was played as a guerilla fighter who awaited the right moment to arouse the people to open revolt against imperialism. This production was not anti-war, but pro-revolution. Candaules' treatment of the people, seen in his treatment of his servant, brought Gyges and the audience (which was to be revolutionized) to a full consciousness of the necessity for rebellion. The whole progress of the uprising in Scene 4, and especially the role of the students in it, acquired new significance. Gyges threw the bomb with the conscious goal of triggering the sequence of events leading to the revolution. He gleefully douses his master with gasoline and invites the audience to enjoy the lighting of the matches. In the driver's seat, figuratively as well as literally from the beginning, this revolutionary Gyges represents the point of view of the radical younger generation who relish the destruction of Candaules and Nyssia.

As the eternal master and servant, Candaules and Gyges can mirror the American liberal and subservient black shaking off the chains of servitude and coming out of his stupor, or they can reflect the benevolent imperialist and the revolutionary out to subvert him.

Baudelaire claimed, "La Révolution a été fait par des voluptueux" (The [French] Revolution has been made by voluptuaries), and "Les livres libertins commentent donc et expliquent la révolution" (Libertine books give a commentary on and an explanation of the revolution). Revolution and sex are also linked in the story of Candaules. The Lydian revolution is made in a bedroom; exposure of the queen's naked body topples the empire. In fact, Herodotus gives an erotic history of the coup d'état and explains history erotically.

Candaules, Commissioner explores the role of voyeurism in furthering the revolution. The Lydian uprising is not made by voluptuaries, but provoked by a repressed bureaucrat who has lost contact with the physical realities of life and a sensual perception of pleasure and pain. Candaules wishes to remove himself as completely as possible from reality and become a total voyeur—invisible to the hostile world around him and to the complete facts of life—whether these .be the cruelties of war or his wife's frustrated sexuality.

Candaules sees without seeing, looking through bullet-proof glass, camera lenses, binoculars, or other people's eyes. At the end of the opening scene, he puts on Gyges' ring to protect himself from contact with the threatening mob. Clothes are used as a similar disguise at the end of the second scene when Candaules and Nyssia go out into the city wearing Gyges' old rags over their own expensive clothes so as not to be seen. Gyges himself puts on his magic ring at the end of Scene 3, making himself invisible to enter Nyssia's bedroom and see her naked. At the end of the final scene, Gyges puts the ring over Nyssia without even looking at her—she has become non-existent. Without her clothes, she loses her identity which was based on social position and wealth. Candaules likewise derives his identity from his clothing and imagines that his humane principles are somehow connected with keeping his pants on.

The ring of invisibility is not an ordinary ring worn on the finger, which would be too small to be seen in the theatre and whose magic properties would seem preposterous, but instead a gold hoop attached to a black bag large enough to cover a person's body. It is used at the end of three of the four scenes, and each of the three characters goes into it. To be a better voyeur, Candaules wishes to be invisible to the surrounding world; Gyges is in fact an invisible man since his true identity and human personality are never seen by his master or mistress; and Nyssia becomes invisible in her nakedness—her true self, which no one ever sees, and which in fact is nothingness.

Nakedness is central to the fable. Although nudity in the legend can be interpreted on a figurative level, it is a literal element in the plot. Any attempt to put it off-stage or gloss it over can only arouse expectations and then frustrate them in a titillating fashion. One aspect of the story that first interested me was the opportunity it offered for a necessary use of nakedness on the stage. That was some years ago. The recent presentation of mass nudity in the theatre is another matter— as though Candaules himself had become a director and were putting on plays for audiences of Candauleses.

Obsession with nakedness in *Candaules, Commissioner* is a form of perversion. Candaules' desire to expose his wife is an aberration of impotence, and Nyssia's need to exhibit herself and be tortured an expression of her guilt. The desire to strip oneself or others publicly is a sickness, the inverse form of which is Candaules' own need to be fully clothed always.

Nyssia's full nakedness is withheld until the final moments of the play where it comes as an unexpected revelation of what she is. At what would be the traditional disrobing, after Candaules has introduced Gyges into the bedroom and she has begun to undress, Nyssia sticks her breast into the light socket in a desperate attempt to put herself in the place of the natives who are tortured and suffer what they suffer.

By this delay, it should be possible to present her final total nakedness at the end of the play as something pathetic, repellent, and sexless, since we already have seen her disintegrating personality and total loneliness. Her body should appear pale and sickly, as though she were dead. The effect should be a sudden shock—Nyssia is nothing but an ugly bag of bones, hair, flesh, and organs that no one cares anything about. Such is the outcome of the wonderful erotic viewing which Candaules had promised. Abandoned and unregarded, stripped and defenseless, Nyssia ceases to exist.

The earlier scene in which Candaules is stripped stops short of total nudity since Nyssia finds his body too repellent to look at. His naked irreducible self is disgusting, and he is as passionate in wanting to conceal it as he is in trying to expose his wife. Gyges always remains clothed and masked, hiding his thoughts even from himself—the most protected of the trio. The one point at which he exposes himself—both his outer and his inner wounds—is when he rolls up his sleeves and shows the burns on his bare arm, his childhood scars as a victim of the bombings and burnings.

Only the demise of Candaules finally frees Gyges, who had been a man asleep and under someone else's control. Now he starts to think and speak for himself. After rejecting the temptation to submit to another form of easy subjugation by his refusal even to look at Nyssia's proferred body, Gyges goes out into the streets to search for his identity. But he is still wearing his master's coat and carrying the gun that Candaules gave him. The Lydian revolution has given Gyges the power, but the forms are still the same as under his oppressors. Gyges is now the *new* king of Lydia.

CANDAULES AMONG THE
FRENCH REVOLUTIONARIES

Jean Duchesne

When I saw the Stanford Repertory Theater production of *Candaules, Commissioner* in January, 1968, I noticed that the public and most critics praised the play highly because they took to heart the moral lesson that it taught. I too was fascinated, although as a visitor from France I thought I could refuse to identify with Americans trapped in the Vietnam war or with other Candauleses caught in Third World snares.

Once I discovered that it would be possible to translate the play into French and produce it at the Ecole Normale Supérieure (the school for the supposed academic elite of the future), I imagined that people in France would not spend much time reflecting on past and present deceits and depravities of colonialism, but would rather be interested in the eternal phenomenon of oppression and revolt. It seemed to me that the play was a brilliant illustration of this equation: oppression-vice. I understood the relations in the master-wife-servant trio in the following way.

In actual fact, Candaules does not reign over Gyges and Nyssia because of his merits or virtues, but because of his vices. The effect of Candaules' power is that those around him become infected by his abnormality. Practically abandoned by Candaules, Nyssia sinks further and further into sophisticated but unsatisfying sado-masochistic perversion. No longer able to enjoy his wife, Candaules tries to find vicarious satisfaction through Gyges. This is actually an attempt to make the young Lydian learn his master's perversion, that is, impotent voyeurism. Candaules' authority would thus be somehow strengthened over both Nyssia (a mere object one can see, but not touch) and Gyges (doomed never to get what he has been taught to want).

Gyges cannot help listening to Candaules. He is therefore subject to temptation; perhaps he is even partially seduced. It is likely that he does not feel basically oppressed and unhappy; we may even believe that he sincerely admires his master when he says that he does. Nyssia too will try to seduce Gyges, perhaps more to win him over to her own perversion than to take revenge on Candaules. However,

Gyges is essentially healthy, and this is why he cannot go along with Nyssia and eventually joins the revolution outside.

The revolution is a revolt against Candaules' (and Nyssia's) insanity and vice. In addition to being a given political situation that can be reproduced many times in many different places, the revolution is a healthy answer to the temptation of hypocrisy and perversion that is characteristic of oppression. Consequently, Gyges must be considered the true hero of the story. All the same, the reason for the revolution is not the revolutionary's determination, but the master's corruption.

We should keep in mind that Candaules is *personally* responsible for the revolution in Lydia. He forces Gyges to watch his wife naked—physically and above all psychologically—and to be seduced by her. Earlier, the same Candaules had unknowingly driven Nyssia to a perversion that will lead her to have Gyges throw the bomb which then causes the police to attack students. Fighting breaks out in the streets, inaugurating the great day of revolution when all the oppressors are defeated and punished. Eventually vice turns oppression into self-destruction.

The play reveals the hidden pretext of revolution. It is a story that history ignores. However, Candaules' domestic failure is mysteriously linked to historical events, which now appear as a new manifestation of an everlasting truth, and not only as the necessary conclusion of a twentieth-century colonial war or the inescapable consequence of class struggle and the internal contradictions of western capitalism. Candaules is responsible for his own fall and that of his fellow countrymen. Even if it seems that his own wife betrays him, he actually makes her desire to see him stumble and fall. Candaules makes history, but official history will ignore him. Only art reveals him and uncovers what governs history.

For this reason, we see the antique legend develop into a myth on the stage. Inasmuch as the spectator himself can watch and even enjoy everything more or less as a voyeur (especially when he expects to catch a glimpse of Nyssia's body), he experiences at his own expense the strength and threat of the myth. In this respect, the spectator does identify with Candaules.

Along with the queen's nakedness, we see unveiled on stage what is behind all oppression: vice, which means self-destruction. In other words, the reason for the revolution is not primarily that the oppressed become conscious of some social injustice; rather the oppressors are doomed because they are no longer able to realize and get rid of their own hypocrisy and vice, and because their power has become absurd. The revolution is above all a reaction. It is therefore not necessarily the universal solution to all problems in life.

Perhaps this interpretation is a bit too subtle. In any case, I discovered during rehearsals that it did not correspond to ready-made ideas about revolution and guerilla warfare.

Most students at the Ecole Normale Supérieure (as well at at the Sorbonne and the University of Nanterre) are anxious to display their political sophistication, which really means intellectual conformism to an old leftist tradition at French universities. Furthermore, because most courses of study are outdated, a student in France today does not learn any definite occupation or acquire any professional qualifications. Belonging to a separate world, French students severely and bitterly criticize middle-class society which they feel oppresses and rejects them. They often see themselves as conscious, aggressive victims. Such a condition is, however, far from being unpleasant: some satisfaction and self-righteousness can be found in talking about the revolution and anticipating it.

In a way, becoming a teacher gives one the opportunity to make this situation last, to keep one's social status, and to avoid making a "dishonorable" change and adaptation to the "bourgeois" way of life. Besides, it is true that most diplomas (especially in the field of the arts, sociology, philsophy, etc.) lead almost exclusively to teaching careers. The Ecole Normale Supérieure is supposed to prepare the best professors, and even tomorrow's scholars, thinkers and leading political figures (from Jean-Paul Sartre to Georges Pompidou, for instance).

Then too, the Ecole Normale Supérieure is the traditional center where the most advanced ideas are debated and shaped. An active pro-Chinese group was born in November, 1966. They have vigorously propagandized in favor of the National Liberation Front and North Vietnam, and posted numerous handwritten "newspapers" on the walls of the dormitories: quotations from Chairman Mao, comments on the proletarian's situation in France, anti-American ("Nixon the Plague Go Home!"; "U.S.-S.S." [Nazis]) and anti-Soviet slogans ("Down with Soviet revisionism!"). Hanoi and Viet-Cong representatives and officials from the Red Chinese Embassy in Paris have been invited several times by a "Cultural Committee" to speak at the Ecole Normale Supérieure. Money has been raised (in the words of the student radicals) "to help the courageous Vietnamese people fight their just struggle against U.S. Imperialism." Other groups challenge the pro-Chinese in the field of ideology: regular French communists, Trotskyites, various socialists, and even "progressive" Christians; but all share the revolutionary ideal.

Even non-Marxist and politically uncommitted students agree to give noisy "moral support" to almost all revolutionary causes and guerilla actions in the whole world. Automatic enthusiasm has recently been generated for the Palestinian Arabs, whose demands are not founded on Marxist grounds. The result of such political attitudes is a kind of Manicheism: all revolutionaries are good; all those who oppose the revolution are oppressors; all oppressors are bad.

Members of the student Theatre Group "L'Aquarium" at the Ecole Normale Supérieure at first thought that *Candaules, Commissioner* would fill a real need (this was in January, 1969), since few plays can be found about twentieth-century revolution. Previously, the group had given successful revisions of Rabelais' *Picrocholian Wars* and Flaubert's *Bouvard and Pécuchet*. *Candaules* was exciting because it seemed to be directly in touch with events that no famous playwright had been able to deal with.

Protest arose, however, when I tried to escape revolutionary Manicheism. First, there were lengthy and fiery discussions about the character of Gyges. Although I asked the actor playing Gyges to interpret his relationship with Candaules at the beginning of the play simply and straightforwardly (in order to suggest that Gyges admired his master), the entire company felt that it was absolutely necessary to stress that Gyges was not taken in by Candaules, but from the beginning was waiting for an opportunity to free himself. They argued that Gyges could not fail to realize that Candaules was trying to rob him of his very personality. Above all, the company felt that the public expected to applaud a revolutionary hero with whom they could readily identify. I objected in vain that the play showed Gyges in the process of becoming conscious of his new social status (it is obvious that, thanks to Candaules, he is one of the more privileged Lydians) and that in any case Gyges is more a victim, since Candaules has made him alienated and perhaps even ridiculous. The group responded that it was unthinkable that even a would-be revolutionary appear obsequious and unintelligent. From the start, they said, Gyges had to be class-conscious. I said that he probably had not read Lenin or Mao, but they argued that there was nothing to prove that Gyges had not planned everything from the beginning and that all he said was cunningly devised to flatter Candaules and force him to show his wife naked. We all agreed on one point: all of these interpretations of the play, as written, remain possible, and the meaning of the play in production depends on how it is directed and acted.

Other discussions revolved around the character of Nyssia. The girl playing the part felt that Nyssia was disillusioned about herself and her world, that she was more lucid than Candaules, and that because she realized western civilization was dying, she had no scruples about betraying it. The actress virtually believed that Nyssia was so aware of everything that was taking place that she deliberately chose to incite the revolution; it was the only honorable course of action left her. According to this interpretation, Nyssia was to some extent a revolutionary herself, and personifies all neurotic capitalists who are ready to sacrifice themselves for the sake of mankind and thus perhaps save their own souls!

Apart from this, the actress felt rather uneasy about Nyssia's sadomasochistic tendencies. She stubbornly refused to appear stark naked and bought skin-color tights. Neither did she want to appear to torture herself with the electric light socket. Instead, four extras, who appeared throughout the play as a kind of chorus of oppressed Lydians, employed a stylized pantomime to suggest that they were torturing her. I concluded that revolutionaries are indeed puritanical in their hatred of vice and that rather than display what they regard as private and personal, they prefer to fall back upon ideology.

Finally, as I could not accept the production becoming a didactic fable, as uninteresting as any official literature ("noble sentiments do not make good literature"), the actors and I reached a compromise: they would follow the directions I had given them, so that some ambiguity would remain and the spectators would realize that things were not as simple and clear-cut as propaganda would have them believe. On the other hand, Gyges would be free to overdo his disgust when he spits out the milk, and to improvise for about thirty seconds at the beginning of the second scene while waiting in the dressing room for Candaules. The actor first showed some interest in the furniture and toilet articles, suddenly seemed to hate all this luxury, and finally stretched out on his master's sofa. When he bumped into it once, Gyges shouted, "Crève, salope!" ("Die, you son of a bitch"), a student slogan against the police and university staff and faculty during the May, 1968, rebellion.

In addition, I could not prevent Gyges from looking bestially cruel and terribly sadistic during the last scene. Moreover, the chorus of Lydians chanted "F.N.L. vaincra" ("The N.L.F. will win"—a pro-Viet-Cong slogan) while they were threatening Candaules at the end of the first scene. They also painted the name "Krivine" (the Trotskyite candidate for president of the republic in June, 1969) on the back of Gyges' old clothes.

Generally speaking, the public thought it was a "good show." They thoroughly enjoyed Candaules' hypocrisy and stupidity. They were more hesitant about the character of Nyssia: "Was it necessary?" "It was so disturbing." Regular revolutionaries supported Gyges vigoroously. Others said, "I wouldn't like to be an American! See what's waiting for them around the corner."

Dan Gerould came to Paris to see the last performance. On the following day, we were both invited for lunch with the Director of the Ecole Normale Supérieure and other college officials. The meal was good, the wines were better. The conversation concerned revolution. We were served by a young staff member who I knew was an active, buoyant figure in the employees' pro-communist union. He wore a white waiter's coat, and his face was an impassive mask. After we left, I told Dan Gerould about the young waiter, and we burst out laughing. Fortunately, the Director's wife had not been present.

The
Black
Revolution

THE SLAVE

The title of LeRoi Jones's play, *The Slave*, refers to the Negro's status when he was brought to this country, to ideas which still bind him, and to his severing those bonds in revolutionary action. The play prophecies racial war in the United States and perhaps in the world.

When the thirteen colonies freed themselves from bondage to England, liberty was not extended to black Americans. The Declaration of Independence promised no independence for the Negro. Quite the contrary, before they accepted the document Thomas Jefferson presented them, the delegates to the Continental Congress made one substantial change (the only important change): they deleted a lengthy clause that denounced slavery as one of the English king's intolerable abuses, a "cruel" and "execrable" violation of the "most sacred rights of life and liberty." In his *Autobiography*, Jefferson, who was chiefly responsible for the draft of the Declaration of Independence, reveals that the deletion was made in compliance with the desires of the delegates from South Carolina and Georgia.

In 1863, Abraham Lincoln issued the Emancipation Proclamation, ending slavery. Nevertheless, economically, socially, and politically, the Negro was still subjugated. Equal rights under law, equal opportunities, and integration became and remain goals. One hundred years after Lincoln's decree, Martin Luther King, Jr., proclaimed, "I have a dream that one day this nation will . . . live out the true meaning of its creed: 'We hold these truths to be self-evident, that all men are created equal'." After a century, this goal is still to be realized.

Whereas Dr. King worked toward a racially integrated society, others rejected this goal. To Stokely Carmichael, for instance, former chairman of SNCC (Student Nonviolent Coordinating Committee), integration in practice means the entry of blacks into white neighborhoods but not the reverse. Therefore, he believes, it insidiously reinforces the conception that white is superior and black inferior. An

169

alternative goal, black separatism,[1] has attracted a number of black Americans who, rejecting white America, advocate black control of black communities as a better method to improve the lives of Negroes in the United States.

In the 1960's, through the efforts of forceful civil rights leaders and integrationists like Dr. King and Ralph Abernathy, and through those of militant separatists like Malcolm X and Elijah Muhammad, leader of the Black Muslims, two paradoxical developments occurred: one, increased desegregation and the accelerated integration of blacks into the mainstream of American life; and two, the growing appeal of black separatism and the greater desire for black control of black communities. Some integrationists, W. H. Ferris, for instance, sadly conclude that the liberal goal is impossible, that separatism is likely to be the course of the future, and that the famous marching song should be changed to "We Shall *Not* Overcome." Others, such as John L. Perry, conclude that the black man has a choice, which is desirable for both whites and blacks. The dual developments are paradoxical rather than contradictory for in one important sense, as Malcolm X observes, the ultimate goals of both integration and separatism are alike: freedom, equality, justice, and dignity.

Like Malcolm X, the Black Panthers regard Negroes in the United States not as Americans but as victims of America, oppressed members of colonies within a mother country which enslaves and exploits them. Like other Third World colonies, they demand independence and self-government. Insisting on freedom, full employment, decent housing and education, and trial of blacks only by blacks, the Panthers list as a "major political objective" a plebiscite supervised by the United Nations, "to be held throughout the black colony in which only black colonial subjects will be allowed to participate, for the purpose of determining the will of the black people as to their national destiny."

Whereas many blacks (notably, Dr. King) adopt the tactic of nonviolence, others (notably, the Panthers) reject this method. Malcolmn X points out that George Washington did not achieve independence for the United States by nonviolent means or by singing "We Shall Overcome." Instead, says Malcolm X in a speech called "The Ballot or the Bullet," nonviolence should only be used against those who themselves use nonviolence, and blacks should fight rather than sing to overcome. He predicts that if blacks do not receive the ballot they will use the bullet.

---

[1] Because black Americans are to a large extent already separated from white Americans, separatism really means independence (political and economic).

Violence, a tactic of white racists who resist integration and fight the extension of civil rights to black Americans, erupted in the 1960's in several black "ghettos" of large American cities. In the wake of extreme violence in the summer of 1967, President Lyndon B. Johnson appointed a National Advisory Commission on Civil Disorders to investigate the problem. In 1968, the commission reported that black violence was an echo of white violence, black racism of white racism. It labeled white racism as the fundamental cause of racial disorders in the United States.

"The limits of tyrants," said Frederick Douglass, a black American, in 1857, "are prescribed by the endurance of those whom they oppress." In the 1960's, it was clear that the endurance of many blacks was about to end. "It isn't that time is running out," warned Malcolm X, "time has run out!" *The Slave*, written in 1964, the same year as "The Ballot or the Bullet" and one year after King's "I have a dream" speech, takes place after the end of endurance and the cessation of time.

THE BALLOT OR THE BULLET

Malcolm X

Mr. Moderator, Brother Lomax,[1] brothers and sisters, friends and
enemies: I just can't believe everyone in here is a friend and I don't
want to leave anybody out. The question tonight, as I understand it,
is "The Negro Revolt, and Where Do We Go From Here?" or "What
Next?" In my little humble way of understanding it, it points toward
either the ballot or the bullet.

Before we try and explain what is meant by the ballot or the
bullet, I would like to clarify something concerning myself. I'm still a
Muslim, my religion is still Islam. That's my personal belief. Just as
Adam Clayton Powell is a Christian minister who heads the Abyssinian
Baptist Church in New York, but at the same time takes part in the
political struggles to try and bring about rights to the black people
in this country; and Dr. Martin Luther King is a Christian minister
down in Atlanta, Georgia, who heads another organization fighting for
the civil rights of black people in this country; and Rev. Galamison,[2]
I guess you've heard of him, is another Christian minister in New York
who has been deeply involved in the school boycotts to eliminate
segregated education; well, I myself am a minister, not a Christian
minister, but a Musilm minister; and I believe in action on all fronts
by whatever means necessary.

Although I'm still a Muslim, I'm not here tonight to discuss
my religion. I'm not here to try and change your religion. I'm not here
to argue or discuss anything that we differ about, because it's time
for us to submerge our differences and realize that it is best for us to
first see that we have the same problem, a common problem—a problem
that will make you catch hell whether you're a Baptist, or a Methodist,
or a Musilm, or a nationalist. Whether you're educated or illiterate,
whether you live on the boulevard or in the alley, you're going to catch
hell just like I am. We're all in the same boat and we all are going
to catch the same hell from the same man. He just happens to be a

[1] Louis E. Lomax, the first speaker.
[2] Milton Galamison.

From *Malcolm X Speaks*, copyright © 1965 by Merit Publishers and Betty Shabazz.
This speech was delivered as part of a symposium, "The Negro Revolt—What Comes
Next?" sponsored by CORE (Congress of Racial Equality) at the Cory Methodist
Church, Cleveland, Ohio, on April 3, 1964.

white man. All of us have suffered here, in this country, political oppression at the hands of the white man, economic exploitation at the
hands of the white man, and social degradation at the hands of the
white man.

Now in speaking like this, it doesn't mean that we're anti-white,
but it does mean we're anti-exploitation, we're anti-degradation, we're
anti-oppression. And if the white man doesn't want us to be anti-him,
let him stop oppressing and exploiting and degrading us. Whether we
are Christians or Muslims or nationalists or agnostics or atheists, we
must first learn to forget our differences. If we have differences, let us
differ in the closet; when we come out in front, let us not have anything
to argue about until we get finished arguing with the man. If the late
President Kennedy could get together with Khrushchev and exchange
some wheat, we certainly have more in common with each other than
Kennedy and Khrushchev had with each other.

If we don't do something real soon, I think you'll have to agree
that we're going to be forced either to use the ballot or the bullet.
It's one or the other in 1964. It isn't that time is running out—time has
run out! 1964 threatens to be the most explosive year America has ever
witnessed. The most explosive year. Why? It's also a political year.
It's the year when all of the white politicians will be back in the so-called
Negro community jiving you and me for some votes. The year when
all of the white political crooks will be right back in your and my
community with their false promises, building up our hopes for a
letdown, with their trickery and their treachery, with their false promises
which they don't intend to keep. As they nourish these dissatisfactions,
it can only lead to one thing, an explosion; and now we have the type
of black man on the scene in America today—I'm sorry, Brother Lomax
—who just doesn't intend to turn the other cheek any longer.

Don't let anybody tell you anything about the odds are against
you. If they draft you, they send you to Korea and make you face 800
million Chinese. If you can be brave over there, you can be brave
right here. These odds aren't as great as those odds. And if you fight
here, you will at least know what you're fighting for.

I'm not a politician, not even a student of politics; in fact, I'm
not a student of much of anything. I'm not a Democrat, I'm not a
Republican, and I don't even consider myself an American. If you and
I were Americans, there'd be no problem. Those Hunkies that just got
off the boat, they're already Americans; Polacks are already Americans;
the Italian refugees are already Americans. Everything that came out
of Europe, every blue-eyed thing, is already an American. And as long
as you and I have been over here, we aren't Americans yet.

Well, I am one who doesn't believe in deluding myself. I'm not going to sit at your table and watch you eat, with nothing on my plate, and call myself a diner. Sitting at the table doesn't make you a diner, unless you eat some of what's on that plate. Being here in America doesn't make you an American. Being born here in America doesn't make you an American. Why, if birth made you American, you wouldn't need any legislation, you wouldn't need any amendments to the Constitution, you wouldn't be faced with civil-rights filibustering in Washington, D.C., right now. They don't have to pass civil-rights legislation to make a Polack an American.

No, I'm not an American. I'm one of the 22 million black people who are the victims of Americanism. One of the 22 million black people who are the victims of democracy, nothing but disguised hypocrisy. So, I'm not standing here speaking to you as an American, or a patriot, or a flag-saluter, or a flag-waver—no, not I. I'm speaking as a victim of this American system. And I see America through the eyes of the victim. I don't see any American dream; I see an American nightmare.

These 22 million victims are waking up. Their eyes are coming open. They're beginning to see what they used to only look at. They're becoming politically mature. They are realizing that there are new political trends from coast to coast. As they see these new political trends, it's possible for them to see that every time there's an election the races are so close that they have to have a recount. They had to recount in Massachusetts to see who was going to be governor, it was so close. It was the same way in Rhode Island, in Minnesota, and in many other parts of the country. And the same with Kennedy and Nixon when they ran for president. It was so close they had to count all over again. Well, what does this mean? It means that when white people are evenly divided, and black people have a bloc of votes of their own, it is left up to them to determine who's going to sit in the White House and who's going to be in the dog house.

It was the black man's vote that put the present administration in Washington, D.C. Your vote, your dumb vote, your ignorant vote, your wasted vote put in an administration in Washington, D.C., that has seen fit to pass every kind of legislation imaginable, saving you until last, then filibustering on top of that. And your and my leaders have the audacity to run around clapping their hands and talk about how much progress we're making. And what a good president we have. If he wasn't good in Texas, he sure can't be good in Washington, D.C. Because Texas is a lynch state. It is in the same breath as Mississippi, no different; only they lynch you in Texas with a Texas accent and lynch you in Mississippi with a Mississippi accent. And these Negro leaders have the audacity to go and have some coffee in the White

House with a Texan a Southern cracker—that's all he is—and then come out and tell you and me that he's going to be better for us because, since he's from the South, he knows how to deal with the Southerners. What kind of logic is that? Let Eastland be president, he's from the South too. He should be better able to deal with them than Johnson.

In this present administration they have in the House of Representatives 257 Democrats to only 177 Republicans. They control two-thirds of the House vote. Why can't they pass something that will help you and me? In the Senate, there are 67 senators who are of the Democratic Party. Only 33 of them are Republicans. Why, the Democrats have got the government sewed up, and you're the one who sewed it up for them. And what have they given you for it? Four years in office, and just now getting around to some civil-rights legislation. Just now, after everything else is gone, out of the way, they're going to sit down now and play with you all summer long—the same old giant con game that they call filibuster. All those are in cahoots together. Don't you ever think they're not in cahoots together, for the man that is heading the civil-rights filibuster is a man from Georgia named Richard Russell. When Johnson became president, the first man he asked for when he got back to Washington, D.C., was "Dicky"—that's how tight they are. That's his boy, that's his pal, that's his buddy. But they're playing that old con game. One of them makes believe he's for you, and he's got it fixed where the other one is so tight against you, he never has to keep his promise.

So it's time in 1964 to wake up. And when you see them coming up with that kind of conspiracy, let them know your eyes are open. And let them know you got something else that's wide open too. It's got to be the ballot or the bullet. The ballot or the bullet. If you're afraid to use an expression like that, you should get on out of the country, you should get back in the cotton patch, you should get back in the alley. They get all the Negro vote, and after they get it, the Negro gets nothing in return. All they did when they got to Washington was give a few big Negroes big jobs. Those big Negroes didn't need big jobs, they already had jobs. That's camouflage, that's trickery, that's treachery, window-dressing. I'm not trying to knock out the Democrats for the Republicans, we'll get to them in a minute. But it is true—you put the Democrats first and the Democrats put you last.

Look at it the way it is. What alibis do they use, since they control Congress and the Senate? What alibi do they use when you and I ask, "Well, when are you going to keep your promise?" They blame the Dixiecrats. What is a Dixiecrat? A Democrat. A Dixiecrat is nothing but a Democrat in disguise. The titular head of the Democrats is also the head of the Dixiecrats, because the Dixiecrats are a part of the Democratic Party. The Democrats have never kicked the Dixiecrats out of the party. The Dixiecrats bolted themselves once, but the Democrats didn't put them out. Imagine, these lowdown Southern segregationists put the Northern Democrats down. But the Northern Democrats have never put the Dixiecrats down. No, look at that thing the way it is. They have got a con game going on, a political con game, and you and I are in the middle. It's time for you and me to wake up and start looking at it like it is, and trying to understand it like it is; and then we can deal with it like it is.

The Dixiecrats in Washington, D.C., control the key committees that run the government. The only reason the Dixiecrats control these committees is because they have seniority. The only reason they have seniority is because they come from states where Negroes can't vote. This is not even a government that's based on democracy. It is not a government that is made up of representatives of the people. Half of the people in the South can't even vote. Eastland is not even supposed to be in Washington. Half of the senators and congressmen who occupy these key positions in Washington, D.C., are there illegally, are there unconstitutionally.

I was in Washington, .D.C., a week ago Thursday, when they were debating whether or not they should let the bill come onto the floor. And in the back of the room where the Senate meets, there's a huge map of the United States, and on that map it shows the location of Negroes throughout the country. And it shows that the Southern section of the country, the states that are most heavily concentrated with Negroes, are the ones that have senators and congressmen standing up filibustering and doing all other kinds of trickery to keep the Negro from being able to vote. This is pitiful. But it's not pitiful for us any longer; it's actually pitiful for the white man, because soon now, as the Negro awakens a little more and sees the vise that he's in, sees the bag that he's in, sees the real game that he's in, then the Negro's going to develop a new tactic.

These senators and congressmen actually violate the constitutional amendments that guarantee the people of that particular state or country the right to vote. And the Constitution itself has within it the machinery to expel any representative from a state where the voting rights of the people are violated. You don't even need new legislation. Any person in Congress right now, who is there from a state or a district where the voting rights of the people are violated, that particular person should be expelled from Congress. And when you expel him, you've removed one of the obstacles in the path of any real meaningful legislation in this country. In fact, when you expel them, you don't need new legislation, because they will be replaced by black representatives from counties and districts where the black man is in the majority, not in the minority.

If the black man in these Southern states had his full voting rights, the key Dixiecrats in Washington, D.C., which means the key Democrats in Washington, D.C., would lose their seats. The Democratic Party itself would lose its power. It would cease to be powerful as a party. When you see the amount of power that would be lost by the Democratic Party if it were to lose the Dixiecrat wing, or branch, or element, you can see where it's against the interests of the Democrats to give voting rights to Negroes in states where the Democrats have been in complete power and authority ever since the Civil War. You just can't belong to that party without analyzing it.

I say again, I'm not anti-Democrat, I'm not anti-Republican, I'm not anti-anything. I'm just questioning their sincerity, and some of the strategy that they've been using on our people by promising them promises that they don't intend to keep. When you keep the Democrats in power, you're keeping the Dixiecrats in power. I doubt that my good Brother Lomax will deny that. A vote for a Democrat is a vote for a Dixiecrat. That's why, in 1964, it's time now for you and me to become more politically mature and realize what the ballot is for; what we're supposed to get when we cast a ballot; and that if we don't cast a ballot, it's going to end up in a situation where we're going to have to cast a bullet. It's either a ballot or a bullet.

In the North, they do it a different way. They have a system that's known as gerrymandering, whatever that means. It means when Negroes become too heavily concentrated in a certain area, and begin to gain too much political power, the white man comes along and changes the district lines. You may say, "Why do you keep saying white man?" Because it's the white man who does it. I haven't ever seen any Negro changing any lines. They don't let him get near the line. It's the white man who does this. And usually, it's the white man who grins at you the most, and pats you on the back, and is supposed to be your friend. He may be friendly, but he's not your friend.

So, what I'm trying to impress upon you, in essence, is this: You and I in America are faced not with a segregationist conspiracy, we're faced with a government conspiracy. Everyone who's filibustering is a senator—that's the government. Everyone who's finagling in Washington, D.C., is a congressman—that's the government. You don't have anybody putting blocks in your path but people who are a part of the government. The same government that you go abroad to fight for and die for is the government that is in a conspiracy to deprive you of your voting rights, deprive you of your economic opportunities, deprive you of decent housing, deprive you of decent education. You don't need to go to the employer alone, it is the government itself, the government of America, that is responsible for the oppression and exploitation and degradation of black people in this country. And you should drop it in their lap. This government has failed the Negro. This so-called democracy has failed the Negro. And all these white liberals have definitely failed the Negro.

So, where do we go from here? First, we need some friends. We need some new allies. The entire civil-rights struggle needs a new interpretation, a broader interpretation. We need to look at this civil-rights thing from another angle—from the inside as well as from the outside. To those of us whose philosophy is black nationalism, the only way you can get involved in the civil-rights struggle is give it a new interpretation. That old interpretation excluded us. It kept us out. So, we're giving a new interpretation to the civil-rights struggle, an interpretation that will enable us to come into it, take part in it. And these handkerchief-heads who have been dillydallying and pussyfooting and compromising—we don't intend to let them pussyfoot and dillydally and compromise any longer.

How can you thank a man for giving you what's already yours? How then can you thank him for giving you only part of what's already yours? You haven't even made progress, if what's being given to you, you should have had already. That's not progress. And I love my Brother Lomax, the way he pointed out we're right back where we were in 1954. We're not even as far up as we were in 1954. We're behind where we were in 1954. There's more segregation now than there was in 1954. There's more racial animosity, more racial hatred, more racial violence today in 1964, than there was in 1954. Where is the progress?

And now you're facing a situation where the young Negro's coming up. They don't want to hear that "turn-the-other-cheek" stuff, no. In Jacksonville, those were teenagers, they were throwing Molotov cocktails. Negroes have never done that before. But it shows you there's a new deal coming in. There's new thinking coming in. There's new strategy coming in. It'll be Molotov cocktails this month, hand grenades next month, and something else next month. It'll be ballots, or it'll be bullets. It'll be liberty, or it will be death. The only difference about this kind of death—it'll be reciprocal. You know what is meant by "reciprocal"? That's one of Brother Lomax's words, I stole it from him. I don't usually deal with those big words because I don't usually deal with big people. I deal with small people. I find you can get a whole lot of small people and whip hell out of a whole lot of big people. They haven't got anything to lose, and they've got everything to gain. And they'll let you know in a minute: "It takes two to tango; when I go, you go."

The black nationalists, those whose philosophy is black nationalism, in bringing about this new interpretation of the entire meaning of civil rights, look upon it as meaning, as Brother Lomax has pointed out, equality of opportunity. Well, we're justified in seeking civil rights, if it means equality of opportunity, because all we're doing there is trying to collect for our investment. Our mothers and fathers invested sweat and blood. Three hundred and ten years we worked in this country without a dime in return—I mean without a *dime* in return. You let the white man walk around here talking about how rich this country is, but you never stop to think how it got rich so quick. It got rich because you made it rich.

You take the people who are in this audience right now. They're poor, we're all poor as individuals. Our weekly salary individually amounts to hardly anything. But if you take the salary of everyone in here collectively it'll fill up a whole lot of baskets. It's a lot of wealth. If you can collect the wages of just these people right here for a year, you'll be rich—richer than rich. When you look at it like that, think how rich Uncle Sam had to become, not with this handful, but millions of black people. Your and my mother and father, who didn't work an eight-hour shift, but worked from "can't see" in the morning until "can't see" at night, and worked for nothing, making the white man rich, making Uncle Sam rich.

This is our investment. This is our contribution—our blood. Not only did we give of our free labor, we gave of our blood. Every time he had a call to arms, we were the first ones in uniform. We died on every battlefield the white man had. We have made a greater sacrifice than anybody who's standing up in America today. We have made a greater contribution and have collected less. Civil rights, for those of us whose philosophy is black nationalism, means: "Give it to us now. Don't wait for next year. Give it to us yesterday, and that's not fast enough."

I might stop right here to point out one thing. Whenever you're going after something that belongs to you, anyone who's depriving you of the right to have it is a criminal. Understand that. Whenever you are going after something that is yours, you are within your legal rights to lay claim to it. And anyone who puts forth any effort to deprive you of that which is yours, is breaking the law, is a criminal. And this was pointed out by the Supreme Court decision. It outlawed segregation. Which means segregation is against the law. Which means a segregationist is breaking the law. A segregationist is a criminal. You can't label him as anything other than that. And when you demonstrate against segregation, the law is on your side. The Supreme Court is on your side.

Now, who is it that opposes you in carrying out the law? The police department itself. With police dogs and clubs. Whenever you demonstrate against segregation, whether it is segregated education, segregated housing, or anything else, the law is on your side, and anyone who stands in the way is not the law any longer. They are breaking the law, they are not representatives of the law. Any time you demonstrate against segregation and a man has the audacity to put a police dog on you, kill that dog, kill him, I'm telling you, kill that dog. I say it, if they put me in jail tomorrow, kill—that—dog. Then you'll put a stop to it. Now, if these white people in here don't want to see that kind of action, get down and tell the mayor to tell the police department to pull the dogs in. That's all you have to do. If you don't do it, someone else will.

If you don't take this kind of stand, your little children will grow up and look at you and think "shame." If you don't take an uncompromising stand—I don't mean go out and get violent; but at the same time you should never be nonviolent unless you run into some nonviolence. I'm nonviolent with those who are nonviolent with me. But when you drop that violence on me, then you've made me go insane, and I'm not responsible for what I do. And that's the way every Negro should get. Any time you know you're within the law, within your legal rights, within your moral rights, in accord with justice, then die for what you believe in. But don't die alone. Let your dying be reciprocal. This is what is meant by equality. What's good for the goose is good for the gander.

When we begin to get in this area, we need new friends, we need new allies. We need to expand the civil-rights struggle to a higher level—to the level of human rights. Whenever you are in a civil-rights struggle, whether you know it or not, you are confining yourself to the jurisdiction of Uncle Sam. No one from the outside world can speak out in your behalf as long as your struggle is a civil-rights struggle. Civil rights comes within the domestic affairs of this country. All of our African brothers and our Asian brothers and our Latin-American brothers cannot open their mouths and interfere in the domestic affairs of the United States. And as long as it's civil rights, this comes under the jurisdiction of Uncle Sam.

But the United Nations has what's known as the charter of human rights, it has a committee that deals in human rights. You may wonder why all of the atrocities that have been committed in Africa and in Hungary and in Asia and in Latin America are brought before the UN, and the Negro problem is never brought before the UN. This is part of the conspiracy. This old, tricky, blue-eyed liberal who is supposed to be your and my friend, supposed to be in our corner, supposed to be subsidizing our struggle, and supposed to be acting in the capacity of an adviser, never tells you anything about human rights. They keep you wrapped up in civil rights. And you spend so much time barking up the civil-rights tree, you don't even know there's a human-rights tree on the same floor.

When you expand the civil-rights struggle to the level of human rights, you can then take the case of the black man in this country before the nations in the UN. You can take it before the General Assembly. You can take Uncle Sam before a world court. But the only level you can do it on is the level of human rights. Civil rights keeps you under his restrictions, under his jurisdiction. Civil rights keeps you in his pocket. Civil rights means you're asking Uncle Sam to treat you right. Human rights are something you were born with. Human rights are your God-given rights. Human rights are the rights that are recognized by all nations of this earth. And any time any one violates your human rights, you can take them to the world court. Uncle Sam's hands are dripping with blood, dripping with the blood of the black man in this country. He's the earth's number-one hypocrite. He has the audacity—yes, he has—imagine him posing as the leader of the free world. The free world!—and you over here singing "We Shall Overcome." Expand the civil-rights struggle to the level of human rights, take it into the United Nations, where our African brothers can throw their weight on our side, where our Asian brothers can throw their weight on our side, where our Latin-American brothers can throw their weight on our side, and where 800 million Chinamen are sitting there waiting to throw their weight on our side.

Let the world know how bloody his hands are. Let the world know the hypocrisy that's practiced over here. Let it be the ballot or the bullet. Let him know that it must be the ballot or the bullet.

When you take your case to Washington, D.C., you're taking it to the criminal who's responsible; it's like running from the wolf to the fox. They're all in cahoots together. They all work political chicanery and make you look like a chump before the eyes of the world. Here you are walking around in America, getting ready to be drafted and sent abroad, like a tin soldier, and when you get over there, people ask you what are you fighting for, and you have to stick your tongue in your cheek. No, take Uncle Sam to court, take him before the world.

By ballot I only mean freedom. Don't you know—I disagree with Lomax on this issue—that the ballot is more important than the dollar? Can I prove it? Yes. Look in the UN. There are poor nations in the UN; yet those poor nations can get together with their voting power and keep the rich nations from making a move. They have one nation—one vote, everyone has an equal vote. And when those brothers from Asia, and Africa and the darker parts of this earth get together, their voting power is sufficient to hold Sam in check. Or Russia in check. Or some other section of the earth in check. So, the ballot is most important.

Right now, in this country, if you and I, 22 million African-Americans—that's what we are—Africans who are in America. You're nothing but Africans. Nothing but Africans. In fact, you'd get farther calling yourself African instead of Negro. Africans don't catch hell. You're the only one catching hell. They don't have to pass civil-rights bills for Africans. An African can go anywhere he wants right now. All you've got to do is tie your head up. That's right, go anywhere you want. Just stop being a Negro. Change your name to Hoogagagooba. That'll show you how silly the white man is. You're dealing with a silly man. A friend of mine who's very dark put a turban on his head and went into a restaurant in Atlanta before they called themselves de-segregated. He went into a white restaurant, he sat down, they served him, and he said, "What would happen if a Negro came in here?" And there he's sitting, black as night, but because he had his head wrapped up the waitress looked back at him and says, "Why, there wouldn't no nigger dare come in here."

So, you're dealing with a man whose bias and prejudice are making him lose his mind, his intelligence, every day. He's frightened. He looks around and sees what's taking place on this earth, and he sees that the pendulum of time is swinging in your direction. The dark people are waking up. They're losing their fear of the white man. No place where he's fighting right now is he winning. Everywhere he's fighting, he's fighting someone your and my complexion. And they're beating him. He can't win any more. He's won his last battle. He failed to win the Korean War. He couldn't win it. He had to sign a truce. That's a loss. Any time Uncle Sam, with all his machinery for warfare, is held to a draw by some rice-eaters, he's lost the battle. He had to sign a truce. America's not supposed to sign a truce. She's supposed to be bad. But she's not bad any more. She's bad as long as she can use her hydrogen bomb, but she can't use hers for fear Russia might use hers.

Russia can't use hers, for fear that Sam might use his. So, both of them are weaponless. They can't use the weapon because each's weapon nullifies the other's. So the only place where action can take place is on the ground. And the white man can't win another war fighting on the ground. Those days are over. The black man knows it, the brown man knows it, the red man knows it, and the yellow man knows it. So they engage him in guerrilla warfare. That's not his style. You've got to have heart to be a guerrilla warrior, and he hasn't got any heart. I'm telling you now.

I just want to give you a little briefing on guerrilla warfare because, before you know it, before you know it—It takes heart to be a guerrilla warrior because you're on your own. In conventional warfare you have tanks and a whole lot of other people with you to back you up, planes over your head and all that kind of stuff. But a guerrilla is on his own. All you have is a rifle, some sneakers and a bowl of rice, and that's all you need—and a lot of heart. The Japanese on some of those islands in the Pacific, when the American soldiers landed, one Japanese sometimes could hold the whole army off. He'd just wait until the sun went down, and when the sun went down they were all equal. He would take his little blade and slip from bush to bush, and from American to American. The white soldiers couldn't cope with that. Whenever you see a white soldier that fought in the Pacific, he has the shakes, he has a nervous condition, because they scared him to death.

The same thing happened to the French up in French Indochina. People who just a few years previously were rice farmers got together and ran the heavily-mechanized French army out of Indochina. You don't need it—modern warfare today won't work. This is the day of the guerrilla. They did the same thing in Algeria. Algerians, who were nothing but Bedouins, took a rifle and sneaked off to the hills, and de Gaulle and all of his highfalutin' war machinery couldn't defeat those guerrillas. Nowhere on this earth does the white man win in a guerrilla warfare. It's not his speed. Just as guerrilla warfare is prevailing in Asia and in parts of Africa and in parts of Latin America, you've got to be mighty naive, or you've got to play the black man cheap, if you don't think some day he's going to wake up and find that it's got to be the ballot or the bullet.

I would like to say, in closing, a few things concerning the Muslim Mosque, Inc., which we established recently in New York City. It's true we're Muslims and our religion is Islam, but we don't mix our religion with our politics and our economics and our social and civil activities—not any more. We keep our religion in our mosque. After our religious services are over, then as Muslims we become involved in political action, economic action and social and civic action. We become involved with anybody, anywhere, any time and in any manner that's designed to eliminate the evils, the political, economic and social evils that are afflicting the people of our community.

The political philosophy of black nationalism means that the black man should control the politics and the politicians in his own community; no more. The black man in the black community has to be re-educated into the science of politics so he will know what politics is supposed to bring him in return. Don't be throwing out any ballots. A ballot is like a bullet. You don't throw your ballots until you see a target, and if that target is not within your reach, keep your ballot in your pocket. The political philosophy of black nationalism is being taught in the Christian church. It's being taught in the NAACP. It's being taught in CORE meetings. It's being taught in SNCC [Student Nonviolent Coordinating Committee] meetings. It's being taught in Muslim meetings. It's being taught where nothing but atheists and agnostics come together. It's being taught everywhere. Black people are fed up with the dillydallying, pussyfooting, compromising approach that we've been using toward getting our freedom. We want freedom *now*, but we're not going to get it saying "We Shall Overcome." We've got to fight until we overcome.

The economic philosophy of black nationalism is pure and simple. It only means that we should control the economy of our community. Why should white people be running all the stores in our community? Why should white people be running the banks of our community? Why should the economy of our community be in the hands of the white man? Why? If a black man can't move his store into a white community, you tell me why a white man should move his store into a black community. The philosophy of black nationalism involves a re-education program in the black community in regards to economics. Our people have to be made to see that any time you take your dollar out of your community and spend it in a community where you don't live, the community where you live will get poorer and poorer, and the community where you spend your money will get richer and richer. Then you wonder why where you live is always a ghetto or a slum area. And where you and I are concerned, not only do we lose it when we spend it out of the community, but the white man has got all our stores in the community tied up; so that though we spend it in the community, at sundown the man who runs the store takes it over across town somewhere. He's got us in a vise.

So the economic philosophy of black nationalism means in every church, in every civic organization, in every fraternal order, it's time now for our people to become conscious of the importance of controlling the economy of our community. If we own the stores, if we operate the businesses, if we try and establish some industry in our own community, then we're developing to the position where we are creating employment for our own kind. Once you gain control of the economy of your own community, then you don't have to picket and boycott and beg some cracker downtown for a job in his business.

The social philosophy of black nationalism only means that we have to get together and remove the evils, the vices, alcoholism, drug addiction, and other evils that are destroying the moral fiber of our community. We ourselves have to lift the level of our community, the standard of our community to a higher level, make our own society beautiful so that we will be satisfied in our own social circles and won't be running around here trying to knock our way into a social circle where we're not wanted.

So I say, in spreading a gospel such as black nationalism, it is not designed to make the black man re-evaluate the white man—you known him already—but to make the black man re-evaluate himself. Don't change the white man's mind—you can't change his mind, and that whole thing about appealing to the moral conscience of America— America's conscience is bankrupt. She lost all conscience a long time ago. Uncle Sam has no conscience. They don't know what morals are. They don't try and eliminate an evil because it's evil, or because it's illegal, or because it's immoral; they eliminate it only when it threatens their existence. So you're wasting your time appealing to the moral conscience of a bankrupt man like Uncle Sam. If he had a conscience, he'd straighten this thing out with no more pressure being put upon him. So it is not necessary to change the white man's mind. We have to change our own mind. You can't change his mind about us. We've got to change our own minds about each other. We have to see each other with new eyes. We have to see each other as brothers and sisters. We have to come together with warmth so we can develop unity and harmony that's necessary to get this problem solved ourselves. How can we do this? How can we avoid jealously? How can we avoid the suspicion and the divisions that exist in the community? I'll tell you how.

I have watched how Billy Graham comes into a city, spreading what he calls the gospel of Christ, which is only white nationalism. That's what he is. Billy Graham is a white nationalist; I'm a black nationalist. But since it's the natural tendency for leaders to be jealous and look upon a powerful figure like Graham with suspicion and envy, how is it possible for him to come into a city and get all the cooperation of the church leaders? Don't think because they're church leaders that they don't have weaknesses that make them envious and jealous—no, everybody's got it. It's not an accident that when they want to choose a cardinal [as Pope] over there in Rome, they get in a closet so you can't hear them cussing and fighting and carrying on.

Billy Graham comes in preaching the gospel of Christ, he evangelizes the gospel, he stirs everybody up, but he never tries to start a church. If he came in trying to start a church, all the churches would be against him. So, he just comes in talking about Chirst and tells everybody who gets Christ to go to any church were Christ is; and in this way the church cooperates with him. So we're going to take a page from his book.

Our gospel is black nationalism. We're not trying to threaten the existence of any organization, but we're spreading the gospel of black nationalism. Anywhere there's a church that is also preaching and practicing the gospel of black nationalism, join that church. If the NAACP is preaching and practicing the gospel of black nationalism, join the NAACP. If CORE is spreading and practicing the gospel of black nationalism, join CORE. Join any organization that has a gospel that's for the uplift of the black man. And when you get into it and see them pussyfooting or compromising, pull out of it because that's not black nationalism. We'll find another one.

And in this manner, the organizations will increase in number and in quantity and in quality, and by August, it is then our intention to have a black nationalist convention which will consist of delegates from all over the country who are interested in the political, economic and social philosophy of black nationalism. After these delegates convene, we will hold a seminar, we will hold discussions, we will listen to everyone. We want to hear new ideas and new solutions and new answers. And at that time, if we see fit then to form a black nationalist party, we'll form a black nationalist party. If it's necessary to form a black nationalist army, we'll form a black nationalist army. It'll be the ballot or the bullet. It'll be liberty or it'll be death.

It's time for you and me to stop sitting in this country, letting some cracker senators, Northern crackers and Southern crackers, sit there in Washington, D.C., and come to a conclusion in their mind that you and I are supposed to have civil rights. There's no white man going to tell me anything about *my* rights. Brothers and sisters, always remember, if it doesn't take senators and congressmen and presidential proclamations to give freedom to the white man, it is not necessary for legislation or proclamation or Supreme Court decisions to give freedom to the black man. You let that white man know, if this is a country of freedom, let it be a country of freedom; and if it's not a country of freedom, change it.

We will work with anybody, anywhere, at any time, who is genuinely interested in tackling the problem head-on, nonviolently as long as the enemy is nonviolent, but violent when the enemy gets violent. We'll work with you on the voter-registration drive, we'll work with you on rent strikes, we'll work with you on school boycotts—I don't believe in any kind of integration; I'm not even worried about it because I know you're not going to get it anyway; you're not going to get it because you're afraid to die; you've got to be ready to die if you try and force yourself on the white man, because he'll get just as violent as those crackers in Mississippi, right here in Cleveland. But we will still work with you on the school boycotts because we're against a segregated school system. A segregated school system produces children who, when they graduate, graduate with crippled minds. But this does not mean that a school is segregated because it's all black. A segregated school means a school that is controlled by people who have no real interest in it whatsoever.

Let me explain what I mean. A segregated district or community is a community in which people live, but outsiders control the politics and the economy of that community. They never refer to the white section as a segregated community. It's the all-Negro section that's a segregated community. Why? The white man controls his own school, his own bank, his own economy, his own politics, his own everything, his own community—but he also controls yours. When you're under someone else's control, you're segregated. They'll always give you the lowest or the worst that there is to offer, but it doesn't mean you're segregated just because you have your own. You've got to *control* your own. Just like the white man has control of his, you need to control yours.

You know the best way to get rid of segregation? The white man is more afraid of separation than he is of integration. Segregation means that he puts you away from him, but not far enough for you to be out of his jurisdiction; separation means you're gone. And the white man will integrate faster than he'll let you separate. So we will work with you against the segregated school system because it's criminal, because it is absolutely destructive, in every way imaginable, to the minds of the children who have to be exposed to that type of crippling education.

Last but not least, I must say this concerning the great controversy over rifles and shotguns. The only thing that I've ever said is that in areas where the government has proven itself either unwilling or unable to defend the lives and the property of Negroes, it's time for Negroes to defend themselves. Article number two of the constitutional amendments provides you and me the right to own a rifle or a shotgun. It is constitutionally legal to own a shotgun or a rifle. This doesn't mean you're going to get a rifle and form battalions and go out looking for white folks, although you'd be within your rights—I mean, you'd be justified; but that would be illegal and we don't do anything illegal. If the white man doesn't want the black man buying rifles and shotguns, then let the government do its job. That's all. And don't let the white man come to you and ask you what you think about what Malcolm says—why, you old Uncle Tom. He would never ask you if he thought you were going to say, "Amen!" No, he is making a Tom out of you.

So, this doesn't mean forming rifle clubs and going out looking for people, but it is time, in 1964, if you are a man, to let that man know. If he's not going to do his job in running the government and providing you and me with the protection that our taxes are supposed to be for, since he spends all those billions for his defense budget, he certainly can't begrudge you and me spending $12 or $15 for a single-shot, or double-action. I hope you understand. Don't go out shooting people, but any time, brothers and sisters, and especially the men in this audience—some of you wearing Congressional Medals of Honor, with shoulders this wide, chests this big, muscles that big— any time you and I sit around and read where they bomb a church and murder in cold blood, not some grownups, but four little girls while they were praying to the same god the white man taught them to pray to, and you and I see the government go down and can't find who did it.

Why, this man—he can find Eichmann hiding down in Argentina somewhere. Let two or three American soldiers, who are minding somebody else's business way over in South Vietnam, get killed, and he'll send battleships, sticking his nose in their business. He wanted to send troops down to Cuba and make them have what he calls free elections— this old cracker who doesn't have free elections in his own country. No, if you never see me another time in your life, if I die in the morning, I'll die saying one thing: the ballot or the bullet, the ballot or the bullet.

If a Negro in 1964 has to sit around and wait for some cracker senator to filibuster when it comes to the rights of black people, why, you and I should hang our heads in shame. You talk about a march on Washington in 1963, you haven't seen anything. There's some more going down in '64. And this time they're not going like they went last year. They're not going singing "We Shall Overcome." They're not going with white friends. They're not going with placards already painted for them. They're not going with round-trip tickets. They're going with one-way tickets.

And if they don't want that non-nonviolent army going down there, tell them to bring the filibuster to a halt. The black nationalists aren't going to wait. Lyndon B. Johnson is the head of the Democratic Party. If he's for civil rights, let him go into the Senate next week and declare himself. Let him go in there right now and declare himself. Let him go in there and denounce the Southern branch of his party. Let him go in there right now and take a moral stand—right now, not later. Tell him, don't wait until election time. If he waits too long, brothers and sisters, he will be responsible for letting a condition develop in this country which will create a climate that will bring seeds up out of the ground with vegetation on the end of them looking like something these people never dreamed of. In 1964, it's the ballot or the bullet. Thank you.

Integration
or
Separation?

FAREWELL TO INTEGRATION
W. H. Ferry
(1968)

My proposition is that racial integration in the United States is impossible. I set forth this proposition without qualification. There are no hidden unlesses, buts, or ifs in it. I shall not deny that—in some remote future—integration may come about. But I do not see it resulting from the actual present trends and attitudes in American society. It can only be produced by some event overturning these trends. There is no denial in this proposition that there will be a steady betterment in the material situation of blacks. This is even likely. My proposition does, nevertheless, contradict the words of President Johnson that "the promise of America" will be extended to all races and peoples in the nation's slums.

My proposition is sad. Like tens of thousands of other Americans I have supported, organized, and taken part in reformist projects, with integration always beckoning at the end of weary labors. Now such activities must be seen as nothing more than acts of good will, rather like Peace Corps expeditions into an undeveloped country that look toward the welfare and material progress of the natives but not to their integration with the homeland.

My proposition, in short, smashes the liberal dream. It eliminates the democratic optimistic claim that we are finding our way to a harmonious blending of the races. It changes the words of the marching song to "We Shall *Not* Overcome," for what was eventually to be overcome was hostility and non-fraternity between black and white. My

Reprinted, by permission, from the September 1969 issue of *The Center Magazine*, Vol. II, Number 5, a publication of the Center for the Study of Democratic Institutions, Santa Barbara, California. The overall title is the present editor's.

proposition dynamites the foundations of the N.A.A.C.P., the Urban League, and similar organizations. It asserts that blacktown U.S.A. and whitetown U.S.A., for all practical purposes and with unimportant exceptions, will remain separate social communities for as long as one can see ahead. I am not sure, but it may also mean that blacktown will become a separate political community.

The proposition, I am aware, lends support to Southerners who have been acting on it for hundreds of years. It would seem to place me in the camp of the bigots and locate me with the hopeless. It puts at ultimate zero the efforts of the tough and high-minded who are giving their lives, in the urban bearpits and hovels of America, to the dream of equality among men.

Yet I am convinced that integration in the United States is a sentimental, not a doctrinal, idea. We came to the idea late in American history, and it disappears readily from the rhetoric of politics—though not from the list of sacred democratic aims—at the first sign of indocility, at the first showing of the rioter's torch. The vast fuss today about improvements in blacktown is not aimed at integration. Few are afflicting us any longer with such a tiresome lie. All these measures are primarily aimed at the prevention of civic commotions, secondarily at assuaging the conscience of whitetown, and finally at helping the blacks. Priorities tell the story. In the last seven years we have spent three hundred and eighty-four billion dollars on war, twenty-seven billion on space, and less than two billion on community development and housing.

In giving up on integration I am not giving up on the blacks but on the whites.

ENTERING WHITE AMERICA
John L. Perry
(1968)

I can tolerate whites on the subject of what whites should do in relation to blacks; it is the license under which I am writing this. I just don't want to hear any more from whites attempting to speak for Negroes. What particularly concerns me are those whites who see the monumental stupidities and outrages committed by white America against black America and wish—out of a sense of guilt or whatever motivates them—to punish white American for its sins.

It does not concern me very much that those despairing whites now want to play Jove and punish their fellow-whites. What bothers me is the temerity of those whites who, in order to gratify whatever is eating them, are willing to prescribe for blacks—in some instances, to prescribe surrender of any hope of black betterment through measures short of violence, or to prescribe self-genocide for blacks, which is precisely how unrelenting black-versus-white violence must end. If a Negro wishes to say farewell to integration or desegregation, or welcome Black Power or violence, then that is the prerogative of that individual —and not just because he is an individual, either, but because he is a black individual.

No one has the right to give up on behalf of another man, least of all when the man giving up is white and the man he is giving up for is black. Blacks in this country have been sold out in a million ways, but this is a new, even less forgiveable, fashion. Vicarious sympathy, empathetic ratiocination, and the most faithful parroting of Negro expressions are no substitute for actually being black. White good will helps. White approximation of Negro sentiment helps. None of it—not even white precise identity with Negro sentiment—is good enough.

Whites probably have as much business looking into the crystal ball as anyone, and if the subject of white-black relations is kept in the area of prognostications I am prepared to listen to whites as well as to blacks. In fact, I have no reluctance to do some predicting of my own. It must be obvious that two things, on the surface diametrically opposed, are going on today. Desegregation *is* taking place. Blacks *are* entering

Reprinted, by permission, from the September 1969 issue of *The Center Magazine*, Vol. II, Number 5, a publication of the Center for the Study of Democratic Institutions, Santa Barbara, California.

white America, in greater numbers and in greater percentages. To discount all that is happening, before the eyes of any who are willing to see, as nothing more than blacks turning into whites because they have made it into white America, is to forfeit the claim to serious consideration. At the same time, black separation is going on.

Those blacks entering white America are making it that much easier for other blacks to follow. Those who remain in the ghetto are, I predict, going to produce some very desirable citizens—desirable to both black and white America, for they will be stronger, more self-assured human beings. With this sort of dual process going on, I have to ask how dare anyone raise a white staying hand to the possibilities of integration? No white has the right to say to a black that he can or cannot, must or must not, enter white America. The black man, and only he, is entitled to decide.

BLACK POWER
Albert Cleage
(1968)

What is now happening in Detroit, I think, is typical in at least one way of black communities throughout America: it represents the determination of the black people to control their own community. This marks a new day for black people. Wherever the black revolution is in progress, specific steps have to be taken to structure a transfer of power from the white community to the black community. The white community apparently finds this painful and distasteful, but it is a necessity if there is to be any peaceful resolution of the kind of conflict that shook America last summer and the two preceding summers. The black community is growing increasingly determined that it must control its own destiny. In the simplest terms this means political control of all areas in which black people are a majority—control of community services, police services, and all the things that go to make up a community and that black people do not now control in Detroit or in any other urban center.

The idea that I would advocate a racist approach to a solution of the black man's problems seemed unthinkable to many respectable, responsible black leaders. But this feeling has grown less and less as the years have gone by. In Cleveland, which is much less organized and much less militant and much less black-conscious than Detroit, all but four per cent of the black community supported a black candidate without any feeling that they were in any way negating the basic principles of American good government.

This indicates to me that something basically important is happening to the black community throughout America: black people have tended to sever their identification with the white community and to become alienated from America. They no longer want to be part of the white man's society; they have ceased to accept the white man's standards of what is good or bad. This is a total rejection of integration as an ideal or an objective. Instead, the black man is trying to recapture a sense of identification with his own cultural heritage. This involves the rediscovery of Africa, the development of black consciousness, black

Reprinted, by permission, from the September 1969 issue of *The Center Magazine*, Vol. II, Number 5, a publication of the Center for the Study of Democratic Institutions, Santa Barbara, California.

pride, black unity, and at least the beginning of the development of black power.

White people killed the myth and the dream of integration, about which Dr. King spoke so eloquently. Black people listened, but then the dream died, because it was not based on reality. Now their dream is to recapture their own past, their own culture, their own history, and to put the race issue on the basis of a power struggle pure and simple.

We will take in this country what we have power enough to take, and what we do not have power enough to take we will stop dreaming about. We will try to build power to take the things we have to have. This is the only kind of equality there is—an equality based on power. We are concerned primarily with our own black community. We are not trying to invade white communities, or take over white communities. But we do insist that white people cannot enjoy the luxury of separating us into black ghettos and also enjoy the privilege of exploiting us in these ghettos they have forced us into.

GUILT AND FORGIVENESS

John Cogley

(1963)

From time to time we hear that one Negro spokesman or another is obsessed, or unbalanced, or hysterical in his approach to the race problem. I have no doubt that there are such cases. But all of us are more or less guilt-ridden, lacking in health, our characters corroded by living in a caste society. If it is hard to be black in such a society, it is also hard to be white. For to be a white man in a segregated society, at least today, is to live in nameless fear and isolation and withdrawal from a whole sector of one's fellow-citizens. Segregation means that the holding back of friendship has become institutionalized. The spiritual unhealthiness in it derives from the fact that it is easier in such a society to withhold love than to give love. This is the definition of a serious sickness. It afflicts all of us.

We are schizophrenic about the claims put forth as our "American" philosophy. Our deed does not match our creed; our history does not fit in with our doctrine; our moral claims do not jibe with our actual traditions. If in textbooks there is a kind of man known as an American who lives in a land where freedom and equality are the heritage of all, the fact is that no such man has ever lived, North or South. This much we have to admit.

But now that the moment of truth has arrived, what will be our reaction? We whites can perhaps learn to live in fear of the violence that may spring up at any hour—and in time our fear will inevitably turn to hate. Negroes can perhaps live with resentment eating away at their natural friendliness. They may even learn to comfort themselves with the strange, foreign doctrines of a reverse racism. They can perhaps learn to live without hope, but with a certain fierce private pride, in a land peopled by "white devils" and satanic forces. But who calls that living? Hatred can be swollen on both sides. We can, both groups, learn to live with each other in a state of permanent hostility. We can, in a word, exist in a kind of racist hell. "Hell is not to love any more" (George Bernanos).

But what, is our best moments, do we seek? The status quo is

Reprinted, by permission, from the September 1969 issue of *The Center Magazine*, Vol. II, Number 5, a publication of the Center for the Study of Democratic Institutions, Santa Barbara, California.

clearly unacceptable. A return to the ugly past is out of the question. We have no choice but to change. How such a change will take place, and what the nature of it will be, depends on leaders, black and white, working together to lead the people, black and white. It is not easy for the dominant whites to acknowledge their ancient guilt, a guilt borne more or less by all. It is not easy for the oppressed blacks to forgive. But what other choice do we have?

BREAKING THE LAW

Bayard Rustin

(1966)

I do not believe that one ever has the *right* to civil disobedience. Rather, one has something much more profound, and that is the *duty* to be a civil disobedient with the objective of revealing inconsistencies in the society and of correcting them. The willingness of a civil disobedient to accept suffering cheerfully is one of the most important ways of getting other people to think about the wrongs of society. Therefore, those who have engaged in civil disobedience have asked their people most of the following questions and have expected a "yes" to each.

Number 1: Are you attempting, rather than merely to break a law, to adhere conscientiously to a higher principle in the hope that the law you break will be changed and that new law will emerge on the basis of that higher principle?

Number 2: Have you engaged in the democratic process and exercised the constitutional means that are available before engaging in the breaking of law? One cannot possibly say that Negroes a hundred years after the Emancipation Proclamation have no right to engage in civil disobedience when every Negro leader for at least fifty years has been struggling to get some semblance of justice for his people, and until the last ten years struggling unsuccessfully. When Negroes engage in civil disobedience they can truthfully answer this question with, "Yes, we have not only used but exhausted every possibility under the law to establish justice."

For the young rebels today a variation of the question must be posed: Is what you conceive so monstrous that you do not believe there is time for dealing with it by constitutional means? Their answer to this question is "yes" because they say that they do not want to see American boys dying who do not understand what is happening in the Far East; they do not want to see American boys burning huts with women and children in them. I have said to these young people that they make too much of American brutality. The Vietcong is equally brutal. Whether one is among the battling Pakistanis and Indians, or

Reprinted, by permission, from the September 1969 issue of *The Center Magazine*, Vol. II, Number 5, a publication of the Center for the Study of Democratic Institutions, Santa Barbara, California.

in Watts, or in warfare anywhere, the law of violence is such that each side becomes equally vicious. To try to distinguish between which is more vicious is to fail to recognize the logic of war. It is war that is the evil, not the Vietcong, not the United States.

Number 3: Have I removed ego as much as it is possible to do so? That is to say, am I on this march because I want to get my picture in the paper, or because I'm just mad at society, or because my mother doesn't want me to do this and I'll show her? Or am I here for impersonal, objective reasons?

Number 4: Do the people whom I ask to rebel feel there is a grievous wrong involved, and does my own rebellion help them to bring to the surface the inner feelings that they have not previously dared to express?

Number 5: Am I prepared to accept the consequences of my acts? Throughout the civil-rights struggle I myself have fought against lying in the streets and being carried off by the police. When the policeman taps me on the shoulder and says, "You are under arrest," I believe I strengthen my ability to educate the people in the South who disagree with me by answering, "Yes, officer, I have broken the law because I believe it is wrong. I am perfectly willing to go with you. I do not want you to carry me." And when I get to the judge I want to say to him, "I have done what society feels is wrong. I accept the punishment."

Number 6: Am I attempting to bring about a new social order by my rebellion, or a new law that is better than the one that now exists?

And the seventh and final question that one must ask springs from Kant's categorical imperative: Would the world be a better place if everybody, not just in my country and not just those who are black, but everyone in the world did likewise? Obviously, if everyone in the world were prepared to burn his draft card, war would not be possible.

WHAT WHITES MUST DO

Grace Lee

(1963)

Hannah Arendt has observed that violence occurs where there are no politics. In the present circumstances the great likelihood is indeed just that—that whites will respond with ugly violence to the Negro struggle. They cannot respond politically or philosophically, much less spiritually, because they have nothing to say about who they themselves are or what they want as free men.

The great, the urgent need is to create a genuine political movement among whites that has the passion of the Negro movement. What the whites need to do is to go into their own communities and organizations and there clash with other whites over the issues, freeing themselves of their whiteness—that peculiar complex ·of guilt, anger, and fear that few whites recognize in themselves and even fewer have begun to explore. Until this happens, the Negro struggle must remain one of Negroes against whites.

Reprinted, by permission, from the September 1969 issue of *The Center Magazine*, Vol. II, Number 5, a publication of the Center for the Study of Democratic Institutions, Santa Barbara, California.

THE BASIC CAUSES OF
RECENT RACIAL DISORDERS

Otto Kerner, John V. Lindsay, *et al.*

. . . we shift our focus from the local to the national scene, from the particular events of the summer of 1967 to the factors within the society at large which have brought about the sudden violent mood of so many urban Negroes.

The record before this Commission reveals that the causes of recent racial disorders are embedded in a massive tangle of issues and circumstances—social, economic, political, and psyhological—which arise out of the historical pattern of Negro-white relations in America.

These factors are both complex and interacting; they vary significantly in their effect from city to city and from year to year: and the consequences of one disorder, generating new grievances and new demands, become the causes of the next. It is this which creates the "thicket of tension, conflicting evidence and extreme opinions" cited by the President.

Despite these complexities, certain fundamental matters are clear. Of these, the most fundamental is the racial attitude and behavior of white Americans toward black Americans. Race prejudice has shaped our history decisively in the past; it now threatens to do so again. White racism is essentially responsible for the explosive mixture which has been accumulating in our cities since the end of World War II. At the base of this mixture are three of the most bitter fruits of white racial attitudes:

Pervasive discrimination and segregation. The first is surely the continuing exclusion of great numbers of Negroes from the benefits of economic progress through discrimination in employment and education, and their enforced confinement in segregated housing and schools. The corrosive and degrading effects of this condition and the attitudes that underlie it are the source of the deepest bitterness and at the center of the problem of racial disorder.

Black migration and white exodus. The second is the massive and growing concentration of impoverished Negroes in our major cities

From Part II, Chapter 4 ("The Basic Causes"), *Report of the National Advisory Commission on Civil Disorders* (1968), Otto Kerner, Chairman; John V. Lindsay, Vice Chairman.

resulting from Negro migration from the rural South, rapid population growth and the continuing movement of the white middle-class to the suburbs. The consequence is a greatly increased burden on the already depleted resources of cities, creating a growing crisis of deteriorating facilities and services and unmet human needs.

Black ghettos. Third, in the teeming racial ghettos, segregation and poverty have intersected to destroy opportunity and hope and to enforce failure. The ghettos too often mean men and women without jobs, families without men, and schools where children are processed instead of educated, until they return to the street—to crime, to narcotics, to dependency on welfare, and to bitterness and resentment against society in general and white society in particular.

These three forces have converged on the inner city in recent years and on the people who inhabit it. At the same time, most whites and many Negroes outside the ghetto have prospered to a degree unparalleled in the history of civilization. Through television—the universal appliance in the ghetto—and the other media of mass communications, this affluence has been endlessly flaunted before the eyes of the Negro poor and the jobless ghetto youth.

As Americans, most Negro citizens carry within themselves two basic aspirations of our society. They seek to share in both the material resources of our system and its intangible benefits—dignity, respect and acceptance. Outside the ghetto many have succeeded in achieving a decent standard of life, and in developing the inner resources which give life meaning and direction. Within the ghetto, however, it is rare that either aspiration is achieved.

Yet these facts alone—fundamental as they are—cannot be said to have caused the disorders. Other and more immediate factors help explain why these events happened now.

Recently, three powerful ingredients have begun to catalyze the mixture.

Frustrated hopes. The expectations aroused by the great judicial and legislative victories of the civil rights movement have led to frustration, hostility and cynicism in the face of the persistent gap between promise and fulfillment. The dramatic struggle for equal rights in the South has sensitized Northern Negroes to the economic inequalities reflected in the deprivations of ghetto life.

Legitimation of violence. A climate that tends toward the approval and encouragement of violence as a form of protest has been created by white terrorism directed against nonviolent protest, including instances of abuse and even murder of some civil rights workers in the South; by the open defiance of law and federal authority by state and local officials resisting desegregation; and by some protest groups engaging in civil disobedience who turn their backs on nonviolence, go beyond the Constitutionally protected rights of petition and free assembly, and resort to violence to attempt to compel alteration of laws and policies with which they disagree. This condition has been reinforced by a general erosion of respect for authority in American society and reduced effectiveness of social standards and community restraints on violence and crime. This in turn has largely resulted from rapid urbanization and the dramatic reduction in the average age of the total population.

Powerlessness. Finally, many Negroes have come to believe that they are being exploited politically and economically by the white "power structure." Negroes, like people in poverty everywhere, in fact lack the channels of communication, influence and appeal that traditionally have been available to ethnic minorities within the city and which enabled them—unburdened by color—to scale the walls of the white ghettos in an earlier era. The frustrations of powerlessness have led some to the conviction that there is no effective alternative to violence as a means of expression and redress, as a way of "moving the system." More generally, the result is alienation and hostility toward the institutions of law and government and the white society which controls them. This is reflected in the reach toward racial consciousness and solidarity reflected in the slogan "Black Power."

These facts have combined to inspire a new mood among Negroes, particularly among the young. Self-esteem and enhanced racial pride are replacing apathy and submission to "the system." Moreover, Negro youth, who make up over half of the ghetto population, share the growing sense of alienation felt by many white youth in our country. Thus, their role in recent civil disorders reflects not only a shared sense of deprivation and victimization by white society but also the rising incidence of disruptive conduct by a segment of American youth throughout the society.

Incitement and encouragement of violence. These conditions have created a volatile mixture of attitudes and beliefs which needs only a spark to ignite mass violence. Strident appeals to violence, first heard from white racists, were echoed and reinforced last summer in the inflammatory rhetoric of black racists and militants. Throughout the year, extremists crisscrossed the country preaching a doctrine of black power and violence. Their rhetoric was widely reported in the mass media; it was echoed by local "militants" and organizations; it became the ugly background noise of the violent summer.

We cannot measure with any precision the influence of these

organizations and individuals in the ghetto, but we think it clear that the intolerable and unconscionable encouragement of violence heightened tensions, created a mood of acceptance and an expectation of violence, and thus contributed to the eruption of the disorders last summer.

The Police. It is the convergence of all these factors that makes the role of the police so difficult and so significant. Almost invariably the incident that ignites disorder arises from police action. Harlem, Watts, Newark and Detroit—all the major outbursts of recent years—were precipitated by routine arrests of Negroes for minor offenses by white police.

But the police are not merely the spark. In discharge of their obligation to maintain order and insure public safety in the disruptive conditions of ghetto life, they are inevitably involved in sharper and more frequent conflicts with ghetto residents than with the residents of other areas. Thus, to many Negroes police have come to symbolize white power, white racism and white repression. And the fact is that many police do reflect and express these white attitudes. The atmosphere of hostility and cynicism is reinforced by a widespread perception among Negroes of the existence of police brutality and corruption, and of a "double standard" of justice and protection—one for Negroes and one for whites.

THE TEN POINT PROGRAM
OF BLACK LIBERATION OF THE
BLACK PANTHER PARTY

1. We want freedom. We want power to determine the destiny of our Black Community.

2. We want full employment for our people.

3. We want an end to the robbery by the Capitalist[1] of our Black Community.

4. We want decent housing, fit for shelter of human beings.

5. We want education for our people that exposes the true nature of this decadent American society. We want education that teaches us our true history and our role in the present day society.

6. We want all black men to be exempt from military service.

7. We want an immediate end to police brutality and murder of black people.

8. We want freedom for all black men held in federal, state, county and city prisons and jails.

9. We want all black people when brought to trial to be tried in court by a jury of their peer group or people from their black communities, as defined by the Constitution of the United States.

10. We want land, bread, housing, education, clothing, justice, and peace. And as our major political objective, a United Nations-supervised plebiscite to be held throughout the black colony in which only black colonial subjects will be allowed to participate, for the purpose of determining the will of black people as to their national destiny.

---

[1] In an earlier version, "by the White Man."

THE REVOLUTIONARY THEATRE

LeRoi Jones

The Revolutionary Theatre should force change; it should be change. (All their faces turned into the lights and you work on them black nigger magic, and cleanse them as having seen the ugliness. And if the beautiful see themselves, they will love themselves.) We are preaching virtue again, but by that to mean NOW, toward what seems the most constructive use of the world.

The Revolutionary Theatre must EXPOSE! Show up the insides of these humans, look into black skulls. White men will cower before this theatre because it hates them. Because they themselves have been trained to hate. The Revolutionary Theatre must hate them for hating. For presuming with their technology to deny the supremacy of the Spirit. They will all die because of this.

The Revolutionary Theatre must teach them their deaths. It must crack their faces open to the mad cries of the poor. It must teach them about silence and the truths lodged there. It must kill any God anyone names except Common Sense. The Revolutionary Theatre should flush the fags and murders out of Lincoln's face.

It should stagger through our universe correcting, insulting, preaching, spitting craziness—but a craziness taught to us in our most rational moments. People must be taught to trust true scientists (knowers, diggers, oddballs) and that the holiness of life is the constant possibility of widening the consciousness. And they must be incited to strike back against *any* agency that attempts to prevent this widening.

The Revolutionary Theatre must Accuse and Attack anything that can be accused and attacked. It must Accuse and Attack because it is a theatre of Victims. It looks at the sky with the victims' eyes, and moves the victims to look at the strength in their minds and their bodies.

Clay, in *Dutchman*, Ray in *The Toilet*, Walker in *The Slave*, are all victims. In the Western sense they could be heroes. But the Revolutionary Theatre, even if it is Western, must be anti-Western. It must show horrible coming attractions of *The Crumbling of the West*. Even as Artaud[1] designed *The Conquest of Mexico,* so we must design *The Conquest of White Eye,* and show the missionaries and wiggly Liberals dying under blasts of concrete. For sound effects, wild screams of joy, from all the peoples of the world.

The Revolutionary Theatre must take dreams and give them a reality. It must isolate the ritual and historical cycles of reality. But it must be food for all those who need food, and daring propaganda for the beauty of the Human Mind. It is a political theatre, a weapon to help in the slaughter of these dim-witted fatbellied white guys who somehow believe that the rest of the world is here for them to slobber on.

This should be a theatre of World Spirit. Where the spirit can be shown to be the most competent force in the world. Force. Spirit. Feeling. The language will be anybody's, but tightened by the poet's backbone. And even the language must show what the facts are in this consciousness epic, what's happening. We will talk about the world, and the preciseness with which we are able to summon the world will be our art. Art is method. And art, "like any ashtray or senator," remains in the world. Wittgenstein[2] said ethics and aesthetics are one. I believe this. So the Broadway theatre is a theatre of reaction whose ethics, like its aesthetics, reflect the spiritual values of this unholy society, which sends young crackers all over the world blowing off colored people's heads. (In some of these flippy Southern towns they even shoot up the immigrants' Favorite Son, be it Michael Schwerner[3] or JFKennedy.)

The Revolutionary Theatre is shaped by the world, and moved to reshape the world, using as its force the natural force and perpetual vibrations of the mind in the world. We are history and desire, what we are, and what any experience can make us.

It is a social theatre, but all theatre is social theatre. But we will change the drawing rooms into places where real things can be said about a real world, or into smoky rooms where the destruction of Washington can be plotted. The Revolutionary Theatre must function like an incendiary pencil planted in Curtis Lemay's cap.[4] So that when

[1] Antonin Artaud (1896–1948), French playwright, actor, and dramatic theorist who proposed a theatre of cruelty.

[2] Ludwig Wittgenstein (1889–1951), German philosopher.

[3] In 1964, in Mississippi, southern white racists shot three northern white civil rights workers: Michael Schwerner, James Earl Chaney, and Andrew Goodman.

[4] Curtis E. Lemay (1906–   ), former head of Strategic Air Command. In 1968 he was the vice-presidential candidate on the third party ticket headed by Alabama politician George Wallace.

the final curtain goes down brains are splattered over the seats and floor, and bleeding nuns must wire SOS's to Belgians with gold teeth.

Our theatre will show victims so that their brothers in the audience will be better able to understand that they are the brothers of victims, and that they themselves are victims if they are blood brothers. And what we show must cause the blood to rush, so that pre-revolutionary temperaments will be bathed in this blood, and it will cause their deepest souls to move, and they will find themselves tensed and clenched, even ready to die, at what the soul has been taught. We will scream and cry, murder, run through the streets in agony, if it means some soul will be moved, moved to actual life understanding of what the world is, and what it ought to be. We are preaching virtue and feeling, and a natural sense of the self in the world. All men live in the world, and the world ought to be a place for them to live.

What is called the imagination (from image, magi, magic, magician, etc.) is a practical vector from the soul. It stores all data, and can be called on to solve all our "problems." The imagination is the projection of ourselves past our sense of ourselves as "things." Imagination (image) is all possibility, because from the image, the initial circumscribed energy, any use (idea) is possible. And so begins that image's use in the world. Possibility is what moves us.

The popular white man's theatre like the popular white man's novel shows tired white lives, and the problems of eating white sugar, or else it herds bigcaboosed blondes onto huge stages in rhinestones and makes believe they are dancing or singing. WHITE BUSINESSMEN OF THE WORLD, DO YOU WANT TO SEE PEOPLE REALLY DANCING AND SINGING??? ALL OF YOU GO UP TO HARLEM AND GET YOURSELF KILLED. THERE WILL BE DANCING AND SINGING, THEN, FOR REAL!! (In *The Slave*, Walker Vessels, the black revolutionary, wears an armband, which is the insignia of the attacking army—a big red-lipped minstrel, grinning like crazy.)

The liberal white man's objection to the theatre of the revolution (if he is "hip" enough) will be on aesthetic grounds. Most white Western artists do not need to be "political," since usually, whether they know it or not, they are in complete sympathy with the most repressive social forces in the world today. There are more junior birdmen fascists running around the West today disguised as Artists than there are disguised as fascists. (But then, that word, *Fascist*, and with it, *Fascism*, has been made obsolete by the words *America*, and *Americanism*.) The American Artist usually turns out to be just a super-Bourgeois, because, finally, all he has to show for his sojourn through the world is "better taste" than the Bourgeois—many times not even that.

Americans will hate the Revolutionary Theatre because it will be out to destroy them and whatever they believe is real. American cops will try to close the theatres where such nakedness of the human spirit is paraded. American producers will say the revolutionary plays are filthy, usually because they will treat human life as if it were actually happening. American directors will say that the white guys in the plays are too abstract and cowardly ("don't get me wrong . . . I mean aesthetically. . . .") and they will be right.

The force we want is of twenty million spooks storming America with furious cries and upstoppable weapons. We want actual explosions and actual brutality: AN EPIC IS CRUMBLING and we must give it the space and hugeness of its actual demise. The Revolutionary Theatre, which is now peopled with victims, will soon begin to be peopled with new kinds of heroes—not the weak Hamlets debating whether or not they are ready to die for what's on their minds, but men and women (and minds) digging out from under a thousand years of "high art" and weak-faced dalliance. We must make an art that will function so as to call down the actual wrath of world spirit. We are witch doctors and assassins, but we will open a place for the true scientists to expand our consciousness. This is a theatre of assault. The play that will split the heavens for us will be called THE DESTRUCTION OF AMERICA. The heroes will be Crazy Horse,[5] Denmark Vesey,[6] Patrice Lumumba,[7] and not history, not memory, not sad sentimental groping for a warmth in our despair; these will be new men, new heroes, and their enemies most of you who are reading this.

[5] Sioux Indian Chief Crazy Horse (1849?–1877) joined Chief Sitting Bull and other Sioux on the Little Big Horn River, where they annihilated the soldiers commanded by Colonel George A. Custer.

[6] In 1822, Denmark Vesey, a free Negro, led an abortive revolt of slaves and free Negroes in South Carolina.

[7] The first Prime Minister of the Republic of the Congo, Patrice Lumumba was killed in 1961 by forces of a political rival, Colonel Joseph Mobutu, who with United Nations approval seized power.

The Brown Revolution

JUSTICE

In his poem "El Grito" ("The Outcry"), Guadalupe de Saavedra, author of *Justice*, contrasts the old Chicano (Mexican-American) with the new:

> until yesterday, you called me a good chicano.
> i was meek, humble, goddamned ignorant.
> i was young, passive,
> > another pawn in a game you play.
> i bent my knee, smiled, echoed,
> > "my country, right or wrong."

As a good Chicano, he "licked the hand that fed me crumbs." Today, however, he is what the *Anglos* (white Americans) call a bad Chicano:

> because i dare to speak of truth,
> because i dare not be silent,
> because i dare destroy the image
> > you have built of me,
> because i choose not to live
> > or end my life in an eternal siesta.
> you point at me as a militant,
> > because i will not crawl,
> > because i seek to uproot the hell
> > > of being the system's dog,
> > patted on the head . . . "NICE BOY, PANCHO,"
> > > while a finger is jammed right up my ass,
> > because i desire to be a man.

The history of Mexican-Americans, whose language (Spanish) white authorities have tried to suppress and whose rights have often been denied—despite American obligations to the contrary (in the Treaty of Guadalupe-Hidalgo, 1848)—has included discrimination, denied opportunities, and virtual peonage. No longer silent or humbly acquiescent, Chicanos today are demanding that wrongs be righted. Seeking an end to discrimination, restitution for mineral and other resources taken from lands they claim were stolen from them, restoration of those lands, community control of police and education, recognition in their schools that Spanish is the first and English the second language, militant Chicanos want not only to affirm their ethnic identity but—in Saavedra's words—"to uproot the hell/of being the system's dog. . . ."

The radical Teatro Chicano, founded by Saavedra in Los Angeles in 1968, aims to achieve these goals as well as to transform the society in which Chicanos live. In their bilingual songs, poetry readings, and *actos* (short, one-act plays), they present the problems of Chicanos of the *barrios* (districts or neighborhoods) in the cities of the southwestern United States, and they offer solutions. As Saavedra explains, the Teatro Chicano is concerned with two types of revolution. "One is a revolution against outside forces: the system, the dominant society, the ideology that's holding us down. There's also another revolution—within our own people." Although the Teatro Chicano uses nonviolent means (education and propaganda) to effect social change, it also dramatizes the failures of nonviolence. The paradox is not lost on Saavedra, who observes in his poem "Dilemma of a Revolutionary Poet,"

> *Words will not stop bullets;*
> *Rhymes offer no protection from a racist club.*
> *Metaphors are useless weapons against brutality,*
> *And*
> *Adjectives will not prevent my being slaughtered,*
> *So*
> *As a pastime*
> *I collect bullets.*

Justice not only dramatizes the futility of nonviolence but also suggests a revolution against "the system." The other revolution consists of the rejection of the *Anglo* way of life and the assertion of Chicano identity —the refusal, as Tony Avallon (an actor in the Teatro Chicano) says, to "let any group, any person, tell you you have to be a certain way and you have to do things a certain way because he got there first."

On May 2, 3, 4, and "Cinco" (5), 1969—May 5 is the anniversary of the Battle of Puebla (1862), in which the Mexicans, led by General Ignacio Zaragoza, under President Benito Juarez, defeated the French invaders—the Mexican-American community of East Los Angeles sponsored a *Fiesta de los Barrios* (Festival of the *Barrios*), in which the Chicanos performed plays, songs, and dances for their community and the city at large. To attract audiences of the poor, as well as of other classes, no admission prices were charged. At this fiesta, the Teatro Chicano gave three and the Teatro Chicano de UMAS (United Mexican-

American Students) gave two performances. The interview with Tony Avallon was conducted on May 3, following an evening performance of *Justice*, in which he played Honkie Sam. The interview with Guadalupe de Saavedra, founder of both Teatro Chicano and Teatro Chicano de UMAS, was conducted the following day.

Interview with GUADALUPE DE SAAVEDRA

Bernard F. Dukore

DUKORE   What is the Teatro Chicano?

SAAVEDRA   The Teatro Chicano is more than a theatre group, which is basically what *teatro* means. It's a concept. It's a concept of having theatres go to the people—bringing the message to the people instead of setting up a theatre and having everybody come to it and having them pay their money to it.

DUKORE   How did it get started?

SAAVEDRA   It happened last August [1968]. We had seen the Teatro Campesino from Delano [California]. We had also seen the effect that they had on the farm workers, and on us—those that supported the farm workers' strike. But the enemy we saw was a limited thing: a union thing, a farm workers' thing, a rural thing. And it's great. But for the people in the urban areas, in the cities—it didn't bring out the problems that exist here. So Teatro Chicano started. There was a need for it. We got some people together and I took some of the things that I had written before as *cuentos* [stories] and just made them into *actos*. An *acto* comes halfway between a skit and a one-act play, like a short act, and it deals with the people in the community—either in this community [East Los Angeles] or the southwest, with the people as a whole.

DUKORE   The Teatro Chicano does more than perform plays. There are songs, readings—

SAAVEDRA   The action switches: bang, bang, bang. It's sort of—you hit them with one thing and then as they're getting used to that you hit them with something else. A song, a poem, a reading. One time I was reading one of my poems, and there was this guy sitting in the third row and he had a guitar. Before I knew it, he was playing background music for me. It sounded beautiful.

DUKORE   Most of the audience yesterday seemed to respond more to the Spanish than to the English, and most of the show was done in Spanish. Does this change, depending on the audience?

SAAVEDRA   The *teatros* are bilingual things. They can be done com-

214

pletely in Spanish, and if it's done in English it's spiced with Spanish. It changes, depending on the audience.

DUKORE   Last night the Teatro Chicano did *Justice*. When you played it before other groups, how did it differ from last night's performance?

SAAVEDRA   Well, for one thing, the narrator was more active . . . before. He would become involved in a dialogue with the audience or with the farmer, Honkie Sam. Or the dog would come over and bite him, he would kick the dog, or something like that. Or he would carry on a conversation with the people behind the stage—like yelling at them, and they would yell back. And one of the major differences was in the ending. I mean, what you saw last night was really two *actos*, one right after another. *Justice* ended when they drove the dog and Sam out. That's one *acto*. Then—

DUKORE   Wait. Justice came out and killed the dog.

SAAVEDRA   Justice came out and killed the dog. Then everybody comes out, they greet each other, and then they say "¡Viva la Justica! ¡Viva la Verdad! ¡Viva la Causa! ¡Viva la Raza!" And they drive the dog out. He was already dead. We don't try to portray realism: we exaggerate.

DUKORE   What was the second *acto*?

SAAVEDRA   The birth *acto*. As soon as they finished the first *acto*, then when the other girl went into labor pains—that's the start of another *acto*.

DUKORE   Is it always played with *Justice* now?

SAAVEDRA   Yes, but it can be added to other plays, too.

DUKORE   Has it been?

SAAVEDRA   Yes.

DUKORE   The end of the nativity scene, the end of *Justice*, was different in last night's performance from the ending in the script. In the script, the girl gives birth to a picture of Che Guevara. Last night—

SAAVEDRA   Last night they put in a picture of Zapata. Now, I admire Zapata very much. I've read about him. I've talked to people in Mexico about him. But I happen to believe that people can get hung up—and I have seen people get hung up—and yell "Viva la revolución," "Viva Zapata," and all that, and they're not relating to the present. They're talking about 1910 and they're still living in 1910. As long as they keep on doing that, they will not be able to relate to now.

DUKORE   And the picture of Che?

SAAVEDRA   It was a way of introducing a new ideology to the people.

DUKORE   Do your audiences always recognize the picture of Che?

SAAVEDRA   There were always some people in the audience who did, and there were always people afterward who came and asked.

DUKORE   Was the point of it to have them come and ask?

SAAVEDRA   It was to start people thinking, "Why Che?"—which would then start them thinking about Latin America as a whole. Those who don't know who Che was, who start asking who Che was—I mean, have them start seeing it in the *barrios*, start exposing the people to a picture of Che, to the ideology or what he stood for, so that they won't have to be afraid. Because a lot of people—they say: "Che—communism. Che—Cuba. Che—bad." But if we make the word Che synonymous with Justice, which is actually what it is, then they start thinking along a different line. I mean, after a performance they have asked about it or have asked where to go to get something more to know about this man, or they'll come and say, "Well, why did you have that communist up there?" and then we'd get into a conversation. The performance may end on stage, but what you do on stage is just plant a seed. It has to be cultivated before you can have any results. So after what we do on stage, we follow it through.

DUKORE   Is this the main goal of the Teatro Chicano, to plant the seed?

SAAVEDRA   Yes.

DUKORE   What do you want to follow?

SAAVEDRA   As far as the Chicano movement goes, the most revolutionary want to change the system and move on to greater things.

DUKORE   Change it to what?

SAAVEDRA   Collective living, socialism, or a combination of things. I mean, we can't say communism is going to be it, or socialism or another concept is going to be it, or that capitalism or democracy is going to be it. More likely, it will be a combination of different things, a combination of the best things that come out of each ideology. Actually, there are two types of revolution going on—if you want to call the second one a revolution. One is a revolution against outside forces: the system, the dominant society, the ideology that's holding us down. There's also another revolution—within our own people. I wrote a real short poem:

I met a revolutionary the other day.
He spoke Chicano,
Slept gabacho.[1]

The girls fool around all night long, so it hits them also. Some of the *actos* attack the things within our own people that have to be corrected. Like one, for example, is called *Jorge el Chingón. El Chingón* can either mean "Big Dick" or "Big Shot." Literally, it means one that's very *macho*, the most *macho* of all. Do you know what *macho* is? Male egoism. It's very prevalent in Latin countries and *El Chingón* is the most *macho* of them. The lights would go up and then the girls would all come up from backstage. They would talk: "Hey, have you heard he's coming?" "Jorge's coming?" "Our leader's coming." I played Jorge. I'd come on with a field jacket, dark sun glasses, cigar, red scarf around my neck— everything that's militant. The girls would start swooning just like they do for a singer. I'd lift my foot and one of them would kiss it. I'd take out a cigar and they would fight with each other to see who would light it, and finally I would grant one of them the privilege. If I raised my hand—like this—they would all shut up, or they would start making a fuss, applaud, things like that. Then I would talk to the people [the audience] with an accent: "You know who I am? My name is Jorge. They call me a *chingón*, man. They call me that because I'm the biggest one of them all. Do you know who these girls are? They're my women. You know why they like me? Because I'm Mexican. I'm a pure Chicano all the way to my toes." And then I would start talking down the *gabachos*, killing them and all that. About this time we would have somebody planted in the audience—the lightest girl in the entire group —and you would hear her voice: "*George!*" No "Jorge": the name in English is "George." "*George!*" At first, George—Jorge—wouldn't pay attention. Then she would get up from the audience and walk to the stage yelling "George!" and she would be draped in an American flag, with a sign that says "Angela."[2] She would get on the stage and say, "Goddam it, George, I told you not to leave home before you washed the dishes." George would be making excuses: "It's a good business." But she would drag him off by the ear: "George, if you want to sleep with me tonight, you'd better come and do the dishes." The girls would look bewildered and make remarks like "What kind of leaders do we have?" and "*Is* this a business?" Then somebody else would say, "Our leaders talk Chicano nationalism all day and sleep white all night." Then they would all point at people in the audience—and there are

---

[1] A *Chicano* is a Mexican-American, a *gabacho* a white American.
[2] In these *actos*, the white woman is frequently named Angela Anglo.

people in the audience guilty of this—and would say, "Are you a white sleeper?" "This is one of them."

DUKORE　*Justice* dealt with an immediate problem, exploitation. The solution at the end—

SAAVEDRA　The problem could have been solved by Sam and the people at any one stage. It could have been solved when they presented their grievances. The ending seemed to happen even though it could have been solved.

DUKORE　There are four possible solutions: one solution is that Sam would have been reasonable and would have stopped doing certain things on his own; another is to organize the people and they would persuade him to stop doing certain things; the third, organize and get rid of the dogs and Sam himself.

SAAVEDRA　Not only get rid of him, but be strong enough to get rid of him in the open, not just one by one from behind.

DUKORE　In the fourth stage, Che, it's more than just organizing, defending yourselves, and getting rid of. It's going a step beyond that. But in the context of the play itself, the first two never seem to matter. It's taken for granted that nothing will happen at those steps.

SAAVEDRA　The people know that nothing is going to happen. You see, the whole thing is that the people know, this community knows, the Chicanos in the southwest know, because they've seen it tried. The only thing is that they haven't got themselves organized to the point where they could put this across. There were a couple of times when a couple of people would get up there and tell us, "Get Sam off. Drive him off."

DUKORE　*Justice* and *Jorge* are about problems the Chicanos are facing today. But what of *The Battle of Puebla*? I haven't seen it yet, but in reading it it comes off as history, period. How does it come off in performance?

SAAVEDRA　It comes off as history. The fifth of May, historically, was the turning point in driving the French off the national lands of Mexico. In a sense, this is the fight against foreign aggression. What the Mexicans were fighting against is no different from what the Vietnamese are fighting against—the Viet Cong—it's the same. The *vendidos*—the sellouts, or whatever you want to call them—bring in outsiders to come in and make it for themselves. There were Mexicans who did this in Mexico, who requested the French to come, and the people rose up and drove them out. In Vietnam it isn't the first time it's happened. *The Battle of Puebla* is an anti-aggression *acto* and it's more than that, it's also a community control of the community interest *acto*.

DUKORE   How do you show this to the audience?

SAAVEDRA   The guys that play the soldiers—they're not going to be dressed like Mexicans over there and they're not going to walk like Mexicans. They're going to walk like *cholos*, like street guys in Los Angeles. Hey, Oreste, show him how Benito Juarez is going to walk in. [Oreste swaggers, walks around the room.] Benito Juarez comes in like a *cholo*, like that, and everybody recognizes him as a guy from the *barrios* as we know it.

DUKORE   And he'll be dressed as Oreste is today, but he'll wear a sign that will say "Juarez," so that the costume will tell the audience that it's today and the sign will tell them that it's 1862?

SAAVEDRA   Yes.

DUKORE   What about the French? Business suits or police uniforms?

SAAVEDRA   The French will wear business suits—and hats. We're going to make paper hats, put feathers on the hats, plumes, and all that.

DUKORE   The group that played *Justice* last night is the Teatro Chicano, but there is another Teatro Chicano, which is going to perform *The Battle of Puebla*.

SAAVEDRA   The original Teatro Chicano [which performed *Justice*] was started last August, and people seem to have identified that as being the only Teatro Chicano. They aren't the only Teatro Chicano. There's going to be, there has to be, more. There's going to be things that one group can't make that another group can make. There are going to be areas that one group can relate to that the other's won't be able to, simply because the locale and the environment are different.

DUKORE   The group putting on *The Battle of Puebla* tomorrow is listed as the Teatro Chicano de UMAS [United Mexican-American Students]. How new is this company?

SAAVEDRA   This is going to be the first *acto* they've put on.

DUKORE   How old are the people in the two companies?

SAAVEDRA   About eighteen to about thirty-five.

DUKORE   How do they support themselves? How do you? I mean, you're not making anything out of this.

SAAVEDRA   By anything. By lecturing on literature or poetry reading. I'm driving a truck at the Grand Central Market.

DUKORE   Why did you leave the original Teatro Chicano?

SAAVEDRA   This was planned. It was planned to work with the Teatro Chicano to bring them up to the point where they would be good, to prove the concept of the *teatros* does work: going out to the people, educating them, planting seeds. They came of age—planning and putting on performances and all that. That was the reason for leaving it. The other reason was that it freed me to work with other groups—start moving around, circulating, and getting other groups together. I don't want the Teatro Chicano for myself. I want a Teatro Chicano in every neighborhood, in every *barrio* in the southwest:[3] California, Texas—it's different there.

DUKORE   How?

SAAVEDRA   For one thing, you have a group called the Texas Rangers. In Spanish they're called *rinches*. *Rinches* have been known to have a long history of discrimination against Mexicans. I don't mean just harassment, but openly lynching Mexicans. Texas has a long history of prejudice against Mexicans. On the whole it's a very, very, ultra-conservative state. I guess New Mexico would follow. Like, let's say, for example, *Justice*. Some kids that saw us went back with *Justice*. They did it and they got arrested. Right after the performance. That's the difference in Texas. The lines are drawn more clearly there. In a lot of the *barrios* in a lot of the cities there, the elected officials are people from *la raza* [of our race], but things don't change. So people come to the conclusion that a Mexican capitalist is worse than a white capitalist: he's exploiting his own people. They see it's not so much the nationality of the person, it's the system on which the economy is based or the wheels function in this country that perpetuates this.

---

[3] As of August 1969 there were nine Teatro Chicanos: three in Texas, three in southern California (two in Los Angeles, one in San Diego), two in Arizona, and one in New Mexico.

Interview with TONY AVALLON

Bernard F. Dukore

DUKORE   Your name is pronounced—

AVALLON   Ava-lon. Or Ava-*yon*: give it the Spanish. That's part of the whole thing: when you have been told something as personal as your name is pronounced with the *l* sound, and then it isn't until you're in your twenties that it is admitted, even by your own mother, for the first time, that it's a Spanish name and that it's pronounced *yon.* My mother wouldn't teach me Spanish. This was America and we speak only English here. The problem among the Mexican-Americans is they want to reject any kind of identification with being Mexican. "Mexican-American," incidentally, can be a put-down, depending on the context. If you use the term "Chicano" all the time—like yourself, because you're white—we would know you were hep. A "Mexican-American" means he's the guy who wants to be white, especially when we pronounce it slowly and carefully—Mex-i-can A-mer-i-can—that means we're putting him down because he wants to be white. Yes, sir, we have lots of those spin people like that. But they're nice people, they're beautiful people. If we get angry at another Chicano, or a Mexican-American—you know, it's a family affair. We would come to his aid at a moment's notice. . . .

DUKORE   You were saying he wants to be white.

AVALLON   "What's wrong with that?" you ask. "After all, they're living in America." But it's a strange psychology to have to pretend to be something that you are not. Inside of you, you've learned as a child that it's an entirely different way of life. No matter how you try to ignore it, it's always going to be there. It's going to be there in the form of kind of a resentment towards your parents, a resentment of where you came from. It's something I've seen men well into their forties and fifties carry with them all their lives. They feel demeaned by the fact they are of a certain ethnic origin. They resent it. I think even in *Portnoy's Complaint* this is what Philip Roth was talking about: this man who was trying to outlive the fact that he was the boy in a Jewish joke. Only it ain't no joke. Wow, that's an incredible condemnation of a man all his life to live like that. I've seen it many times and this is one of the reasons I'm militant.

DUKORE   A militant wants something. What do you want?

AVALLON   I want to live in a community where I never have to have any man tell me he's Spanish, not Mexican. You see, I'm not Mexican. I'm Spanish and Italian. But I grew up in that *barrio* [district or neighborhood]. My mother always insisted, "You are Spanish, not Mexican"—all that poor unfortunate baloney. I don't want to have any man live like that. That's chains and slavery.

DUKORE   But why shouldn't your mother have said that? You *are* Spanish, you're *not* Mexican.

AVALLON   Yeah. Well, I'm making up for the *conquistadores*. Pizarro's apology. "Gee, we're sorry, gang."

DUKORE   How does Teatro Chicano help you get what you want?

AVALLON   Theatre: it's like comic strips for the people. It entertains them. It explains. "Why should I want to be Mexican, man? I want to be white." The Browns right now, a lot of them, could slip into white society. Just forget you're dark, and accept the jibes and the jokes about tortillas for a little bit, and white society will accept you, unless you're really Indian looking; then you may have trouble. We explain this by entertaining. Our heroes are exaggerated. Our villains are exaggerated. Our actions are very simple. With humor, with this very broad humor, we find that we have a message that people are able to grasp.

DUKORE   What is the message?

AVALLON   "Organize." Don't let any group, any person, tell you you have to be a certain way and you have to do things a certain way because he got there first. What is the validity of a man's authority over you? In this country, the community is supposed to be the government. O.K., Mexican—O.K., Black—O.K., whoever—organize yourselves to fight back when you think something wrong is being done to your community. Also, look around to see what is wrong. In the *actos* [short, one-act plays], we point out things that are wrong. Like that school we did the *actos* in tonight. That hasn't been changed in thirty years. And Fairfax High School has got one of the most ultra-modern complexes in the world. It happens to be within a Jewish community. Now, we all talk about what we can learn from the Jews. Hey, man, the first thing to learn is "Get organized." Money isn't the power that community's got. It's the organization of that community. They have their ways of doing it. We will have our way. The Blacks will have their way. And it can happen in white communities too. They'll come over and screw you in your own streets, your street lighting, anything. Seriously, it's getting the government back to the people. We have something to add, the Blacks have something to add, and it's not being added because the assumption of all authority is that they're right, otherwise they wouldn't be in authority. Political pressure—that's the way. Political power comes from masses of people. No matter what illegal rackets have been done, the people who are pulling the dirty game still want popular support. That wonderful word, "popular support." That's our strength. This is what brings the government back.

DUKORE   When we left the theatre tonight, you called Teatro Chicano a revolutionary group. At the beginning of the interview, you called yourself a militant. But the way you've been talking, you seem reformist rather than revolutionary.

AVALLON   I'm being very gentle with you. I let it out a little at a time. The next thing is literally to change the form of the government. This representative government is obviously faulty because representatives can be had. And they are had by property owners. They are had by the most economically influential people in the state or in the nation. We really don't want that any more. This American revolution was a revolution of aristocrats. Study Mexican history. None of their revolutions was a really popular, people's revolution until the revolution in which Emiliano Zapata and the man they call Pancho Villa partook. That's not his real name: his real name was Doroteo Arango. We have to look to what a real revolution is. That's what we really want. Historically, it's got to come: that governments are really run by the people. I could go into a whole rap about political theory on this, but not now.

DUKORE   What is Teatro Chicano?

AVALLON   It's a name given to a theatre of the *barrio* of the East side of L.A. It came from the Teatro Campesino [Farm Workers' Theatre], which arose out of the Delano grape strike. It was a means of communicating the problems inherent in their lives and in the strike, and what the strike was all about. It did it by exaggeration. The villain was always very villainous. The heroes were at first cowardly and then they got their *machismo* and became heroic. *Machismo* means balls, but it really means manhood. The Teatro Campesino used placards hanging around the neck—one placard to represent the field worker, one placard to represent the bad *vendido*, the man who is a Mexican-American who works for the white man and sells out his brothers, the Uncle Tom of the Mexicans, the man who wears the white shirt and the nice tie of his boss, yet is used as a go-between between the boss's power and the Mexicans, who may resist and resent a white man dealing with them.

Our stories, our *actos*, come out of the city *barrios*, the city ghettos, and we have had this reaction from kids all over: "We like the Campesino, but you guys really know where it is." Our best audiences are the young high school kids who are just learning about *chicanismo*, who do not know anything about the Brown Revolution or Brown Power, but are still just high school kids aware of being Mexican and they want to find out more about it. They catch on to every one of our lines. They react beautifully. Our toughest audience is the one you've seen tonight. They're hard core militants.

DUKORE Your *toughest* audience?

AVALLON I mean our hardest, because they already know the whole line and they're ready to come into the *acto* with us.

DUKORE Why does this make them so tough? One of the things I caught tonight, which I've caught very few times from other theatre groups, was a sense of your belonging to your audience. The actors weren't divided from them by any magical line. The audience felt free to interrupt and call things to you, and they did it in a friendly way, and the actors were just as friendly with them. One of the actors yelled something like "Viva la Huelga [strike]," and everyone in the audience yelled, "Viva la Huelga." Then someone from the audience yelled "Viva Cesar Chavez [leader of the grape workers' strike]," and the actors picked it up. They fielded comments from the audience, tossed comments back to them, as if to say, "Yes, we're with you, and we'll take thirty seconds or a minute or two to join you in this and then go back to our thing."

AVALLON I think you've said it.

DUKORE But why does this make them a tough audience? They're a sympathetic audience.

AVALLON "Toughest" should be in quotes. It's hard for us to keep a division between us, and we aren't trying to do that—ever. What I'm really trying to say is because we want to start laughing too, with them, it cuts into our professionalism. The hardest audience of all, right: the "hardest" audience of all.

DUKORE Except for you, the people in Teatro Chicano haven't had professional experience or training as actors.

AVALLON You know, it's really funny you say that, because it's a hard trip for me. I have to keep my mouth shut sometimes when I want to say things. I have to let these people grow to my level, or what I think is my level, or maybe beyond. So I go to them as a student and I keep my mouth shut. I learn. All I do is contribute a little more organization, technical experience, smooth things out when they start getting rough. Like today, I was the one who thought, "Oh my God, I'd better go up front to find out who knows we're here, what lighting we've got, what microphoning," because I knew about these things. But raw ideas, impetus—no. I let them teach me about that. Yeah, sometimes I have to sit there and really swallow my pride, swallow my desire to be the leader, but screw it, Jack, it isn't important. I'm there to learn and I'm also there to function within this group, and to help this limited group—from my position I think it's limited, right?—find its limitless-ness. That first, then from beyond that I can apply what is personally mine. That will come next. We've had problems within our group. Like, one girl doesn't like another because she isn't Mexican enough, and all this garbage. Another girl doesn't listen. Another girl keeps pushing people. Oddly enough, the guys get along beautifully.

DUKORE   Has there been any turnover since the group started [August, 1968]?

AVALLON   No. We're devoted people. You see, it's less of an ego thing —it really is. There's a little bit of that ego in there, but it's all absorbed by your audience because you all feel the way revolutionaries are sup-posed to feel: really one with the community. The big secret of the coming revolution—here it is—is that you still can be an individual and relate your work and your efforts to the larger community. A very strange trip, baby, because you've always been brought up thinking that it's individual success and the gathering of individual material that makes you an individual, and it could be true, but when you find out that you can relate to the larger community, you can actually swallow that ego a little bit.

DUKORE   One final question. At the end of *Justice*, in the script, the girl gives birth to a picture of Che Guevara. In tonight's performance, you substituted a picture of Zapata. Why?

AVALLON   If I go down to the *barrio* where a man is struggling to keep the dirt out of his house, I'm not going to come on with Che Guevara. I'm sorry, I'm going to give him his hero, Emiliano Zapata. Maybe it's out of date but it's still valid to him. My God, the symbology, the rela-tionship between the revolution and what we're trying to do in the *barrio*—that's significant!

'his book may be kept

FOURTEEN DAYS